Paul's SAT® Writing

저자 Paul Kim(김동현)

For the Redesigned SAT

Contributors

Written and edited by the talented test prep professionals at
✓ PaulAcademy

PaulAcademy is the publishing arm of one of the industry-leading test prep organizations in Asia. PaulAcademy is a dedicated test prep organization that has helped thousands of students to realize their potentials and achieve their dreams. As a leader in test prep & strategy development specializing in SAT, ACT and AP preparation, PaulAcademy teaches pragmatic problem-solving skills that will ultimately help students obtain successful academic results. PaulAcademy aims to spread its expert knowledge to students worldwide.

Editor-in-Chief
Paul Kim

Head of Publishing
Saeyeun Kim, Sieun Lee

Material Development & Editing
Jaewoo Lee

Marketing
Byeong Kook Kim, Paul Jae Woo Jung

Email: books@paulacademy.net   Website: http://www.paulacademy.net

Copyright © 2016 All rights reserved by PaulAcademy.
The contents of the book may not be copied or reused without the expressed written consent of PaulAcademy.

SAT® is a registered trademark of the College Board, which is not affiliated with and does not endorse this product.

ISBN : 979-11-86461-10-5

Paul's SAT® Writing

Paul Academy

Paul's SAT Writing 서문

10여 년 전 "한국의 Test Prep이 세계 최고"라는 가능성을 보고 유학길에 올라 공부를 마치고 귀국 후 강남의 모 SAT 학원 팀장으로 매년 20%씩 성장을 이룬 후, 그 학원을 나와서 '친절한 폴샘'의 SAT 서문을 쓴 지도 이제 2년이 지났다. 그 당시에는 "아마존 Test Prep 분야 넘버원"이라는 꿈을 위해서 한국의 SAT 교재 1등을 달성한 후에 미국에 진출하고 싶다"고 이야기했는데, 그 2년 간 수많은 동역자들의 도움으로 한국 SAT 교재 베스트셀러(교보문고 기준)를 달성했고, 미국 Amazon.com에 진출하여 SAT Grammar 분야 4위, SAT Math 분야 15위를 기록했다. (2015년 5월 25일 기준) 글로벌 시장 진출을 위해서 시리즈 제목도 '친절한 폴샘의 SAT' 시리즈에서 'Paul's SAT', 'Paul's ACT' 시리즈로 정비하고 본격적인 미국 진출에 박차를 가하고 있다.

저자의 고교 시절에는 교과서, 학교 수업과 참고서만으로도 충분히 자기주도학습이 가능했지만, 지금은 학원에서 공부하지 않으면 효율적인 학습과 시험준비가 불가능하다는 견해가 이 사회에 팽배해 있는 것 같다. 저자는 좋은 교재와 콘텐츠를 만들어 사교육에 의존하지 않고도 자기주도학습이 가능하다는 것을 증명하고, 학습에 대한 잘못된 사회인식을 바로잡고, 더 나아가 미국 아마존의 Test Prep 분야에서 세계최고가 되어 '교육한류'의 한 축이 되고 싶다.

만일 누군가 독학이 힘들어 학원의 도움이 필요하다면, 폴아카데미에서 도움을 받기를 바란다. 폴아카데미에서는 본 교재를 사용하여 학생들이 빠른 시간 내에 고득점을 받을 수 있도록 도와주고, 혼자서 해결하기 힘든 부분들에 대한 해결책을 제시해 주고 있다.

이 책은 2016년 3월부터 시행되는 Redesigned SAT를 효과적으로 대비할 수 있게 해 주는 Writing 교재이다. 새로운 SAT Writing은 Passage를 기반으로 한 Evidence-based 형태로, 기존의 문법 위주 시험에서 Reading 능력까지 갖추어야 할 시험으로 변화하였다. 이를 반영해 교재를 두 섹션으로 나누어 문법 숙지를 쉽게 하고 Writing 고득점을 위한 기본적인 Reading 능력까지 갖출 수 있도록 유형화하여 구성하였다. 각 주제마다 One-Point Lesson과 기초를 다질 수 있는 Practice Question들이 포함되어 있고, CollegeBoard 공식 가이드라인을 참고하여 만들어 실제 시험과 매우 유사한 난이도를 가진 4개의 Full-length practice test 역시 포함되어 있다. 이 교재 하나로 SAT Writing 학습을 처음부터 끝까지 마무리 지을 수 있다.

본 교재와 콘텐츠를 통해 단기간에 고득점을 가능하게 하고, 그렇게 확보된 소중한 시간을 본인이 진정으로 하고 싶은 것을 하면서 사는 세상을 만드는데 기여하는데 이 책이 좋은 첫걸음이 되길 바란다. "Paul's SAT Writing"가 빛을 볼 수 있도록 많은 사람들이 도움을 주었다. 내게 "best place to work"의 꿈을 심어주신 하늘에 계신 사랑하는 아버지, 못난 아들을 위해 항상 기도해 주시는 사랑하는 어머니, 부족한 남편임에도 열심히 섬겨주는 사랑하는 아내, 그리고 바쁘다는 이유로 함께 시간을 갖지 못해도 바르게 자라주고 있는 사랑하는 두 아들 영준, 경준에게 너무나 고맙고 사랑한다는 말을 전하고 싶다. 마지막으로 길가의 돌멩이보다 못한 나에게 비전을 주시고 여건을 허락해 주신 하나님께 감사를 드린다.

Paul Kim

NYU에서 영어교육을 전공하였으며 실력 있는 SAT, ACT 부문 최고의 전문강사로서 세한아카데미에서 수많은 학생을 가르치며 큰 명성을 쌓아온 Paul Kim은 현재 Test Prep 전문기관 Paul Academy의 대표로 재직하고 있다. Paul Academy에서는 SAT 및 ACT 교재 시리즈 출간, 온라인 교육 콘텐츠 개발, 자기주도학습과 수험생을 위한 영어교육 전반에 힘을 쏟고 있다.

CONTENTS

A. 서문 4

B. 목차 5

C. Redesigned SAT 소개 6

D. Part I : Standard English Conventions 13
    1. Number Agreement 14
    2. Pronouns 24
    3. Parallelism 42
    4. Comparisons 48
    5. Modifiers 57
    6. Punctuation 66
    7. Structure 81
    8. Tense 96

E. Part II : Expression of Ideas 103
    9. Usage 104
    10. Style, Tone and Syntax 123
    11. Insertion/Deletion/Replacement/Content Order 145
    12. Graphs & Charts 156

F. Practice Question Answers & Explanations 161

G. Chapter Test Answers & Explanations 189

H. 4 Practice Tests 205

J. Practice Test Answers & Explanations 265

SAT 시험, 이렇게 바뀐다!

2016 Redesigned SAT 소개

시행일시 : 2016년 3월부터 시행될 예정

1. Redesigned SAT 주요변화

A. 점수
- 전체 2,400점 만점 → 1,600점 만점 (Reading+Writing & Language 800점, Math 800점)
- 에세이는 선택사항으로 변경되고 점수도 독자적으로 매겨진다. Reading, analysis, writing 각 항목에 대해서 2~8점 배점되고 총점은 24점
- 에세이가 선택사항으로 바뀌었지만 상위권 대학을 희망하는 학생들은 필수적으로 점수를 받아놓아야 한다.

B. 영역
Essay, Critical Reading, Writing, Math 였던 영역구분이
→ Evidence-based Reading & Writing(Reading+Writing & Language), Math, Essay(선택사항) 으로 변경됨

C. 시험시간

전체 3시간 45분이었던 것이 3시간으로 축소. (에세이를 선택할 경우에는 3시간 50분)

1. Evidence-based Reading & Writing: 65분 reading, 35분 writing

2. Math: 55분 계산기 허용, 25분 계산기 사용불가

D. 시험 문제수
- Critical Reading: 67문제 → 52문제
- Writing: 49문제 → 44문제
- Essay: 1문제 그대로
- Math: 54문제 → 58문제

E. 시험 출제방식
- 오지선다에서 사지선다 방식으로 변경
- 지필시험방식을 유지

F. 채점방식 및 기준
- Essay: 글의 일관성보다는 학생의 분석능력과 논증과정을 중시
- 오답에 대한 감점제도 폐지: 틀린 문제와 풀지 않은 문제가 성적에 영향을 주지 않음

G. 기존 SAT와 새로운 SAT 비교표

현재 SAT			Redesigned SAT			
과목	시험시간	문제 수	과목	시험시간	문제 수	시험방식
Critical Reading	70분	67문제	Reading	65분	52문제	4 LP 1 DP
Writing	60분	49문제	Writing & Language	35분	44문제	4 Passages
Essay	25분	1문제	Essay	50분	1문제	1 EP 1 RP
Math	70분	54문제	Math	80분	58문제	계산기/ 38문제 NO계산기/ 20문제
계	225분	171문제	계	180분 (에세이 포함시 230분)	154문제 (에세이 포함시 155문제)	

※참고 – LP: Long Passages, DP: Double Passages, EP: Essay Prompt, RP: Reading Passage

2. 과목별 구체적인 변화

A. Reading Test (독해)
1. 단어의 난이도 보다는 context에 집중
   - 기존의 단어 뜻 모르면 풀 수 없는 obscure한 문제 폐지
   - Extended context에서 단어 톤 찾기
     예) how word choice shapes tone/impact
   - Sentence Completion 폐지
   - 단편적인 정보, 직접적으로 단어 뜻을 물어보는 문제는 축소

2. Analysis & evidence use (분석, 근거 사용)
   - 답을 찾아내는 것뿐 아니라 텍스트의 어느 부분이 그 답을 support하는지 찾아야 한다
     예) Which portion of the passage best supports the answer to the text?
     CB: "There will be at least one question asking them to select a quote from the text that best supports the answer they have chosen in response to the preceding question."

3. Real-world에 관한 지문
   - 기존의 임의적인 토픽의 essay와 fiction은 나오지 않음
   - 차트, 그래프, 인포그래픽이 포함된 지문 (reading, writing, math 모두 동일하게 적용됨)
   - 1개의 역사/사회 지문과 1개의 과학지문

4. 새로운 지문
   - 미국, 세계문학 유지, 역사/사회/과학 지문 추가
   - Founding Documents (미국 건국자들에 관한 문서), Global conversation 지문 포함

> **학습전략**
>
> Redesigned SAT는 Evidence-based reading을 강조하므로 글의 paragraph summary, main idea, tone을 꼼꼼히 체크해가면서 글을 읽고 이해를 하며, 리딩문제를 풀 때 더 이상 '감'에 의존해서 푸는 것이 아니라 몇 번째 line을 통해서 답을 유추했는지를 항상 확인하면서 공부를 해야 한다. 혼자 하기 어려운 학생은 친절한 폴샘의 기출 해설서의 CR 영역을 공부하면 된다.
>
>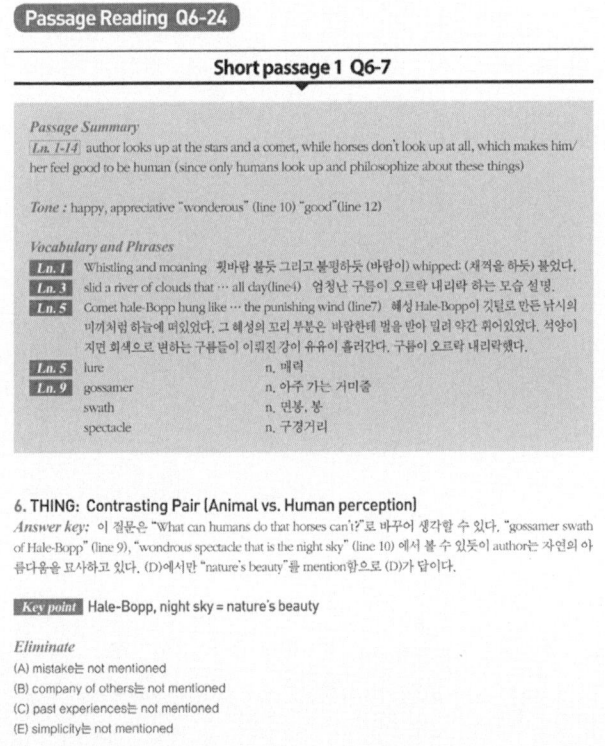
>
> 특별히 CR이 600점대 이하의, 유학 3년차 이하의 학생들은 찍기 식으로 가르치는 학원보다는 지문을 잘 이해시켜 주는 curriculum을 제공하는 학원과 교재를 선정하여 공부하는 것이 좋다. 그리고 SAT는 미국대학에 진학하려는 학생을 위한 시험이므로, 평소에 미국적 사고에 필요한 역사, 문학, 사회이슈들에 대한 배경지식을 잘 정리해 놓으면 지문을 이해하고 문제풀이 시간을 줄이는데 도움이 된다.

B. Writing and Language Test (문법)

1. Real-world에 관한 지문
- 역사/사회, 과학, 인문학, Career 관련 지문
- 그래프, 도표 문제 한 개 이상 출제: 주어진 정보들을 어떻게 잘 연결해서 자연스럽고 논리적인 글로 만들어낼 수 있는가에 대한 문제 출제

2. 문법적 오류 관련문제는 크게 변화 없음
- Development of idea
  - 예) adding relevant supporting details, improving focus and cohesion
- Careful & purposeful use of words
  - 예) improving precision or concision
- Rhetoricals and conventions
  - 예) fragments & run-ons, parallel structure, modifier, tense, pronoun & number, verb agreement, logical comparison, idiom, punctuation
- Diction

3. 주어진 텍스트와 차트 또는 도표 간의 연관 찾기
예) 차트에 대한 잘못된 해석 고치기

4. 지문 길이 증가
- 기존의 한 문장 짜리 문법 문제 폐지
- Extended context를 제공하는 문단 제공

> **학습전략**
> 기존 SAT Grammar 섹션에서 나오는 Improving Paragraph 유형에 Grammar 요소가 조금 더 가미되었다고 보면 된다. 너무 걱정하지 말고 조만간 출간될 Paul's SAT Writing and Language 로 준비하면 된다. 아직 교재가 출간되지 않아 조바심이 나는 경우는 친절한 폴샘의 SAT Grammar 기본서로 공부를 해도 대부분 커버할 수 있으니 너무 걱정하지 말자.

C. Essay (에세이)

1. 요구사항에서 선택사항으로 변경

2. 짧게 자신의 의견을 요구하는 prompt 폐지
- 기존의 prompt는 배경지식과 경험에 의존; 논리구조만 맞으면 fact는 상관 없었지만 새로운 SAT Essay에서는 600~700 단어로 주어진 글을 읽고 그 주장을 분석해서 설명해야 함 → 자기 마음대로 예시를 쓰거나, 단순히 자신의 주장을 펼치는 것이 아니라는 점에 주의
  - 예) 작가가 어떻게 주장을 이끌어 나가는지 텍스트 속 객관적 근거를 제시하여 설명하여야 하며, 자신의 의견은 쓰지 않음

- 글쓴이의 주장과 논리를 분석하여 그 논리전개에 대하여, 또한 그 주장에 대한 찬성 또는 반대의 관점을 어떻게 자기의 말로 잘 풀어내는지가 포인트

3. 채점방식 및 기준
    - 기존의 0~12점대의 scale은 폐지되고 criteria에 따른 점수로 0~24점까지 채점
    - Reading: Source text와 main idea에 대한 이해가 중요하며, 얼마나 디테일이 정확한지, 텍스트 속의 근거를 얼마나 잘 사용하는지 등이 중요한 포인트
    - Analysis: 주어진 과제를 얼마나 잘 이해했는지, 작가가 논거를 펼치며 사용한 각종 element가 얼마나 효과적인지, 그리고 자신의 주장에 대한 근거를 잘 제시하고 있는지 부분에 중점
    - Writing: Central claim 사용, 효과적인 organization과 progression이 되고 있는지, 문장구조가 varied한지, 정확한 뜻의 단어를 사용하는지, 그리고 consistent한 스타일과 톤을 유지하는지, 문법적인 오류는 없는지 등이 중점채점사항

4. 에세이 시간이 25분에서 50분으로 길어졌기 때문에, 체계적인 논리와 전개과정이 필수적이다. 시간이 길어지면서 그만큼 평가도 정확하고 가혹하게 될 것이라 예상된다.

> **학습전략**
>
> 기존 SAT는 내용을 '지어낼' 수 있었던 반면, Redesigned SAT는 fact-based essay이다. 2016 Redesigned Reading처럼 저자의 main idea와 argument를 잘 파악하여 fact-based argument를 하는 연습이 매우 중요해졌다. 이 연습만 잘 된다면 해외고 유학생들이 국내대학의 영어특기자 입시를 준비할 경우에 많은 도움이 될 것이다.

D. Math Test (수학)
*출제범위 및 비중이 조정되었기 때문에 일단 전반적으로 수학문제의 난이도가 올라가게 되며, 일부 문제는 AP 시험유형과 수준의 문제라고 생각하고 준비해야 한다.

1. Data Analysis에 중점
    - Reading과 Writing에서 Real-world에 중점을 둔 것과 같은 맥락
    - 실제 상황에 적용해서 푸는 문제들이 출제된다는 뜻

2. Real-world context 사용한 문제 출제
    예) 사회/역사/과학과 관련된 시나리오를 보여준 후 그것에 대한 문제 여러 개 출제

3. Pre-Calculus 영역이 추가됨
    - Trigonometry, Complex Number, Radians 등의 상급개념 추가

4. 일부 섹션에서 계산기 사용이 제한됨
   - 복잡한 계산은 아니고 유리수 산술계산 정도의 수준
   - Grid-ins 형태의 주관식이 총 12문제 출제

〈출제범위〉

범위	문제 개수	출제비중
Heart of Algebra (Creating, Solving, Interpreting Linear Expressions)	21	36%
Problem Solving and Data Analysis	16	27%
Passport to Advanced Math (Quadratic/Exponential Functions)	15	26%
Additional Topics (Area/Volume Calculation, Investigation of Lines, Angles, Triangles and Circles Using Theorem, Working with Trigonometric Functions)	6	11%
계	58	100%

〈계산기 사용에 따른 구분〉

구분	유형	시험시간
계산기 사용가능	객관식 30문제 Grid-ins 8문제	55분
계산기 사용불가	객관식 15문제 Grid-ins 5문제	25분
계	총 58문제	총 80분

> **학습전략**
>
> Pre-Calculus 영역을 중점 학습하고, 특히 trigonometry(삼각함수), complex number(복소수), radians(호도법) 등의 개념학습을 충실히 한다. 그리고 계산기를 사용할 수 없는 section이 하나 있으므로 평소 계산연습을 많이 해 두도록 하고, real-world situation에 입각한 문제에 대비하기 위해 관련 응용문제 풀이를 많이 하도록 한다. 여름방학에 2016 SAT 학원수강을 하게 되면 꼭 Math수업을 수강하여서 고득점의 발판을 마련하여야 한다. 더 이상 SAT 1 Math는 유학생들에게 쉬운 과목이 아니라는 점을 꼭 명심하도록 하자.

Part I

Standard English Conventions

Number Agreement

1-1. Subject-Verb Agreement

One-Point Lesson

Ensure that the plurality of the **verb** matches the plurality of the **subject**.

Plurality of subject	Verb
Singular	is, was, has, walks, talks
Plural	are, were, have, walk, talk

Example 1: The dogs that bit Abraham <u>is</u> resting. (×)

    is → are

Example 2: The tower of bricks <u>were</u> quickly demolished by the baby. (×)

    were → was

    The **subject** here is 'tower of bricks', which is singular. Therefore, use the singular verb 'was'.

A. In order to find the subject and verb of a sentence, you need to **get rid of the modifiers** that make the sentence complex. Make sure to check the following three first:

<u>1. Delete the prepositional phrases.</u>

A prepositional phrase acts as a modifier and is not a crucial constituent of a sentence - delete it. A preposition is a word that sits before a noun to indicate the place, time, or direction.

    Types of prepositions
        1) Prepositions of place : on, beneath, over, under, above
        2) Prepositions of time : at, in, on, by, for, during
        3) Prepositions of direction : into, out of, across, along, through, from, to
        4) Other prepositions : like, despite, in spite of

    Example)
The dogs in the cage <u>was</u> large (×)

    was → were

    (delete the prepositional phrase 'in the cage', then you are left with 'the dogs' as the subject. The verb must take the plural form)

2. Delete phrases placed between two commas if they serve to modify the subject or any other noun.

Example)

The team of advisors, arriving ahead of schedule, were met at the airport by the team leader. (✗)

    were → was

    'of advisors' is a prepositional phrase - delete it.

    'arriving ahead of schedule' is a phrase placed between two commas - delete it.

    Then you are left with 'The team' as the subject. The verb must take the singular form.

3. Delete the adjectives and adverbs.

Adjectives and adverbs are both modifiers that are not necessary to constitute a sentence. Delete them.

What is an adjective?

An adjective is a word that modifies a noun. It explains or limits the state or traits of the noun.

    Types of adjectives

    1) Original adjective: pretty, handsome, kind, ...

    2) Verb + ing: I saw a flying bird.

    3) Verb + ed: There are two guards posted at the door.

    4) to + Verb: I have many friends to help me.

    5) who(m), which, whose + incomplete: I like a chair which has four legs.

What is an adverb?

An adverb modifies all parts of speech except nouns - verbs, adjectives, other adverbs, phrases, clauses, or whole sentences.

    Types of adverbs

    1) Original adverbs: carefully, closely,...

    2) to + Verb: I went abroad to study English.

    3) Adverb clause: When I was young, I used to play baseball.

B. The gerund/present participle form (Verb+ing) acts a **singular noun**. So in a sentence, it must be paired with a singular verb form.

Example)

Running makes you healthy.

    'Running (Run+ing)' acts as a singular noun, so pair it with a singular verb 'makes.'

Verb forms

Cannot act as a verb		**Can** act as a verb	
Gerund/present participle (Verb+ing)	going	Be + Verb+ing	is going
Past participle	gone	Be + past participle	is gone
To infinitive (to + Verb)	to go	Present, past perfect (have + past participle)	has gone

SAT-Style Example

Choose the answer that best replaces the underlined part:

Dissociative identity disorder is a psychological condition in which the sufferer <u>possess</u>$_1$ at least two distinct identities or is in a dissociated personality state that heavily influences a person's behavior. Quite often, the side effect of possessing two or more separate personalities <u>is</u>$_2$ severe memory deterioration. Diagnosis is often questionable as there is no clear consensus with regards to symptoms or treatment. A well-known literary example of this disorder is the *Strange Case of Dr. Jekyll and Mr. Hyde*.

1. A) NO CHANGE
   B) possesses
   C) are seen possessing
   D) are being possessed with

2. A) NO CHANGE
   B) are
   C) were
   D) have been

Explanation:
The correct answers are (B) and (A).
Pay close attention to the subject that the verb is referring to. For the first question, the subject, 'sufferer', is singular, so the verb should be singular as well. Therefore, the answer is (B).
For the second question, you might think that the subject is 'personalities.' However, the actual subject is 'side effect,' with the bit about 'personalities' merely being a distraction. The subject is singular, so the verb should be singular as well. Therefore, the answer is (A).

Practice Questions

Change the underlined verb to the correct form if necessary.

1. Kim <u>were</u> stepping on the brakes gently, like when it was snowing. "Taking this route might not have been the best idea," he muttered to himself. <u>No error</u>

2. Everyone in the class <u>believe</u> that the teacher is going to let the class out early today. <u>No error</u>

3. The printing press <u>are</u> invented by Gutenberg around 1440 A.D., allowing for rapid spread of information. <u>No error</u>

4. After discovering a family of dwarfs in Ecuador immune to cancer, researchers <u>has been trying</u> to isolate the gene that results in this protection. <u>No error</u>

5. Although he had an excellent sense of creativity, Kyle's career as a screenwriter <u>was</u> handicapped by his dyslexia. <u>No error</u>

6. Tyler and his sister Ellie <u>have won</u> the national spelling bee competition for elementary school students.
    A) NO CHANGE
    B) has won
    C) was winning
    D) is winning

7. "We have less than two weeks before the deadline for our spring issue!" <u>shout</u> Anna to the Science Now Magazine editors who are slacking.
    A) NO CHANGE
    B) have shouted
    C) shouts
    D) were shouting

8. Anyone who travels overseas frequently <u>understands</u> never to ignore immunization shots.
    A) NO CHANGE
    B) understand
    C) were understanding
    D) have understood

9. Awarded the Pulitzer Prize, *To Kill a Mockingbird* <u>have been</u> the heartwarming story of the author's childhood mixed with fictional details.
    A) NO CHANGE
    B) is
    C) are
    D) were

10. With the help from Baseball Training Center for Youth, high school students in Busan, Korea pitch faster and <u>hits</u> harder.
    A) NO CHANGE
    B) has hit
    C) is hitting
    D) hit

1-2. Noun Agreement

One-Point Lesson

Ensure that the plurality of the **subject or the object** matches the plurality of **the other**, or the **adjective**.

Example 1: His grades in Math and English tests were just two <u>illustration</u> of how he failed the final exams.
  illustration → illustrations ('two' is plural.)
Example 2: One of David's uncles became <u>politicians</u>.
  politicians → a politician ('One' is singular)

SAT-Style Example

Choose the answer that best replaces the underlined part:

From Abingdon, Oxfordshire, <u>the English rock band</u>₁ "Radiohead" made its debut with the famous single Creep in 1992. Radiohead is known for its alternative style of incorporating experimental electronic sounds with rock. My favorite song by far is *Paranoid Android* in the *OK Computer* album, which received numerous <u>rewards</u>₂ for its creativity. Radiohead sold over 30 million albums worldwide, and its members were ranked 3rd best British <u>artist</u>₃ of all time. The band members Thom Yorke and Jonny Greenwood are also known for promoting human rights; they have participated in the movement for more than twenty years.

1. A) NO CHANGE
   B) the English rock bands
   C) the English singers
   D) the English rock artist

2. A) NO CHANGE
   B) awards
   C) prize
   D) reward

3. A) NO CHANGE
   B) artists
   C) figureheads in the musical arena
   D) performer

Explanation:

The correct answers are (A), (B), and (B).
For the first question, "Radiohead" is a group of musicians as illustrated in the rest of the passage. The plurality of the underlined part should also match the possessive pronoun 'its' in the first sentence. The only singular noun that implies a group of musicians in the answer choices is (A). The second question is asking which of the answer choices denotes recognition for an achievement. The adjective modifying the underlined part, 'numerous', is plural, so the noun should also be plural. For the third question, the subject is 'members' and thus plural. The most concise answer is (B).

Practice Questions

Change the underlined noun to the correct form if necessary.

1. Boxing champion Travis King considers three <u>opponents</u> powerful enough to provide him with a challenge. <u>No error</u>

2. Fast food such as hamburgers, and processed meats such as bacon and sausage, are just two <u>examples</u> of food guaranteed to cause your cholesterol level to skyrocket. <u>No error</u>

3. "Counter-Strike" and "Call of Duty" seem like <u>an easy computer game</u> to play, but they actually take hours and days to completely master. <u>No error</u>

4. All five of Liam's childhood friends became <u>a doctor</u>; Liam became a stand-up comedian. <u>No error</u>

5. Isaac Newton and Albert Einstein were both <u>a scientist</u> that innovated the field of physics one step further. <u>No error</u>

6. Instagram and Snapchat are just two <u>mean</u> to let your friends see your photographs the moment you take them.
   A) NO CHANGE
   B) method
   C) ways
   D) technique

7. Although Luna usually enjoyed her celebrity status, there were times she dreaded passing through crowds of <u>fan.</u>
   A) NO CHANGE
   B) supporter.
   C) devotee.
   D) admirers.

8. "I first met your mother in the most unlikely <u>venues,</u>" their father said—"inside a patient's ward in a Bosnian hospital."
   A) NO CHANGE
   B) locations
   C) sites
   D) place

9. Alfonso and Bernadette were both <u>gourmets</u> who loved tasting new dishes cooked with various exotic ingredients.

    A) NO CHANGE
    B) epicure
    C) connoisseur
    D) gastronome

10. The professional gamers, who are both <u>ranker</u> in the AOS genre, vowed to make Korea's name shine in the upcoming international match.

    A) NO CHANGE
    B) top player
    C) veteran
    D) experts

Chapter Test

Passage 1

Choose the answer that best replaces the underlined part:

The analytic critic and the casual listener often engage in heated debates as to which artist did what first. Some debates are easily settled – most people involved in music <u>agree</u>₁ that The Kinks played the first hard rock <u>songs</u>₂, with its searing *You Really Got Me*, that The Velvet Underground first harmonized noisy dissonance with mellifluous tunes, and that Bob Dylan pioneered the incorporation of grating social commentary and political criticism into music. However, musical historians break bones and spit blood as to who first invented rock and roll. Many point to a myriad of recordings in the 1940s that went quietly unnoticed, while still others point as far back to 1920 blues in which, they argue, the first seeds of the genre <u>was</u>₃ sown.

1. A) NO CHANGE
   B) agrees
   C) is in agreement
   D) were agreeing

2. A) NO CHANGE
   B) song
   C) musics
   D) melodies

3. A) NO CHANGE
   B) is
   C) had been
   D) were

Passage 2

Choose the answer that best replaces the underlined part:

Great works of literature <u>is</u>₄ often subjected to filmographic representations. Mary Shelley's *Frankenstein* came to life by the hands of James Whale in 1931, and Anthony Burgess' *A Clockwork Orange* became an ultraviolent hit when Stanley Kubrick cast it on the silver screen in 1971. However, one endearing classic that has yet to hit the cinemas is J.D. Salinger's *The Catcher in the Rye*. The relentless director and the clamoring fans <u>wasn't</u>₅ able to change the tenacious author's mind as Salinger refused, even up to his death, to agree to a movie about teenage angst that would surely be, in the words of Holden Caulfield, phony.

4. A) NO CHANGE
   B) is notable for
   C) are
   D) was

5. A) NO CHANGE
   B) isn't
   C) weren't
   D) had success to be

Passage 3

Choose the answer that best replaces the underlined part:

Studies show that drivers distracted by text messaging causes₆ a greater number of accident₇ than drivers under the influence of alcohol. Researchers monitored drivers on a closed course and found that the texting drivers performed worse than the drunk ones. Many texting drivers were unable to pay much attention to the obstacles, while the drunken ones could exert just a modicum of concentration. The lesson? Drunk driving is bad, but driving with phones in our hands are₈ equally bad, if not worse!

6. A) NO CHANGE
   B) is causing
   C) had caused
   D) cause

7. A) NO CHANGE
   B) incident
   C) crash
   D) accidents

8. A) NO CHANGE
   B) hand are
   C) hands is
   D) hands were

Passage 4

Choose the answer that best replaces the underlined part:

Many Americans tend to discard fish heads, preferring to dine upon a platter of faceless meat. What we don't know is that the heads of fish has₉ a wonderfully savory taste to placate our taste buds! Every fish head contain₁₀ bountiful amounts of valuable fillets encased in the cheeks, forehead, and collar. Some even find joy in sucking at the eyes! If you have a problem with eating a face off, then keep in mind that fish heads also make excellent stock. These fish heads are the truly marginalized treasure₁₁ of meat.

9. A) NO CHANGE
   B) had
   C) is
   D) have

10. A) NO CHANGE
    B) contains
    C) are containing
    D) were containing

11. A) NO CHANGE
    B) jewel
    C) item
    D) treasures

Passage 5

Choose the answer that best replaces the underlined part:

Many researchers have been₁₂ perplexed for decades by the lack of vitamin C production in humans. Most members of the animal kingdom are able to create their own vitamin C, but most primates as well as us homo sapiens lacks₁₃ the ability to do so. Even stranger is the fact that we clearly possess the gene that allows for the synthesis of the essential vitamin.

12. A) NO CHANGE
    B) are
    C) has been
    D) was

13. A) NO CHANGE
    B) lacking
    C) lack
    D) have lacked

2 Pronouns

2-1. Pronoun Agreement

One-Point Lesson

Always pay attention to the **plurality** of the original noun that the pronoun indicates (the antecedent).

	Person	Thing
Singular	He/She	It
Plural	They	They

Tip: Even when a pronoun is not used, always pay attention to the **number agreement of nouns** within a sentence.
Example 1: I have two sons, and he is a doctor. (×)
   he is a doctor → they are doctors

Example 2: My mechanical keyboard is very expensive, but they are worth the price. (×)
   they are → it is

SAT-Style Example

Choose the answer that best replaces the underlined part:

John Stuart Mill is commonly regarded as the founder of utilitarianism. Adapting the hedonistic characteristics of Bentham's philosophy, they believed₁ that a morally appropriate action was one that resulted in the greatest happiness for the greatest number of individuals. One common criticism against such thinking was that the theory was "a doctrine only worthy of swine," since it did₂ not recognize the greater worth of some nobler pleasures, such as poetry and art. Mill counters this argument in his book by noting that intellectual pleasures are superior to physical ones.

1. A) NO CHANGE
   B) he believed
   C) we believed
   D) it believed

2. A) NO CHANGE
   B) since they did
   C) since he did
   D) since them did

Explanation:

The correct answers are (B) and (A).

You must be able to find the antecedent for each pronoun.

For the first question, you can see that the pronoun should be referring to 'John Stuart Mill,' so the pronoun 'they' is wrong. Therefore, the answer is (B).

For the second question, the pronoun should be referring to the 'theory,' so the right pronoun 'it' is used. Therefore, the answer is (A).

Practice Questions

Change the underlined noun to the correct form if necessary.

1. The white alligator greatly increased the amount of patrons for the zoo, for they had never been seen in the city before. No error

2. In the past, office position often required unskilled labor, and they did not require new employees to possess a university education. No error

3. Economic depressions, like a recession, a downturn, or any other period of negative growth, can be identified by both the length and severity of its effects. No error

4. Economic development was prevented by the country's high rate of taxation, and so now the nation is attaining its maximal rate of growth. No error

5. By analyzing soil layers to ascertain the rate of Yellowstone volcanic eruption throughout history, geologists have estimated that they happen once every 280,000 years. No error

6. When the taxi driver suddenly said "Yes, I'll be home for dinner," Emmet realized with embarrassment that he was talking on the phone and not to them.
    A) NO CHANGE
    B) Alfred
    C) Emmet and Alfred
    D) DELETE the underlined portion.

7. Sometimes, babysitters use TV shows to keep the kids quiet because the children love watching them.
    A) NO CHANGE
    B) an entertainment channel
    C) a TV show
    D) DELETE the underlined portion.

8. When McDonald's <u>packets</u> of burgers and fries arrived at my house, I called my friend to share it.
- A) NO CHANGE
- B) packages
- C) delivery
- D) containers

9. Universal Studios Florida, a world famous theme park, was my <u>niece's</u> number one choice as the location for the celebration of his 10th birthday.
- A) NO CHANGE
- B) nephew's
- C) protegees'
- D) cousins'

10. <u>Every member</u> of Wizard's Duel Club fidgeted nervously and made sure he brought his wand to the first practice.
- A) NO CHANGE
- B) All
- C) All the members
- D) DELETE the underlined portion.

2-2. Pronoun case

One-Point Lesson

The most typical pronouns have several cases: the **subjective, objective, possessive adjective**, and **possessive pronoun**.

Subjective Pronoun	Objective Pronoun	Possessive Adjective	Possessive Pronoun
I / We	Me / Us	My / Our	Mine / Ours
You	You	Your	Yours
He / She / They	Him / Her / Them	His / Her / Their	His / Hers / Theirs
It / They	It / Them	Its / Their	Its / Theirs

Here are some key tips to help you select the right cases:

1. Look at the **Verb**
2. Look at the **Preposition**
3. Try omitting "**Noun and**"
4. Use the **Possessive adjective** when there is an "**-ing**"
5. Try separating a comparison sentence into two
6. "It is I"

The SAT frequently tests you on telling **possessive adjectives** and **possessive pronouns** apart. The difference is that possessive **adjectives** cannot act as nouns on their own. They are used alongside nouns to indicate that the noun is in possession of someone. However, possessive **pronouns** are used to indicate both the **object that is in possession** and the **entity that possesses the object**.

Let's look at some examples to clarify:

Example 1: I found <u>he</u> stupid. (×)
  he → him
  The verb, 'found' needs an object. Therefore, use the objective case, 'him.'

Example 2: Everyone except <u>I</u> will attend. (×)
  I → me
  The preposition, 'except' needs an object. Therefore, use the objective case, 'me.'

Example 3: The purple gift box is yours, but the yellow one is <u>mine</u> present. (×)
  mine → my
  'mine' can only be used when there is no noun after it, because it is a pronoun used to refer to the noun itself. A possessive adjective, 'my' must be used.

SAT-Style Example

Choose the answer that best replaces the underlined part:

Many fans consider film adaptations of their favorite novels and comic books disappointing at best. I myself am a fan of the Harry Potter series, but <u>between you and I, I find them</u>₁ quite horribly depicted on screen. I see nothing wrong with the creative interpretations of the original series, but if the movie-makers ignore the author's original intent, then I would find <u>theirs portrayals</u>₂ not appropriate at all.

1. A) NO CHANGE
   B) between you and me, I find them
   C) between you and I, I find they
   D) between you and they, I find they

2. A) NO CHANGE
   B) them portrayals
   C) its portrayals
   D) their portrayals

Explanation:
The correct answers are (B) and (D).
Always remember the 6 things to look for when dealing with pronouns.
For the first question, you can see the preposition, 'between.' Therefore, what comes after must be an object, so it has to be 'you and me.' You can also see the verb, 'find,' which needs an object as well. Therefore, 'them' should follow the verb. Therefore, the correct answer is (B).
For the second question, it can be inferred that 'portrayals' needs to be in possession of the 'movie-makers.' Since movie-makers is in the third person plural, we need to use some form of 'they.' Since the noun 'portrayals' is already present, it makes sense to use the possessive adjective, and not the possessive pronoun. Therefore, the correct answer is (D).

Practice Questions

Correct any errors, if present, for the underlined word in the sentence below.

1. Films by Christopher Nolan are known for <u>theirs</u> amazing plot—or scale, depending on what film you're watching. <u>No error</u>

2. I don't have any problem with my own work, but I do think the public will prefer <u>your</u> to mine. <u>No error</u>

3. Critics evaluating the output of director Wes Anderson have become more and more aware of the level of collaboration between his stable of actors and <u>he</u>. <u>No error</u>

4. When we went hiking last fall, my brother and <u>me</u> ran into a grizzly bear. <u>No error</u>

5. Graham's book was dedicated to <u>she</u>, who unwaveringly supported his literary endeavors throughout their marriage. <u>No error</u>

6. The day after Valentine's Day is <u>mine</u> favorite day of the year, as remaining chocolates from the previous day are sold at lower prices.
    A) NO CHANGE
    B) me
    C) my
    D) it's

7. Stephen King's novels are characterized by <u>theirs</u> meticulous details and eerie plots, often featuring supernatural creatures or real-life dangers.
    A) NO CHANGE
    B) its
    C) their
    D) it's

8. There is no community of interests between <u>he</u> and her; they are enemies.
    A) NO CHANGE
    B) his
    C) him
    D) she

9. Everyone except <u>I</u> will attend the meeting scheduled at 2PM.
    A) NO CHANGE
    B) my
    C) me
    D) mine

10. Although Jason borrowed the book from Jane only a week ago, he couldn't remember that it belonged to <u>she</u>.
    A) NO CHANGE
    B) her
    C) she's
    D) he

2-3. Pronoun Shift

One-Point Lesson

Often, SAT Writing questions try to confuse you by using the wrong pronoun case or perspective. You should always be aware of **Perspective** changes and **Case** changes to figure out the right antecedent.

Perspective	Subjective	Objective	Possessive
1st Person	I / We	Me / Us	My / Our
2nd Person	You	You	Your
3rd Person	He / She / They	Him / Her / Them	His / Her / Their
Impersonal	It / They	It / Them	Its / Their

Example 1: If a student wants to study for the SAT, you should read this book. (✗)
  you → he or she

Example 2: Mike bought some apples but it dropped them on the ground. (✗)
  it dropped them → he dropped them
  Be careful of what noun each pronoun is referring to.
  So in this case, **Mike** bought **apples**, but **he** dropped **them** on the ground.

SAT-Style Example

Choose the answer that best replaces the underlined part:

"Breaking Bad" is a commonly used expression in the American Southwest to refer to someone who has deviated from the right path. Hence, it would be fair to say that a cancer-ridden chemistry teacher, who decides to turn into a drug dealer by producing and selling crystal meth, is breaking bad in <u>its life. This,</u>₁ of course, is the description of the main character in the popular TV series, *Breaking Bad*. <u>It aired for 6 years, with their</u>₂ fifth and final season among the most watched cable shows. The thrilling crime drama is regarded as one of the best TV shows of all time, and it holds the Guinness World Record for highest rated show ever.

1. A) NO CHANGE
   B) their life. This,
   C) his life. This,
   D) their lives. This,

2. A) NO CHANGE
   B) It aired for 6 years, with them
   C) They aired for 6 years, with its
   D) It aired for 6 years, with its

Explanation:

The correct answers are (C) and (D).

You should pay attention to the change of pronoun cases along with the perspective shifts.

For the first question, the subject of the long sentence is 'chemistry teacher,' and he is 'breaking bad.' Therefore, it should be a person's life, and the pronoun should be 'his.' Therefore, the correct answer is (C).

For the second question, the TV series, *Breaking Bad* is the antecedent. Therefore, 'it' should be used and 'its' season should be the subject. Therefore, the correct answer is (D).

Practice Questions

Correct any errors, if present, for the underlined word in the sentence below.

1. The ability to manage our willpower is a skill, studies have found, that we can exercise if <u>you</u> wish to end bad habits or make major life changes. <u>No error</u>

2. To understand classical music, <u>we</u> must be sufficiently exposed to Haydn and Mozart, whether one enjoys them or not. <u>No error</u>

3. Students in a class learn as much as they can during a school year but often forget a large amount of knowledge during <u>our</u> summer vacation. <u>No error</u>

4. It would be much more fun for you and me to drive together to the wedding than for each of <u>them</u> to fly separately. <u>No error</u>

5. Once *Seinfeld* made its debut, other television shows began to take on a tone of ironic detachment similar to <u>his</u> tone. <u>No error</u>

6. Seeing the flashing lights of the police cars, Jonathan, Denise and I were so startled that <u>they</u> ran out of the park at once.
    A) NO CHANGE
    B) we
    C) she
    D) us

7. When you are preparing for a job interview, <u>they</u> must be aware of the company's history.
    A) NO CHANGE
    B) one
    C) you
    D) your

8. According to behavioral psychologists, we feel a need to reward ourselves and recharge our willpower; therefore, they overcompensate with treats after an exercise.

   A) NO CHANGE
   B) we
   C) us
   D) them

9. My new coworkers are the most welcoming people I have ever met, and my main hobbies, sports and music are similar to theirs.

   A) NO CHANGE
   B) yours
   C) his
   D) ours

10. As the park ranger escorted us through the park, he told stories about his own explorations of the forest, giving you interesting additional background.

    A) NO CHANGE
    B) your
    C) we
    D) us

2-4. Ambiguous Pronoun

One-Point Lesson

Ambiguity in pronouns can be solved by simply being "**clear**."
It is considered ambiguous when there is no **antecedent** in the sentence or when you **cannot figure out what the exact antecedent is**.

Let's look at a few examples:

Example 1: I like Mexican culture because I have been there. (×)
    'Mexico' is never mentioned; only the 'culture' is mentioned. Therefore, assuming 'there'
    to be 'Mexico' is an ambiguity problem.

Example 2: I like Tom and John because he's kind to me. (×)
    Even though 'Tom' and 'John' is mentioned, you cannot figure out who exactly 'he' is indicating.

SAT-Style Example

Choose the answer that best replaces the underlined part:

As a kid, I wanted to be remembered for generations like Buddy Rich or Elvin Jones; he was practically$_1$ a God of Drums to me. However, fate played its part. On a family trip, I broke my wrist and could not play the drums for weeks. During that time, I gained an interest in studying Roman culture, and as of now, I'm planning a backpacking trip there.$_2$ Who knows, maybe I could have gone on to play in front of a crowd of thousands at Carnegie Hall. However, I can safely say that I am perfectly satisfied at being one of the thousands, simply appreciating the music instead.

1. A) NO CHANGE
   B) it was practically
   C) they were practically
   D) Elvin Jones was practically

2. A) NO CHANGE
   B) trip to Italy.
   C) there.
   D) trip over there.

Explanation:
The correct answers are (D) and (B).
Both questions are typical pronoun ambiguity problems that relate to the context, so keep an eye out for hints in context nearby.
For the first problem, the pronoun could refer to not only 'Buddy Rich' or 'Elvin Jones' but also to them both. Therefore, the answers are narrowed down to (C) and (D). However, if you see the next part, 'a God of Drums', notice the 'God' is singular. Therefore, the pronoun should refer to a singular noun. The answer is (D).

For the second problem, you can infer that the author is taking a backpacking trip somewhere related to 'Roman culture.' However, there is no actual mention of any specific 'place' related to Roman culture in the passage. Therefore, the pronoun is ambiguous, and the clearest mention of the 'place' — 'Italy' — is in (B).

Practice Questions

The underlined pronoun makes the sentence ambiguous. Change it so that the ambiguity is reduced.

1. Suzie and Charlotte are not here because <u>she</u> is at the doctor's office. <u>No error</u>

2. Bill can't find his keys and his wallet after leaving <u>it</u> in the taxi. <u>No error</u>

3. Someday I will go to Paris because I have always wanted to go <u>there.</u> <u>No error</u>

4. Susan, Bill, and Charlie stayed at the office because <u>he</u> had some work to do. <u>No error</u>

5. When Darla and Marie went to the post office, <u>she</u> noticed that the lobby had been cleaned and that their favorite stamps were no longer being offered. <u>No error</u>

6. Peter Hwang and Jake Yoo showed up at the premiere for the newly released movie "Veteran." <u>He</u> voiced his excitement for the film and encouraged his fans to support it.
    A) NO CHANGE
    B) Hwang
    C) The actor
    D) The man

7. Daniel and Prahlad complemented each other on their presentations for which they both chose Abraham Lincoln as the topic. However, <u>he</u> later told his parents that the teacher liked his presentation more.
    A) NO CHANGE
    B) the boy
    C) Daniel
    D) one

8. Kendra and her sister looked very similar except for one major difference; <u>she</u> had dyed her hair blonde.
    A) NO CHANGE
    B) a sister
    C) the female
    D) Kendra

9. Principal Hendricks did a survey on the students' satisfaction with the current teaching staff, and Principal Howard personally interviewed over a dozen teachers to recruit the best men or women for the job. <u>His</u> efforts were crucial for making this school as renowned as it is today.

- A) NO CHANGE
- B) Their
- C) This Principal's
- D) The later Principal's

10. Although watching a documentary and studying for an exam are both equally boring, <u>it</u> is arguably more rewarding.

- A) NO CHANGE
- B) studying for an exam
- C) that activity
- D) the one

2-5. Relative Pronouns

One-Point Lesson

Relative Pronouns **relate** the **relative clause** to the precedent they modify.

Like all pronouns, relative pronouns have various cases:

	Person	Place	Time	Thing
Subjective	Who / That	Where	When	Which / That
Objective	Who / Whom / That	Where	When	Which / That
Possessive	Whose	Of which / Whose / In which		

Note that relative pronouns can act as **conjunctions**, which we will focus on more later in the book. Let's look at some examples on how to use the relative pronouns.

Example 1: The thief, <u>when</u> escaped through the window, left his fingerprints all over the place. (✗)

when → who

Because the thief is a person, use 'who.'

Example 2: Laura, <u>which favorite thing to do</u> is eating ice-cream, had a severe toothache. (✗)

which → whose

the pronoun should refer to Laura's 'favorite thing to do.' Therefore, use 'whose.'

SAT-Style Example

Choose the answer that best replaces the underlined part:

Pluto was stripped of its title as a planet in 2006. In order for a celestial body to be considered a planet, it must pass the qualification <u>that it</u>₁ must not be under any other gravitational force other than the star it's revolving around. Pluto is currently classified as one of many dwarf planets in the outer Solar System. With a radius of approximately about 750 miles, <u>who is</u>₂ roughly one-fifth the size of Earth's, Pluto is indeed a modest celestial body. However, should the official definition change, it is plausible that Pluto will be reinstated as a planet.

1. A) NO CHANGE
   B) when it
   C) who it
   D) where it

2. A) NO CHANGE
   B) in which is
   C) which is
   D) where is

Explanation:

The correct answers are (A) and (C).

If you know what type of pronoun should be used for each antecedent, you should be able to solve these easily.

For the first question, the antecedent is 'qualification.' Therefore, 'that' can be used in this case. Answer is (A).

For the second question, the antecedent is 'radius.' Therefore, 'who' cannot be used, and 'which' should be used. Answer is (C).

Practice Questions

Correct any errors, if present, for the underlined word in the sentence below.

1. At the end of the championship game, the coach congratulated the players <u>which</u> had given the most effort. <u>No error</u>

2. Metal moveable type, thought to have come into existence in Korea, came into use around 1450 in Germany, <u>where</u> the sudden wide availability of information eventually led to social upheaval. <u>No error</u>

3. We peered out of the window of the news helicopter, <u>who</u> flew over a massive flood of the Mississippi river washing away efforts to contain it. <u>No error</u>

4. Renowned 19th century naturalist John Muir, <u>which</u> advocated for the preservation of the natural resources of the United states, was the founder of the Sierra Club. <u>No error</u>

5. Prior to the linking of the North and South American continents, the species of South America exhibited a dazzling amount of biodiversity - much of <u>which</u> would soon be lost to resource competition. <u>No error</u>

6. Instead of travelling the world, Jake had to make do with visiting Las Vegas, <u>where</u> replicas of world's famous structures can be found.
    A) NO CHANGE
    B) but
    C) wherever
    D) although

7. Seoul appeared in the film "Avengers: Age of Ultron", <u>which</u> it became a stage for the Avengers to fight Ultron for the Mind Gem.
    A) NO CHANGE
    B) wherever
    C) whereas
    D) where

8. *Carrie*, written by Stephen King, is the story of a telekinetic girl <u>whom</u> faces a nightmare at the school prom due to unfortunate happenings.

   A) NO CHANGE
   B) she
   C) who
   D) which

9. Gravitational waves, predicted by Einstein in 1916, were finally detected by scientists observing a region of space <u>in which</u> two black holes collided and merged into one.

   A) NO CHANGE
   B) and where
   C) which
   D) OMIT the underlined portion

10. America was originally inhabited by the Native Americans <u>from which</u> the settlers took away their home and built the United States of America.

    A) NO CHANGE
    B) from whom
    C) by them
    D) from who

Chapter Test

Passage 1

Choose the answer that best replaces the underlined part:

Prosopagnosia is a psychological condition in which you are unable to recognize faces already in <u>yours</u>₁ memory. Cases of this disorder were documented as early as the 19th century, including the case studies by John Hughlings Jackson and Jean-Martin Charcot. The term "prosopagnosia" was first coined by Joachim Bodamer, a German neurologist, <u>who put</u>₂ together "prosopon," meaning "face" in Greek, and "agnosia," meaning "non-knowledge." The study of prosopagnosia has been crucial to the development of face perception and <u>it</u>₃ implications in modern cognitive psychology.

1. A) NO CHANGE
   B) one's
   C) your
   D) my

2. A) NO CHANGE
   B) whom put
   C) which put
   D) in which put

3. A) NO CHANGE
   B) them
   C) his
   D) its

Passage 2

Choose the answer that best replaces the underlined part:

Hemingway was raised in Oak Park, Illinois and left for the Italian Front to enlist in World War I. Based on <u>him war experiences, he</u>₄ wrote the famous novel *A Farewell to Arms* in 1929. In 1952, after the second World War, he published *The Old Man and the Sea* and went on to safari Africa. That was when he was almost killed in two plane crashes <u>that left him</u>₅ in pain for the rest of his life. In the end, in the summer of 1961, Hemingway committed suicide, a tragic death for the literary genius.

4. A) NO CHANGE
   B) he war experiences, he
   C) his war experiences, he
   D) their war experiences, he

5. A) NO CHANGE
   B) in which left him
   C) who left him
   D) where left him

Passage 3

Choose the answer that best replaces the underlined part:

Many people believe in the existence of Atlantis, the lost ancient civilization mentioned in Plato and Solon's dialogues, *Timaeus* and *Critias*. Although he had₆ supposedly mentioned the existence of the civilization, one crucial question is yet to be answered: Where was it located? The most popular theory is that the City is under the Mediterranean Sea near Crete and Santorini in Greece, as inferred from Solon and Plato's dialogue. Since they are₇ quite likely that Greek people were fully aware of volcanoes and it₈ effects, this is considered the most probable theory to where Atlantis is.

6. A) NO CHANGE
   B) them had
   C) it had
   D) Plato had

7. A) NO CHANGE
   B) he is
   C) it is
   D) they were

8. A) NO CHANGE
   B) their
   C) his
   D) them

Passage 4

Choose the answer that best replaces the underlined part:

An infamous series of experiments conducted in the 1950s by Solomon Asch provided a shocking revelation on the human tendency to conform. In the experiments, they were₉ brought into a room full of actors playing the role of other participants. Then, the participants were asked to make a simple perceptual judgment — to figure out which line, of three vertical lines varying in length, was of the same length as a target line. Surprisingly, when all the other actor-participants gave blatantly wrong answers, actual participants went along with the consensus, instead of following theirs₁₀ own judgment.

9. A) NO CHANGE
   B) participants were
   C) he was
   D) they had been

10. A) NO CHANGE
    B) their
    C) its
    D) one's

Passage 5

Choose the answer that best replaces the underlined part:

There were many scientists and mathematicians who contributed to modern computer science, but Alan Turing was arguably the most influential one among them. He$_{11}$ introduced the principles of modern computer technology and it$_{12}$ insisted that if a computing machine is presented with a representable algorithm for a task, then it is$_{13}$ capable of performing that task through set mathematical computations. This breakthrough ultimately led to the advent of digital computation and electronic data processing.

11. A) NO CHANGE
    B) they. He
    C) them. They
    D) they. Him

12. A) NO CHANGE
    B) they
    C) he
    D) them

13. A) NO CHANGE
    B) one is
    C) he is
    D) they are

3 Parallelism

One-Point Lesson
To ensure that a sentence or phrase follows a parallel structure, check to see if the articles in the sentence are all of the same form. Articles can be quite varied, ranging from gerunds (words that end with –ing) to to-infinitives (verbs with 'to' before them).

Example 1: My wife is good at running, writing, and <u>she also excels in saving money</u>. (×)
   she also excels in saving money → saving money

Example 2: Darcy, whom Elizabeth initially despised, is a man of solitude, sophistication, and <u>he is kind, too</u>. (×)
   he is kind, too → kindness

Example 3: Send me your reply by mail, <u>fax</u>, or <u>by text</u>. (×)
   fax → by fax **OR** by text → text
   Changing 'fax' to 'by fax' ensures that every article has 'by' before it, maintaining a parallel structure. *Alternatively,* changing 'by text' to 'text' also ensures that every article is parallel, as the 'by' before 'mail' can collectively refer to 'mail,' 'fax,' and 'text.'

SAT-Style Example

Choose the answer that best replaces the underlined part:

A dog barks, a cat meows, and <u>the cow goes moo</u>$_1$. But what does the fox say? The comedy duo Ylvis raised this interesting question in its hit single *The Fox*. Listeners may be surprised to find out that the fox does not say 'ring-ding-ding' or 'hatee-hatee-hatee-ho' in rapid succession. Rather, foxes communicate in yips, <u>barks, and they also howl</u>$_2$ — much like their canine relatives, the more familiar dogs.

1. A) NO CHANGE
   B) the cow moos
   C) cows moo
   D) a cow moos

2. A) NO CHANGE
   B) in barks, and howls
   C) barks, and howls
   D) barks, and in howls

Explanation:

The correct answers are (D) and (C).

For the first question, 'the cow goes moo' is not parallel with the preceding two articles, which contain 'a' and lack 'goes.' Therefore, the answer is (D).

For the second question, the articles must follow the format of either 'yips' or 'in yips'. (B) and (D) may seem correct, but if you are going to add 'in' in front of the articles, make sure you add it for all the articles to maintain a parallel structure. (C) follows a parallel structure as it omits 'in' in front of the articles (remember, the 'in' in front of 'yips' can collectively refer to all three articles). Therefore, the answer is (C).

Practice Questions

Correct any errors, if present, for the underlined word in the sentence below.

1. Although her husband made promises both to take out the garbage and <u>make an attempt</u> to repair the leak in the bathroom, he failed to keep either of them a month later. <u>No error</u>

2. Cryptozoology, a science that investigates the origins of mythical and legendary beasts, helps cultures both understand their mysteries and <u>reconnecting</u> with their pasts. <u>No error</u>

3. The protesters' demands were boiled down to three: transparent government, fair play, and <u>to have them be pardoned</u> for public disturbances. <u>No error</u>

4. Voter participation in the United States might be increased by improving education, <u>facilitate</u> registration, and reforming outdated processes for voting and nominations. <u>No error</u>

5. It is a challenge to imagine what kinds of fears will be prevalent decades from now, as circumstances evolve and people either resolve or <u>they lose interest in</u> the important issues of today. <u>No error</u>

6. In order to prove their superiority, bullies usually resort to hitting, threatening, and <u>mock</u> their victims.
    A) NO CHANGE
    B) mocking
    C) they mock
    D) can mock

7. Juan aims to get good grades, to join a new club, and <u>finding</u> a girlfriend in his first semester of college.
    A) NO CHANGE
    B) will find
    C) find
    D) to find

8. After watching all four *Final Destination* films back to back, Sonja wanted nothing more than to call a friend, hug tightly onto her, and to whimper in terror.
    A) NO CHANGE
    B) she hugs
    C) hugging
    D) to hug

9. The process of planting, watering, and to grow a tree can take years.
    A) NO CHANGE
    B) growing
    C) grow
    D) growth

10. For her 18th birthday, Holly could not decide whether she should have a party, go travelling, or spending time at home quietly.
    A) NO CHANGE
    B) she should spend
    C) spend
    D) to spend

Chapter Test

Passage 1

Choose the answer that best replaces the underlined part:

A comedy should be light and entertaining, a drama should be deep and serious, and <u>action film should be non-stop explosions</u>₁. However, modern genres of cinema are not separated by such clear boundaries. Comedies produce tension by combining the amusing with the tragic, <u>melancholy is alleviated by dramas that fuse poignancy with the humorous</u>₂, and even action films halt chaos by marrying the exciting with the poetic. Concrete categorization becomes harder and harder as the lines distinguishing genres turn increasingly indistinct. It is far more important than ever for scriptwriters and directors to learn how to strike the perfect chord between <u>comedy and the drama</u>₃, action and meditation, and entertainment and art.

1. A) NO CHANGE
   B) a film with action elements should be filled with explosions
   C) an action film should be exhilarating and thrilling
   D) action film should be exhilarating and exploding

2. A) NO CHANGE
   B) dramas fuse poignancy with the humorous to alleviate melancholy
   C) poignancy is fused with the humorous by dramas to alleviate melancholy
   D) dramas alleviate melancholy by fusing the poignant with the humorous

3. A) NO CHANGE
   B) the comedic and the dramatic
   C) the comedy and the drama
   D) comedy and drama

Passage 2

Choose the answer that best replaces the underlined part:

One of the most influential directors of the late 20th century is Steven Spielberg. His films have reached people around the world and inspired countless artists with their rapid pacing, vivid imagery and <u>stories on the human condition</u>₄. His career has not been without missteps, however. Following the great success of *Close Encounters of the Third Kind* in 1977, he made the comedy *1941*, which was widely panned by critics, <u>by fans</u>₅, and casual moviegoers.

4. A) NO CHANGE
   B) humanitarian stories
   C) their human-based stories
   D) stories of human

5. A) NO CHANGE
   B) the fans
   C) his fans
   D) fans

Part I : Standard English Conventions | 45

Passage 3

Choose the answer that best replaces the underlined part:

My neighborhood places a great emphasis on color. Visitors often remark that the moment they turn the corner, they feel as if they've stepped into the world of Cream's *Disraeli Gears*, or Aldous Huxley's *A Door to Perception*, or <u>*Spirited Away* directed by Hayao Miyazaki</u>₆. We have green apartments, pink condominiums, and <u>we have blue bungalows</u>₇. Everything flashes with an intense burst of color — rainbow colored roads, splashy streets, and <u>walls painted whimsically</u>₈. In fact, the only colorless feature is a white room near the station.

6. A) NO CHANGE
   B) Hayao Miyazaki's *Spirited Away*
   C) the *Spirited Away*
   D) *Spirited Away*

7. A) NO CHANGE
   B) bungalows that are blue
   C) bluest bungalows
   D) blue bungalows

8. A) NO CHANGE
   B) walls that are whimsical
   C) whimsically painted walls
   D) walls

Passage 4

Choose the answer that best replaces the underlined part:

The African savannah is home to a wealth of fauna that are otherwise only in the flesh at zoos — lions, <u>the giraffes</u>₉, gazelles. Of them all, though, the most recognizable may just be the fashionable zebra. But is its fancy black and white coat simply for show? Zoologists have come up with several plausible functions, such as camouflaging themselves, communicating with each other, and <u>for the purpose of confusing their predators</u>₁₀. However, recent research suggests that the stripes actually decrease infections from fly bites, as flies find it harder to land on stripes.

9. A) NO CHANGE
   B) long-necked giraffes
   C) some giraffes
   D) giraffes

10. A) NO CHANGE
    B) predators are confused by them
    C) confusing predators
    D) confusion

Passage 5

Choose the answer that best replaces the underlined part:

Alexander Pope is, perhaps, one of the most celebrated poets in the history of literature. He often incorporated the satirical into his works, from poking fun at such trivial matters as cutting off a lock of hair in *The Rape of the Lock* to <u>lampooning both bad writing and bad criticism in *An Essay on Criticism*</u>₁₁. Less-known, however, are his translations of famous literary works — *The Illiad*, *The Odyssey*, and <u>also Shakespearean works</u>₁₂.

11. A) NO CHANGE
    B) *Essay on Criticism*'s lampooning of both bad writing and bad criticism
    C) bad writing and bad criticism lampooning in *Essay on Criticism*
    D) *Essay on Criticism* is well-lampooned

12. A) NO CHANGE
    B) Shakespearean works
    C) works by Shakespeare, too
    D) Shakespeare

4 Comparisons

4-1. Countable vs. Uncountable nouns

One-Point Lesson
Countable Nouns are nouns that can be counted, and have singular/plural forms.
Uncountable Nouns are nouns that cannot be divided into separate elements.
Always consider which type of noun is being compared, and apply the comparatives and superlatives accordingly:

Countable	Uncountable
Many	Much
Few / Fewer / Fewest	Little / Less / Least

Note that 'More' and 'Most' can be used for both countable and uncountable nouns.

Example 1: I have fewer courage than Andy. (×)
   fewer → less

Example 2: I have more money than Bob. (○)

SAT-Style Example

Choose the answer that best replaces the underlined part:

Much species₁ of the animal kingdom suffer from the introduction of a foreign species into their habitat, and such a phenomenon is one that can also be found amongst humans. The indigenous civilizations of Mesoamerica of the Aztec empire, ruled at the time by Montezuma, encountered Europeans for the first time in the 16th century. He welcomed the Spanish party and treated them as guests. However, many tension₂ resulted between him and the Aztec nobility, who frowned upon the fact that a large Spanish army was staying at Tlaxcalteca, the capital city. Eventually, the Aztec Empire was conquered by the Spanish with the help of smallpox, and Montezuma was killed.

1. A) NO CHANGE
   B) Many species
   C) Less species
   D) Least species

2. A) NO CHANGE
   B) few tension
   C) much tension
   D) least tension

Explanation:

The correct answers are (B) and (C).

Differentiating countable nouns and uncountable nouns is the key factor in solving these questions.

The first question is pretty straightforward; 'species' is the noun being modified, so 'much' cannot be used. Of the answer choices, 'many' is the only acceptable comparative, so the answer is (B).

The second question can be more complicated. 'tension' is the noun being modified, so 'many' cannot be used. 'few' is used for countable nouns, and is not a viable answer. 'least' is inappropriate because there is no comparison in the sentence. Therefore, the only available option is (C).

Practice Questions

Correct any errors, if present, for the underlined word in the sentence below.

1. There are <u>fewer</u> complex traffic problems. <u>No error</u>

2. There are <u>less</u> complex traffic problems. <u>No error</u>

3. The FBI has <u>few information</u> about the suspect who tried to bomb the White House. <u>No error</u>

4. As they must face significant competition from online retailers, the owners of record stores know that they are unlikely to make <u>many</u> money in the future. <u>No error</u>

5. The folk history of <u>much</u> cultures is based on non-scientific explanations for natural phenomena and an attempt to explain that which frightened them. <u>No error</u>

6. Unlike his contemporaries, who gained widespread fame and success, Van Gogh was able to sell only <u>little</u> paintings in his lifetime.
    A) NO CHANGE
    B) less
    C) few
    D) fewer

7. There are <u>much</u> songwriters who incorporate personal experience with evocative melodies.
    A) NO CHANGE
    B) many
    C) most
    D) little

8. In 1949, no <u>fewer</u> than 12 nations had signed on to NATO, a defensive alliance that styled itself as a deterrent to Soviet ambitions and provided political cover for US military actions abroad.
    A) NO CHANGE
    B) less
    C) little
    D) least

9. The US added <u>little</u> territories in area in the 1800s than in the 1700s.
    A) NO CHANGE
    B) less
    C) least
    D) fewer

10. In New Orleans and Chicago, the musicians named responsible for the origins of hip hop are <u>less</u> than those named responsible for the origins of jazz.
    A) NO CHANGE
    B) fewer
    C) little
    D) least

4-2. Logical Comparisons

One-Point Lesson

In a comparison, the things being compared must be **logically of equal value**.
Be aware of some of the comparative expressions other than 'than', since they might confuse you in the SAT.
　　ex) as, similar to, exceed, equal, match, etc.

Example 1: My <u>snoring</u> is probably louder than a <u>yeti</u>. (×)
　　yeti → yeti's
　　comparing 'snoring' is the case here, so 'yeti's (snoring)' is the right answer.

Example 2: My <u>SAT scores</u> exceed <u>Matt</u>. (×)
　　Matt → Matt's OR 'those of Matt'
　　You can also say 'that of' or 'those of' to imply possession.

SAT-Style Example

Choose the answer that best replaces the underlined part:

Numerous species have been driven to extinction owing to the arrival of human settlers. A good example of this occurred in New Zealand, when the Maori arrived in the 14th century. The number of bird species in the 14th century was far <u>greater than today</u>$_1$. Including the infamous moa, these exotic birds were hunted and their habitats were threatened due to deforestation. However, one type of bird that escaped extermination was the kiwi. The Maori traditionally believed that kiwis were under the protection of their god and as a result, their existence was more valued <u>than the other birds'</u>$_2$. Since then, the kiwi has become a national symbol.

1. A) NO CHANGE
   B) much than today's
   C) greater than today's
   D) more than today

2. A) NO CHANGE
   B) than the others
   C) than the other bird's
   D) than the other birds

Explanation:

The correct answers are (C) and (A).
Be sure to know what each comparison is referring to.
For the first question, the noun being compared is the 'number' of species. Therefore, the 'number' is greater than 'today's.'
The answer is (C).
For the second question, the noun being compared is the 'existence.' Therefore, the possessive case should be used here. Even though the 'existence' is being compared, various other birds' existence is being compared. Therefore, the plural possessive, 'birds'' should be used. The answer is (A).

Practice Questions

Correct any errors, if present, for the underlined word in the sentence below.

1. Unlike many <u>documentaries</u>, Michael Moore does not hide his political leanings. <u>No error</u>

2. Clothing made from synthetic materials is more durable than <u>natural materials</u>. <u>No error</u>

3. Everything in the play was so well done that it appeared more the production of a professional theater <u>than that of an amateur class</u>. <u>No error</u>

4. Traditionally, London's buses, <u>unlike New York City</u>, are more luxurious in their appearance, and generally more reliable, as well. <u>No error</u>

5. The Amazon Basin has many indigenous amphibians, one of which is smaller <u>than the size of a penny</u>. <u>No error</u>

6. Beowulf's group of great warriors slew more monsters than <u>a country.</u>
   A) NO CHANGE
   B) the armies of an entire country.
   C) a castle.
   D) the city of Danes.

7. If I had to compare the works of Van Gogh <u>and Picasso, I'd say Van Gogh's are best.</u>
   A) NO CHANGE
   B) to Picasso, I'd say Picasso's are best.
   C) to that of Picasso, I'd say Picasso's are better.
   D) to those of Picasso, I'd say Picasso's are better.

8. Many audience feel that Christopher Nolan's later films are grander in scale than <u>those produced at the beginning of his career.</u>
   A) NO CHANGE
   B) his early career as a film director.
   C) the money he invested in his early film.
   D) the time he spent previously on his movie.

9. The superpower countries stockpile nuclear weapons for power play rather than <u>insuring.</u>
   A) NO CHANGE
   B) insure.
   C) for insurance.
   D) to insure.

10. There's a debate about whether cigarettes or <u>using nicotine patches</u> are worse.

    A) NO CHANGE
    B) nicotine patches
    C) wearing nicotine patches
    D) the usage of nicotine patches

Chapter Test

Passage 1

Choose the answer that best replaces the underlined part:

Nobody likes to floss, but dentists say it is one of the most important things we can do to keep our teeth in healthy shape. Why is it more difficult to motivate people to floss than brushing their teeth daily₁? Part of the explanation may be in the fact that many people₂ are not confident that they are doing it correctly. It seems that many public₃ education may be necessary to turn flossing into a more widely accepted part of the daily bathroom ritual.

1. A) NO CHANGE
   B) to motivate them to brush their teeth daily
   C) for them to brush their teeth daily
   D) motivate people to brushing their teeth daily

2. A) NO CHANGE
   B) the most people
   C) more people
   D) much people

3. A) NO CHANGE
   B) many publics
   C) more public
   D) much publics

Passage 2

Choose the answer that best replaces the underlined part:

An increasing number of people all over the world are learning to appreciate coffee, more so than any other beverage₄ in history. Consumers in places that have no cultural history of the drink, such as Korea and Japan, are beginning to see it as a necessary part of the daily routine, and much₅ other places that have enjoyed it for hundreds of years, like Europe and North America, maintain their daily consumption and purchasing habits. Indeed, consumers everywhere see coffee as a luxury and a necessity simultaneously. Will it be possible for coffee growers to keep up the production?

4. A) NO CHANGE
   B) others
   C) other people
   D) those

5. A) NO CHANGE
   B) and many
   C) and more
   D) and less

Passage 3

Choose the answer that best replaces the underlined part:

Gestures are often thought to be universal, making it easy to communicate between cultures and languages. In much₆ cases, this is actually true. The sign for choking in a Paris restaurant is the same as an Indian hospital₇. This comes from biological necessity, since if people could not recognize someone in distress, then they wouldn't be able to help. However, some gestures widely thought to be universal actually have exceptions. For example, in Bulgaria and many other regions in the Mediterranean, a nod of the head signals an answer completely different from other nations₈. It signals 'no' instead of the expected 'yes'.

6. A) NO CHANGE
   B) many
   C) many most
   D) most many

7. A) NO CHANGE
   B) same as it of an Indian
   C) same as those of an Indian
   D) same as that of an Indian

8. A) NO CHANGE
   B) different from the gestures of other nations
   C) different from that of other nations
   D) different from the nod of other nations

Passage 4

Choose the answer that best replaces the underlined part:

In history, there are only a few events less₉ controversial than Columbus' arrival to America. When Christopher Columbus landed on Hispaniola, there was no way he could have been aware of the massive exchange of life that was about to take place. The "Columbian Exchange" was an exceptionally disruptive event to the world's ecosystem, comparable to the more recent era₁₀. Crops from the New World made their way everywhere: potatoes to Ireland, chili peppers to Asia, tobacco to the middle east. Animals and diseases came the other way, including cow and horses. Diseases endemic to the Old World killed more Native Americans, in fact, than killed by European warlords₁₁ seeking to conquer the New World civilizations.

9. A) NO CHANGE
   B) few events fewer
   C) less events less
   D) fewer events less

10. A) NO CHANGE
    B) comparable to the later days
    C) comparable to the events of the more recent era
    D) comparable to the ecosystem of the more recent era

11. A) NO CHANGE
    B) the European warlords
    C) the Native Americans killed by European warlords
    D) the number of European warlords

Passage 5

Choose the answer that best replaces the underlined part:

Is rock and roll dead? <u>Many most people</u>₁₂ would say yes, given the trends in popular consumption. The masses show a distinct preference for hip hop and electronic music <u>rather than the elements of rock and roll</u>₁₃. Things have never looked bleaker for the long-lived genre. There is still hope, however. Those who had claimed the death of a genre were often proven wrong. Other genres, such as industrial and new wave of the 80's, are continually being rediscovered by the later generations. Since rock and roll holds a more popular appeal <u>than industrial or new wave</u>₁₄, we could look forward to a resurgence of the genre in the future.

12. A) NO CHANGE
    B) Much
    C) Much most
    D) Many

13. A) NO CHANGE
    B) rather than rock and roll
    C) rather than the resemblance to rock and roll
    D) rather than rock and roll artists

14. A) NO CHANGE
    B) than the popularity of other genres
    C) than the popular appeal of industrial or new wave
    D) than the resurgence of industrial or new wave

5 Modifiers

5-1. Front Modifiers

One-Point Lesson

Front Modifiers modify the **Subject** and are placed at the beginning of the sentence. Make sure the modifier modifies the subject and nothing else.

Example 1: Walking across the sitting room, the television is turned off by me. (×)

    the television is turned off by me → I turned off the television

    The television is not the one walking across the sitting room, but rather I, the subject.

Example 2: This squirming dog must fetch my slippers under the control of my finger. (×)

    Under the control of my finger, this squirming dog must fetch my slippers.

    'Under the control of my finger' modifies the 'squirming dog,' not 'slippers,' and must therefore be placed at the front of the sentence to maintain an active voice.

Example 3: Despite adopting a healthy diet, Mark's weight still exceeds 250 pounds. (×)

    Mark's weight still exceeds → Mark still weighs more than

    The error here is not with placement, but rather, the logical subject to be modified. Mark adopts a healthy diet, not his weight.

SAT-Style Example

Choose the answer that best replaces the underlined part:

Aiding the recovery of our wounds since we were children, the band-aid's usage covers₁ just about every wound — from cuts to burns to bite marks. But few actually know the story behind the plaster. In 1921, Earle Dickson noticed that the cuts on his wife's fingers weren't healing properly because she was constantly injuring herself while cooking. Worried for his wife, the very first band-aid was invented by Earle₂ — a strip of tape sterilized in crinoline with a piece of gauze stuck to its center. It is perhaps heartwarmingly fitting that the humble invention was spurred not out of corporate greed but rather out of genuine compassion and concern for the well-being of a loved one.

1. A) NO CHANGE
   B) we use band-aids
   C) band-aids cover
   D) young people use band-aids

2. A) NO CHANGE
   B) Earle's very first band-aid was made
   C) Earle invented the very first band-aid
   D) the invention of the band-aid was done by Earle

Explanation:

The correct answers are (C) and (C).

For the first question, band-aids are what have been 'aiding... our wounds,' not 'the band-aid's usage.' The subject 'band-aids' should be placed at the front of the phrase. Therefore, the answer is (C).

For the second question, Earle was the one who was concerned for his wife, not 'the very first band-aid.' The subject 'Earle' should be at the front of the phrase. Therefore, the answer is (C).

Practice Questions

1. Despite John telling him to stop, <u>the mailman was continuously terrorized by Garfield.</u>

   A) NO CHANGE

   B) the postman was scared by Garfield the cat.

   C) the postal carrier was terrorized by Garfield.

   D) Garfield continued to terrorize the mailman.

2. Shocked and curious, <u>the giant they had found was examined cautiously by the Lilliputians as they tied him up.</u>

   A) NO CHANGE

   B) the Lilliputians tied up and cautiously examined the giant they had found.

   C) an examination was needed as the Lilliputians tied up the giant they had found.

   D) the finding of the giant led the Lilliputians to tie him up and examine.

3. Mesmerized by the girl in a mini-skirt, <u>Joshua failed to hear his friend calling his name.</u>

   A) NO CHANGE

   B) the call of his friend was unheard by Joshua.

   C) Joshua's ears failed to catch his friend's call.

   D) everyone saw Joshua failing to hear his friend calling his name.

4. First published in 1997 as Harry Potter and the Philosopher's Stone, <u>generations of ardent fans have followed the book and its sequels.</u>

   A) NO CHANGE

   B) ardent fans have followed the book and its sequels for generations.

   C) the book and its sequels have raised an ardent following for generations.

   D) the following of the book and its sequels have risen over the generations with an ardent fan base.

5. Not carefully watching the clock, <u>there was not enough time for the instructor to completely describe the process for turning off the device.</u>

   A) NO CHANGE

   B) the instructor did not have enough time to completely describe the process for turning off the device.

   C) the process for turning off the device was not completely described by the instructor due to the lack of time.

   D) there was not enough time for the process for turning off the device to be completely described by the instructor.

6. Peering out the window of the news helicopter, the Mississippi River and its massive flood washing away efforts to contain it.

   A) NO CHANGE
   B) the efforts to contain a massive flood of the Mississippi River was washed away.
   C) a massive flood of the Mississippi River was seen washing away efforts to contain it.
   D) we saw a massive flood of the Mississippi River washing away efforts to contain it.

7. While long believed to have a limited ability for consciousness, the chimpanzee, some researchers now think, may have higher cognitive functions than previously suspected.

   A) NO CHANGE
   B) some researchers now think the chimpanzee may have higher cognitive functions than previously suspected.
   C) cognitive functions of chimpanzees may be higher than previously suspected by some researchers.
   D) some researchers may have higher cognitive functions than previously suspected the chimpanzee.

8. Though usually about serious themes and situations, with an eye for humor and humanity are Coen brothers' movies directed.

   A) NO CHANGE
   B) directed with an eye for humor and humanity the Coen brothers' movies are.
   C) the Coen brothers' movies are directed with an eye for humor and humanity.
   D) the Coen brothers direct their movies with an eye for humor and humanity.

9. By challenging outright the sensibilities and tolerances of the industry he was a part of, Johnny Cash's iconoclasm was a distinctive impact.

   A) NO CHANGE
   B) the iconoclastic Johnny Cash left a distinctive impact.
   C) distinctive impact was left by Johnny Cash's iconoclasm.
   D) iconoclasm of Johnny Cash left a distinctive impact.

10. Only after driving it for a few days, felt comfortable with the new car did I.

    A) NO CHANGE
    B) days did a feeling of comfort was given to me by the car.
    C) days did the new car begin to feel comfortable to me.
    D) days did I begin to feel comfortable with the new car.

5-2 Back Modifier

One-Point Lesson

Back Modifiers modify the **Object** and are placed at the end of the sentence.

Be aware, however, that the following two structures are both grammatically correct.

SVO + Incomplete Phrase: The Incomplete Phrase here acts as a **modifier**.

SVO**,** + Incomplete Phrase: The Incomplete Phrase here **provides additional information**.

Let's look at these in more detail in the examples:

Example 1: I found my key <u>walking</u> through the parking lot. (✗)

　　　walking → while I was walking

　　　Since there is no comma here, the incomplete phrase 'walking through the parking lot' acts as a modifier. A key cannot walk through the parking lot.

Example 2: I failed the tests, making my parents angry. (○)

　　　Since there is a comma here, the incomplete phrase 'making my parents angry' provides additional information, rather than actually modifying the object 'tests.'

Example 3: <u>Excitedly wagging her tail as she licked her owner's face, Winona greeted her ecstatic German Shepherd, Samantha.</u> (✗)

　　　Winona greeted her ecstatic German Shepherd, Star, who was excitedly wagging her tail as she licked her owner's face. 'Excitedly wagging… face' modifies the dog Star, not Winona, and must therefore be placed at the back of the sentence to maintain an active voice.

Example 4: Mrs. Tate was greatly disappointed in <u>her son's wrongdoings</u>, who stole money from a blind man. (✗)

　　　her son's wrongdoings → her son

　　　The error here is not with placement, but rather, the logical object to be modified. Mrs. Tate's son stole money from a blind man, not his wrongdoings.

SAT-Style Example

Choose the answer that best replaces the underlined part:

I love raiding the fridge and using the loot from my plunder to cook up something new and wacky. Last week, I fried some old <u>tomatoes spreading</u>₁ melted brie cheese all over its plump, juicy wedges. I also boiled instant noodles and mixed them into <u>a yogurt can</u>₂ that was nearing its expiration date. Not only are my recipes innovative and scrumptious, but they also solve the problem of leftovers crowding the fridge!

1. A) NO CHANGE
   B) tomatoes that spread
   C) tomatoes, while spreading
   D) tomatoes, which spread

2. A) NO CHANGE
   B) a can of yogurt
   C) some yogurt in a can
   D) can

Explanation:

The correct answers are (C) and (B).

For the first question, tomatoes cannot spread 'melted brie cheese' all over itself on its own. Something must be added to clearly state that 'I' am both frying and spreading the tomatoes with melted cheese. Therefore, the answer is (C).

For the second question, it is not physically possible for a can to near an expiration date. The object used must have 'yogurt' directly preceding the back modifier 'that was nearing its expiration date'. Therefore, the answer is (B).

Practice Questions

1. The human body, an organ, contains the kidney, which removes toxic materials from the body.
    A) NO CHANGE
    B) human body contains the kidney, which removes toxic materials, an organ, from the body.
    C) human body contains the kidney, an organ which removes toxic materials from the body.
    D) human body, which removes toxic material from the body, contains the kidney, an organ.

2. Oculus Rift is one of the first virtual reality headsets eager for the most realistic gaming experience possible that allows gamers to step into the gaming world itself.
    A) NO CHANGE
    B) Rift is one eager for the most realistic gaming experience possible of the first virtual reality headsets that allows gamers to step into the gaming world itself.
    C) Rift, eager for the most realistic gaming experience possible, is one of the first virtual reality headsets that allows gamers to step into the gaming world itself.
    D) Rift is one of the first virtual reality headsets that allows gamers, eager for the most realistic gaming experience possible, to step into the gaming world itself.

3. Banksy, a graffiti artist from England, which combine dark humor with graffiti, is known for his satirical street arts.
    A) NO CHANGE
    B) Banksy is known for his satirical street arts, a graffiti artist from England, which combine dark humor with graffiti.
    C) Banksy, a graffiti artist from England, is known for his satirical street arts, which combine dark humor with graffiti.
    D) Banksy, combining dark humor with graffiti, is a graffiti artist from England who is known for his satirical street arts.

4. Issues which were not addressed in the debates of the last election were more than covered by this year, which has seemed to focus endlessly on them.
    A) NO CHANGE
    B) this year's debates, which have seemed to focus endlessly on them.
    C) the focus given endlessly to this year's debates.
    D) the endless focus given his year.

5. Dr. Magnusson, who likes inviting his colleagues to his place for Christmas, served, dressed in a Santa Claus outfit, his classic eggnog.

   A) NO CHANGE
   B) served his classic eggnog dressed in a Santa Claus outfit.
   C) dressed in a Santa Claus outfit to serve his classic eggnog.
   D) dressed, served his classic eggnog, in a Santa Claus outfit.

6. In 1976, David Bowie, one of the most successful recording artists of the day, relocated to Berlin, there he discovered the city's burgeoning electronic music scene and introduced it to a wider audience.

   A) NO CHANGE
   B) he discovered the city's burgeoning electronic music scene and introduced it to a wider audience.
   C) where discovered and introduced by him was the city's burgeoning electronic music scene.
   D) where he discovered the city's burgeoning electronic music scene and introduced it to a wider audience.

7. Robert Adler invented the eventually ubiquitous remote control and directs electronics when buttons are pressed.

   A) NO CHANGE
   B) control when buttons pressed the electronics are directed.
   C) control, directing electronics when buttons are pressed.
   D) control, which directs electronics when buttons are pressed.

8. The management is not responsible for the property of people who are in the stadium.

   A) NO CHANGE
   B) while in the stadium.
   C) the stadium.
   D) where in the stadium.

9. The supervisor must make sure of the belongings of employees while in the restroom.

   A) NO CHANGE
   B) who are in the restroom.
   C) the restroom.
   D) where in the restroom.

10. Germanic peoples employed writing systems called runes, which linguists believe were used before the widespread adoption of the Latin alphabet around 700 AD.

    A) NO CHANGE
    B) linguists believe they were used before the widespread adoption of the Latin alphabet around 700 AD.
    C) which came before the widespread adoption of the Latin alphabet around 700 AD, linguists believe.
    D) used before the linguists believed the widespread adaptation of the Latin alphabet around 700 AD.

Chapter Test

Passage 1

Choose the answer that best replaces the underlined part:

One of nature's most precious gifts, we have been cultivating honey, for the past 8000 years. There is far more to this liquid gold than just its saccharine taste, however. Keep some of your honey in the medicine cabinet! Raw honey gives off hydrogen peroxide, which possesses antiseptic qualities. Not only that, but honey also does not contain much water creating a dehydrated environment, where few bacteria can thrive, if any. This is also the reason honey never has an expiry date — food-spoiling bacteria don't survive long in the gloopy desert. Slathering our wounds and satisfying our sweet tooths, jars of honey are, perhaps the most versatile food to ever bless mankind.

1. A) NO CHANGE
   B) honey has been cultivated
   C) cultivation of honey has gone on
   D) by us, honey has been cultivated

2. A) NO CHANGE
   B) water that creates a dehydrated environment
   C) water, creating a dehydrated environment
   D) water, a dehydrated environment is created

3. A) NO CHANGE
   B) this jar of honey is
   C) bottles of honey are
   D) honey is

Passage 2

Choose the answer that best replaces the underlined part:

Have you ever wondered how a taxi driver always knows the fastest way around the city? It isn't just a matter of practice and memory. Since they are required to drive the quickest path they know, taxi routes are usually thoroughly researched by taxi drivers. "The Knowledge", administered in London, is an example of a grueling training course for taxi drivers. Like the back of their hands, London taxi drivers are required to know every street route and place of interest, before they receive a license that recognizes them as true masters of the London labyrinth.

4. A) NO CHANGE
   B) taxi drivers thoroughly research taxi routes
   C) research of taxi routes are done thoroughly by taxi drivers
   D) thorough research of taxi routes are done by taxi drivers

5. A) NO CHANGE
   B) London taxi drivers are required to know every street route and place of interest like the back of their hands
   C) Every street route and place of interest is known by London taxi drivers like the back of their hands
   D) Required to know them like the back of their hands, every street route and place of interest is memorized by London taxi drivers

Passage 3

Choose the answer that best replaces the underlined part:

The next time you take a walk in Wonderland Park, take a seat down on the bench and observe everyone around you. You will see many strange things. Skis strapped on his back, people giggle "Wrong season!" as an old man awkwardly trudges ahead₆. A woman, impeccably dressed, sniffs away at trash cans with her eager Gold Retriever, striding alongside her₇. A man in a black suit throws apples at a duck with only one leg. Sure, taking a walk in the park does wonders to refresh your body, but it is the lushness of people and their tendencies that never fail to soothe your soul.

6. A) NO CHANGE
   B) "Wrong season!" people giggle as an old man awkwardly trudges ahead
   C) giggling people say "Wrong season!" as an old man awkwardly trudges ahead
   D) an old man awkwardly trudges ahead as people giggle, "Wrong season!"

7. A) NO CHANGE
   B) Sniffing away at trash cans, an impeccably dress woman strides with her eager Golden Retriever
   C) An impeccably dressed woman strides with her eager Golden Retriever which is sniffing away at trash cans
   D) Impeccably dressed, an eager Golden Retriever sniffs at trash cans while her owner, an impeccably dressed woman

Passage 4

Choose the answer that best replaces the underlined part:

The elderly woman made her way to the chest remembering₈ the bittersweet moments of her past. With utmost tenderness, a picture was taken out from the chest by her₉. Presented in a bright pink tutu, innocence was exhibited by the girl in the photograph₁₀ as she began to pirouette on the stage for her first recital. The elderly woman closed her eyes and smiled as she remembered the days of jubilant shouts, crispy leaves and dribbling ice cream and, most of all, the inextinguishable feeling of self-assurance and certainty that one loses with age.

8. A) NO CHANGE
   B) chest, which remembered
   C) chest while remembering
   D) chest that remembered

9. A) NO CHANGE
   B) the chest gave out a picture
   C) she took out a picture from the chest
   D) taken-out picture from the chest

10. A) NO CHANGE
    B) the girl exhibited her innocence in the photograph
    C) exhibition of her innocence
    D) the girl's innocence was exhibited in the photograph

Passage 5

Choose the answer that best replaces the underlined part:

Three stories high and filled with all sorts of fascinating things, the dreams and imaginations of people are captured in the History of the Future Museum₁₁. The museum's most interesting piece is undoubtedly the model kitchen from the 50s, which cleans its own oven when pulling a lever₁₂. Other items range from a display of Leonardo Da Vinci's sketches of flying machines to a whole wing devoted to the Space Race of the 1960s.

11. A) NO CHANGE
    B) people capture their dreams and imaginations in the History of the Future Museum
    C) the History of the Future Museum captures people's dreams and imaginations
    D) capture of people's dreams and imaginations is done by the History of Future Museum

12. A) NO CHANGE
    B) oven pulled a lever
    C) oven pulls a lever
    D) oven when a lever is pulled

6 Punctuation

6-1. Period, Semi-colon vs. Comma

One-Point Lesson

Periods and **Semi-colon** can connect two independent clauses **without** conjunctions.
Commas can only connect two independent clauses **with** a conjunction.
Watch out for transitions or conjunctive adverbs. These are not conjunctions and can only be used with periods and semi-colons.

Example 1: Jane wants to be a doctor; therefore, she will apply for the medical school program. (○)
Jane wants to be a doctor. Therefore, she will apply for the medical school program. (○)

Example 2: Jane wants to be a doctor, so she will apply for the medical school program. (○)

SAT-Style Example

Choose the answer that best replaces the underlined part:

Sirius is known to be the brightest star in the Earth's night sky. The name itself sheds light on this trait, because it is derived from the Greek word *Seirios; which*₁ can be translated as "glowing" or "scorcher." Its luminosity can be accounted for by its proximity to our home planet. However, what many people are not aware of is the fact that it is actually a binary star system. Although perceived as a single star to the naked eye, "the Dog Star" actually consists of two separate stars, Sirius A and Sirius B; the₂ latter is considered to be the supplementary star to the main astrological body.

1. A) NO CHANGE
   B) *Seirios*, which
   C) *Seirios*. Which
   D) *Seirios,* which;

2. A) NO CHANGE
   B) Sirius B, the
   C) Sirius B. The;
   D) Sirius B, the,

Explanation:

The correct answers are (B) and (A).
You should be able to use the proper punctuation depending on the functions each punctuation mark serves.
In the first question, the relative pronoun 'which' necessitates the use of a comma since the punctuation must introduce a conjunction. Therefore, the answer is (B).
The second question may seem tricky, but if you look closely at the sentence, you can see that the sentence needs to be finished with a punctuation mark. Therefore, either a period or a semi-colon is needed. The only logical answer is (A).

Practice Questions

Which punctuation mark (semicolon, period, or comma) should be inserted in the blank below?

1. The mining industry involves processing ore into raw materials and of turning those materials into transportable objects___ after this those materials must be shipped across the world.

2. My best friend thinks she can lift more weight than any other person at her gym___ and she has the bicep muscles to prove it.

3. Most visitors are welcomed at the Buddhist temples in Bangkok___ but anyone wearing short pants or a skirt must be covered by clothing they can purchase in the streets before entering.

4. Though home to only about 47 million people, Canada is the second largest nation in the world___ it is as large as India, Argentina, Kazakhstan, and Algeria combined.

5. According to behavioral psychologists, many people feel a need to reward themselves and recharge their willpower___ therefore they overcompensate with treats when they exercise.

6. Life isn't a video game, it doesn't have a save and load feature that allows someone to try something over and over again.
    A) NO CHANGE
    B) game: it doesn't,
    C) game; it doesn't
    D) game it doesn't

7. In the novel *Ready Player One*, James Halliday's Egg Hunt includes a Copper Key, a Jade Key, and a Crystal Key, as well as the corresponding Gates for all three keys; he spent his last years tirelessly creating the ultimate quest to see who will inherit his vast fortune.
    A) NO CHANGE
    B) includes a Copper Key a Jade Key and a Crystal Key as well as the corresponding Gates for all three keys; he spent his last years tirelessly creating
    C) includes a Copper Key, a Jade Key, and a Crystal Key; as well as the corresponding Gates for all three keys; he spent his last years tirelessly creating
    D) includes a Copper Key; a Jade Key; and a Crystal Key; as well as the corresponding Gates for all three keys; he spent his last years tirelessly creating

8. Although there are roughly 6500 spoken languages in the <u>world today; the</u> most widely spoken is English.

    A) NO CHANGE
    B) world today. The
    C) world today the
    D) world today, the

9. In order to solve the mysterious <u>crime Inspector</u> Lestrade turned to Sherlock Holmes, a "consulting detective" of unparalleled skills.

    A) NO CHANGE
    B) crime, Inspector
    C) crime; Inspector
    D) crime. Inspector

10. The Hubble Space Telescope makes observations of a quality impossible for ground based <u>telescopes: it</u> records images never before seen of the furthest reaches of the universe.

    A) NO CHANGE
    B) telescopes, it
    C) telescopes and it
    D) telescopes. It

6-2. Colons and Dashes

One-Point Lesson
Colons are used to introduce or list a series of items in a clause.
Dashes are used to provide an interruption or emphasis within a clause.

After a colon or a dash, it is possible to use not only **complete sentences**, but also **incomplete sentences and phrases.**

Example 1: The following were on my son's wish list for <u>Christmas: a laptop</u>, a car, and an iPhone. (○)
 simple listing done with phrases (incomplete sentences)

Example 2: I've known her my entire life <u>— 25 years —</u> and she's definitely the right one for you. (○)
 Here, the information between the two dashes provides supplementary information for the main clause.

SAT-Style Example

Choose the answer that best replaces the underlined part:

Out of the Galilean moons orbiting Jupiter, Io is located closest to the giant planet. Io consists of hundreds of active <u>volcanoes — some</u>$_1$ higher than Mount Everest — and thus is considered the most geologically active object in the Solar System. Discovered in 1610 by Galileo Galilei, the moon was named after a character in Greek <u>mythology; the</u>$_2$ priestess of goddess Hera, to be precise. It played a significant role in astronomy, because it reinforced the Copernican model of the Solar System as opposed to the geocentric notion that placed our home planet at the center of the universe.

1. A) NO CHANGE
   B) volcanoes; some
   C) volcanoes: some,
   D) volcanoes. Some

2. A) NO CHANGE
   B) mythology. The
   C) mythology: the
   D) mythology, the:

Explanation:
The correct answers are (A) and (C).
Remember the usage of dashes and colons to solve these kinds of problems.
For the first question, additional information is placed between the two dashes. Therefore, there is no error in using a dash there. The answer is (A).
For the second question, the punctuation is supposed to introduce a piece of information. Therefore, you should use the colon there, and the answer is (C).

Practice Questions

1. Some chameleons have adapted an unusual way of _____
   A) seeing, they move both eyeballs independently of each other.
   B) seeing — they move both eyeballs independently of each other.

2. Despite having died out as a living language more than 1,500 years ago, Latin is still being _____
   A) taught — lessons are offered in the curriculums of high schools and universities around the world.
   B) taught, lessons are offered in the curriculums of high schools and universities around the world.

3. The two young friends found navigating their way through the city to be more difficult than either had _____
   A) expected, they had to be picked up by their mothers not long after being dropped off.
   B) expected — they had to be picked up by their mothers not long after being dropped off.

4. The railroad was the first industry to be subjected to a _____
   A) "trust busting" they were a company that was consumed by illicit business practices and bound by the government to submit to regulation.
   B) "trust busting" — they were a company that was consumed by illicit business practices and bound by the government to submit to regulation.

5. _____ is being accomplished today, but the technology is being stymied by persistent ethical concerns.
   A) Cloning: the process of exactly replicating organisms using their own DNA,
   B) Cloning — the process of exactly replicating organisms using their own DNA —

6. Despite having fought countless villains, Batman would undoubtedly choose only one as his <u>archenemy. The</u> Joker.
   A) NO CHANGE
   B) archenemy;
   C) archenemy
   D) archenemy: the

7. When faced with a life-or-death situation, people act in one of the two <u>ways,</u> fight or flee.
   A) NO CHANGE
   B) ways
   C) ways—
   D) ways;

8. Medical experts say that PTSD—an acronym for Post Traumatic Stress Disorder—poses a serious social threat and must be given more attention.
   A) NO CHANGE
   B) PTSD,
   C) PTSD
   D) PTSD)

9. Toby—who put a dollar in a jar every time he got dumped—ended up buying a car.
   A) NO CHANGE
   B) dumped
   C) dumped,
   D) dumped)

10. Earliest records of the "liger"—a hybrid cross between a male lion and a female tiger: date back to the early 19th century in India.
    A) NO CHANGE
    B) tiger,
    C) tiger—
    D) tiger;

6-3. Various Comma Usages

One-Point Lesson

In this section, we will review all notable comma usages that frequently appear on the SAT. Remember these grammatical structures when using commas:

1. SVO, Coordinating Conjunction SVO

→ Always use a comma before a **coordinating conjunction** connecting two **independent clauses**.

2. Incomplete Phrase, SVO

→ Always use a comma after the **front modifier** that modifies the subject.

3. SVO, Incomplete Phrase

→ Use a comma before the back modifier, **only if** the incomplete phrase **provides additional information**.

4. S, Incomplete Phrase, VO

→ Use commas at the **beginning** and the **end** of an insertion modifying the **subject**.

Let's look at the following examples:

Example 1: I like him, but I don't love him. (○)
   The coordinating conjunction, 'but' is placed between two independent clauses. Therefore, a comma should be placed there.

Example 2: Feeling tired, Tom slowly walked home. (○)
   'Feeling tired' describes 'Tom' and is an incomplete phrase placed in front of an independent clause. Therefore, a comma should be placed there.

Example 3: I'm not a girl, not yet a woman. (○)
   'not yet a woman' provides additional information about the subject and is an incomplete phrase. Therefore, a comma should be placed at its front.

Example 4: Martin Scorsese, known for his trademark style of using long shots, directed the movie *Taxi Driver*. (○)
   'known for his trademark style of using long shots' describes the subject, 'Martin Scorsese'. Therefore, use 2 commas to denote the insertion.

SAT-Style Example

Choose the answer that best replaces the underlined part:

My <u>grandfather; whom</u>₁ I admire very much, had been in the Marine Corps during the Korean War Era. What was fascinating to me was that he had actually been in the battles that we read about in our history books. He was there on the front lines when General Douglas MacArthur successfully took over <u>Incheon, when</u>₂ he took a bullet to his thigh that eventually had him honorably discharged from the Corps.

1. A) NO CHANGE
   B) grandfather. Whom
   C) grandfather, whom
   D) grandfather — whom

2. A) NO CHANGE
   B) Incheon, when;
   C) Incheon; when
   D) Incheon. When

Explanation:
The correct answers are (C) and (A).
Both questions are typical SAT-type questions that test you on comma usage.
In the first question, 'whom I admire very much' is supposed to be inserted between the subject 'grandfather' and the verb 'had been.' Therefore, the comma should be used. Answer is (C).
In the second question, the first part of the sentence 'He was there ... Incheon' is a complete sentence by itself, and the rest is connected by a conjunction 'when'. Therefore, the comma is appropriately placed. The answer is (A).

Practice Questions

For the sentence below, indicate whether a comma is necessary and explain why.

1. While efforts are underway to curb its production___ heroin is Afghanistan's most valuable export and the number of acres turned over to its cultivation grows every year.

2. Russia's Lake Baikal___ containing more than 23,000 square kilometers of water___ is the world's oldest freshwater lake.

3. The Pacific Northwest___ which encompasses all of northern California___ Oregon and Washington, has a host of unique trees, one of which is larger than some buildings.

4. The giant anteater can devour thousands of termites at once___ as well as demolish a massive termite mound in minutes.

5. It was clear that all of the participants had trained extensively for the dancing competition___ for each performance during the initial rounds showed indications of having been meticulously prepared.

6. The inchworm, easily mistaken for a tree twig; remains still most of the time to trick its predators.
   A) NO CHANGE
   B) twig
   C) twig—
   D) twig,

7. Midsummer marks the day of the year with the longest period of daylight. It occurs at the time when the Earth's semi-axis is most inclined toward the sun; also known as the summer solstice.
   A) NO CHANGE
   B) sun. Also
   C) sun also
   D) sun, also

8. Watson was much more likeable as a person than Holmes expressing actual sympathy before engaging the victim's family in a conversation.
   A) NO CHANGE
   B) Holmes, expressing
   C) Holmes; expressing
   D) Holmes. Expressing

9. Although Forrest claims to have scored higher in the SAT than anybody else, Gina, with the score of 1,600, actually scored higher.
   A) NO CHANGE
   B) else; Gina,
   C) else. Gina,
   D) else: Gina,

10. The Tiger might have also gotten the chance to become human. Had he not gotten tired of eating only mugwort and garlic and ran out of the cave.
    A) NO CHANGE
    B) human; had
    C) human, had
    D) human: had

6-4. Apostrophes

One-Point Lesson
Apostrophes are used in 2 ways:
1. To indicate possession
2. To create contractions

Here are some tips on telling the two apart:

1. Look for the verb: lawnmower is (verb) or lawnmower's (possession)
2. Look at the plurality: member's (single) or members' (plural)

Let's look at some examples to clarify:

Example 1: This lawnmower's Jane's. (○)
   This lawnmower is Jane's (lawnmower).

Example 2: This lawnmower's Jane's families'. (✕)
   families' → family's
   the lawnmower belongs to the family of Jane, so you should use the singular noun and a possessive determiner (apostrophe).

Example 3: Your free to choose whether to drink out of a cup or a straw. (✕)
   Your → You're
   Here the subject is 'You' and the verb 'are.' Therefore, the contraction 'You're' should be used instead of the possessive case 'Your.'

SAT-Style Example

Choose the answer that best replaces the underlined part:

Graphene is a two-dimensional allotrope of carbon that is effectively an atomic scale honeycomb lattice. It's$_1$ the basic structural element of several other carbon allotropes that are more complex, such as graphite and charcoal. Although not yet applied for commercial uses, environmentalists have shown a keen interest in the allotrope due to it's$_2$ potential in energy storage. In fact, some experts have hinted that graphene may be able to replace fossil fuels as the main source of energy in the future.

1. A) NO CHANGE
   B) Its
   C) Its'
   D) It

2. A) NO CHANGE
   B) its'
   C) its
   D) it

Explanation:

The correct answers are (A) and (C).

The most typical type of problem that asks about the use of apostrophe is the 'its' versus 'it's' problem. Many students tend to confuse 'its' with 'it's,' so it is important to take a close look at these problems before the test.

For the first question, the sentence should start with 'it is,' since 'it' is referring to 'graphene.' Therefore, the answer is (A).

For the second question, the sentence is talking about graphene's 'potential,' so the answer is (C).

Practice Questions

1. Nadine asked for something small and shiny for her birthday, and her <u>boyfriends</u> gift was a piece of glitter paper. <u>No error</u>

2. The triplets eagerly awaited their <u>father</u> return from the ice cream truck with their favorite Triple Banana Split Sundae. <u>No error</u>

3. The <u>boys'</u> decision to bring his car to school wasn't a smart one because, as a freshman, he wasn't allowed to use the school parking lot. <u>No error</u>

4. Temmie couldn't believe it when she got a call from her professor telling her that she won the scholarship; <u>Temmies</u> first reaction to the news was a shocked silence. <u>No error</u>

5. To escape the deadly clutch of the Cyclops, <u>Odysseus</u> crew tied themselves to the underside of the giant rams. <u>No error</u>

6. The illusionist and escapologist Harry Houdini is famous for <u>he's</u> Chinese Water Tank trick, which is also falsely rumored as the cause of his death.
   A) NO CHANGE
   B) its
   C) it's
   D) his

7. A <u>chipmunks</u> cheek pouch can stretch to fit four or more acorns at a time.
   A) NO CHANGE
   B) chipmunks'
   C) chipmunk's
   D) chipmunk

8. While Alan lost he's nerve to continue through the *Saw* marathon after the first film, Katie was determined to watch all the films until the end.

   A) NO CHANGE
   B) one's
   C) its
   D) his

9. Faker and Madlife are both Korean professional gamers who many fans adore for they're amazing skills.

   A) NO CHANGE
   B) his
   C) its
   D) their

10. The gamers most dreaded quest was Slaying the Horntail because they had to kill over a thousand monsters just to fight the Horntail.

    A) NO CHANGE
    B) gamer
    C) gamers'
    D) gamer's

Chapter Test

Passage 1

Choose the answer that best replaces the underlined part:

The most familiar image associated with a nuclear blast is that of the mushroom cloud, and during the Cold War many around the world feared that one day they would <u>see one however,</u>$_1$ the most destructive aspect of the atomic bomb is not the initial blast, as represented by the cloud. In fact, the fallout is far, far more harmful. The result of nuclear <u>decay; gamma</u>$_2$ rays are so penetrative that it takes a lead wall 15 centimeters thick to prevent exposure. Exposure to such penetrative energy can result in radiation <u>poisoning; its</u>$_3$ symptoms include severe drop in blood cell count, constant vomiting and intestinal pain.

1. A) NO CHANGE
   B) see one. However,
   C) see one, however,
   D) see one — however,

2. A) NO CHANGE
   B) decay. Gamma
   C) decay, gamma
   D) decay gamma

3. A) NO CHANGE
   B) poisoning. It's
   C) poisoning; it's
   D) poisoning, its

Passage 2

Choose the answer that best replaces the underlined part:

Dark matter is one of the most interesting and elusive subjects faced by physicists in the 21st century. Scientists believe it accounts for a vast proportion of the mass of the <u>universe, but</u>$_4$ it has so far proven completely undetectable. This is the reason for its name; "dark" refers to the fact that we cannot perceive it. Furthermore – in addition to dark <u>matter, scientists</u>$_5$ also speculate about the existence of dark energy. If the puzzle of these "dark" forces can be solved, our understanding of the universe will be dramatically enhanced.

4. A) NO CHANGE
   B) universe. But
   C) universe; but
   D) universe; but,

5. A) NO CHANGE
   B) matter: scientists
   C) matter; scientists
   D) matter — scientists

Passage 3

Choose the answer that best replaces the underlined part:

The argument of nature versus nurture dates back as far as the ancient Greeks; scholars₆ in both the Eastern and Western traditions have attempted to draw a line between these two factors: circumstances,₇ we are born into and the decisions we make for ourselves, and how much each of them impacts our lives. These questions seem to have intensified recently as DNA and genetic research have progressed. Scientists continue to find new genetic explanations for medical phenomena; but₈ they raise new questions as well.

6. A) NO CHANGE
   B) Greeks. Scholars,
   C) Greeks, scholars,
   D) Greeks, scholars

7. A) NO CHANGE
   B) factors — circumstances
   C) factors, circumstances
   D) factors; circumstances

8. A) NO CHANGE
   B) phenomena. But
   C) phenomena, but
   D) phenomena; but,

Passage 4

Choose the answer that best replaces the underlined part:

The city of Rome has a long and interesting history: its₉ been both the most important place in the world as well as a festering swamp that people couldn't wait to leave. For Julius Caesar, who brought an entire army across the Rubicon to capture the cities halls₁₀ of power, Rome held a symbolic place as the ultimate goal to be attained in his campaign. For Emperor Claudius, whose hometown was Gaul, the courts of Rome were an obligation he couldn't wait to leave behind. Popes in the 11th century moved to France to get away from the filth of the city's streets.₁₁

9. A) NO CHANGE
   B) history, it's
   C) history: it's
   D) history; its

10. A) NO CHANGE
    B) city's hall's
    C) cities' hall's
    D) city's halls

11. A) NO CHANGE
    B) cities' street's.
    C) city's streets'.
    D) city's street's

Passage 5

Choose the answer that best replaces the underlined part:

Recorded sound, since its invention at the turn of the 20th century; has$_{12}$ enjoyed many different mediums. From wax cylinders to streaming audio, the modern music listener has many options. Of the many possible ways to listen to music, vinyl$_{13}$ records are the most desirable to audiophiles in general because there is a certain 'warmth' of sound that results from the imperfections in the record. What medium to utilize all depends on what the listener prefers, however,$_{14}$ others might prefer a lossless audio file on a specialized electronic audio player which, contrary to popular perception, is actually the most immaculate way to deliver processed sound.

12. A) NO CHANGE
    B) century has
    C) century. Has
    D) century, has

13. A) NO CHANGE
    B) music; vinyl
    C) music. Vinyl
    D) music vinyl

14. A) NO CHANGE
    B) prefers. However,
    C) prefers however,
    D) prefers — however,

7   Structure

7-1. Incomplete Sentences

One-Point Lesson
Usually, incomplete sentence problems ask you to find these kinds of errors:
1. No **Subject**
2. No **Verb**

Also, these problems usually overlap with each other.
Let's look at the following examples to shed light on these errors:

Example 1: My dog running towards me excitedly as she saw me come through the door. (×)
　　running → ran
　　This would be the case of **no verb**

Example 2: Expanding universe since the Big Bang 14 billion years ago. (×)
　　Expanding universe → The universe has been expanding
　　This would be the case of **no subject, no verb**

SAT-Style Example

Choose the answer that best replaces the underlined part:

The haka is a traditional war dance performed by the Maori people of New Zealand. It involving$_1$ vigorous movements accompanied by rhythmic and loud shouting. Although originally performed by warriors before a battle, the haka still holds value in contemporary times with the All Blacks — the New Zealand national rugby team — being the most notable performers. Various types of haka existing and they$_2$ can be performed even by women and children.

1. A) NO CHANGE
   B) Involving
   C) Involving it
   D) It involves

2. A) NO CHANGE
   B) existing they
   C) exist and they
   D) existing, and they

Part I : Standard English Conventions | 81

Explanation:

The correct answers are (D) and (C).

The questions are pretty straightforward; simply make the sentences have proper subject-verb structures.

For the first question, 'It involving' is missing a verb. Therefore, the answer is (D).

For the second question, 'existing' is not a verb, so the verb is missing. Therefore, the answer is (C).

Practice Questions

Correct any errors, if present, for the underlined words in the sentence below.

1. Though now heralded as the progenitor of modern science, <u>Galileo Galilei once being imprisoned</u> by the Catholic church for his observation that the Earth revolves around the sun. <u>No error</u>

2. Followers of Judaism <u>emigrating</u> from nation to nation since the beginnings of the religion, and communities established in cities by the end of the Middle Ages. <u>No error</u>

3. Old town records <u>showing</u> that food production was not significantly impacted by the Little Ice Age, refuting the claim that sudden climate changes immediately impact daily life. <u>No error</u>

4. A combination of rampant insect infestation and greater frequency of forest fires<u>, adding</u> to deforestation in the Rocky Mountains. <u>No error</u>

5. The taxi ride, which was full of close calls and dangerous turns, <u>kept</u> Daniel's face hidden behind his hands. <u>No error</u>

6. The beginnings of the Industrial Revolution <u>taking place</u> due to the inventions of English, American and French scientists.
    A) NO CHANGE
    B) takes place
    C) took place
    D) which took place

7. Watson, Crick and Wilson, winners of the 1962 Nobel Prize for Biology, <u>and who is describing</u> the fundamental nature of DNA.
    A) NO CHANGE
    B) described
    C) who described
    D) describing

8. Paganini, an Italian violinist of the Romantic era and a leading force in the popularization of virtuosic playing, who originated many of the stylistic choices common among solo musicians.
    A) NO CHANGE
    B) originated from
    C) originating
    D) originated

9. A contingent of freshly credentialed, ambitious college graduates embarking each year from universities to enter a workforce already saturated by their unemployed predecessors.
    A) NO CHANGE
    B) entering
    C) who enter
    D) enter

10. Red blood cells, also known as erythrocytes, which carry the hemoglobin that living cells need to process oxygen and maintain life.
    A) NO CHANGE
    B) carrying
    C) carry
    D) which is carrying

7-2. Conjunction Errors — General

One-Point Lesson

Conjunctions are words that connect parts of sentences.
Coordinating Conjunctions connect **two independent clauses**.
→ Example: And, But, For, Nor, Or, So, Yet
Subordinating Conjunctions connect a **dependent (subordinate) clause** to an independent clause.
→ Example: After, Whether, When, Who, etc.

Usually, conjunction problems are about a sentence having the wrong number of conjunctions. No matter how complicated the sentence is, the following equation is always true:

$$\text{No. of subjects} - \text{No. of conjunctions} = 1$$

Let's look at some examples:

Example 1: <u>Before</u> I found my current job, <u>where</u> I spent many years working in a bakery. (×)
where → omit the 'where'
No. of subjects = 2, No. of conjunctions = 2 → 2-2 = 0. Therefore, this sentence is wrong.

Example 2: I wanted to go there, <u>but</u> I had other work to do. (○)
No. of subjects = 2, No. of conjunctions = 1 → 2-1 = 1. Therefore, this sentence is correct.

SAT-Style Example

Choose the answer that best replaces the underlined part:

Since breaking into Hollywood with accolade winning movie *Bottle Rocket* in 1996, Wes Anderson has gained the attention of many cinema-goers with his distinctive visual style. Although some consider his films to be ostentatious, <u>but most</u>$_1$ find his cinematography to be aesthetically pleasing. This can be credited to his near obsession with symmetry as well as his exquisite taste in color. Such aspects can be easily noticed in *The Grand Budapest Hotel*, <u>which received</u>$_2$ 9 nominations in the 87th Academy Awards.

1. A) NO CHANGE
   B) and most
   C) most
   D) yet most

2. A) NO CHANGE
   B) received
   C) it has received
   D) has received

Explanation:

The correct answers are (C) and (A).

Remember the equation above to figure out how many conjunctions are necessary to complete a sentence.

For the first question, there are two conjunctions — 'although' and 'but.' However, there are only two subjects — 'some' and 'most.' Therefore, 2-2 = 0, meaning that there are too many conjunctions. The answer is (C), which has no conjunction and logically fits in the sentence.

For the second question, 'which' is the conjunction. There are 2 subjects – 'aspects' and 'The Grand Budapest Hotel.' Therefore, 2-1 = 1, so the appropriate number of conjunctions is used. The answer is (A).

Practice Questions

Correct any errors, if present, for the underlined words in the sentence below.

1. ID badges are ready for distribution at the main <u>office, they</u> can be picked up by department managers after lunch today. <u>No error</u>

2. J.S. Bach was once dismissed by younger musicians due to his insistence on adhering to unfashionable music <u>forms, his work</u> was later regarded a high point in the history of composition. <u>No error</u>

3. George Lucas has said that his Star Wars films were shaped greatly by classic Greek storytelling <u>forms, but that</u> the pop culture of his youth guided his vision. <u>No error</u>

4. As a painter, Georgia O'Keeffe catalogued the beauty of the American <u>Southwest, she</u> used it as her work's inspiration. <u>No error</u>

5. Our National Park Service, established in 1916, was inspired by <u>Romanticism, stands</u> as an example to many other nations. <u>No error</u>

6. The ferocity of the Russian winter halted Napoleon's advance in 1912, and his army retreated to more hospitable <u>areas, the army</u> was unable to supply itself.
   A) NO CHANGE
   B) areas, however the army
   C) areas, but the army
   D) areas: the army

7. Patients suffering from depression often do not respond to <u>counseling, they</u> are usually treated with a mixture of cognitive therapy and drugs.
   A) NO CHANGE
   B) counseling,
   C) counseling, yet
   D) counseling, so

8. The traditional Japanese diet contains a lot of healthy options and contains basically no saturated <u>fats, it</u> does not cause the kind of health problems associated with Western diets.
    A) NO CHANGE
    B) fats, so it
    C) fats,
    D) fats, but it

9. The museum curator adjusted the artifacts in the <u>display, she</u> went on to inform us of the history of each one.
    A) NO CHANGE
    B) display, but
    C) display and she
    D) display

10. A new study shows that birds caused more than 1.2 billion dollars in damage last <u>year, they</u> collide with aircraft.
    A) NO CHANGE
    B) year for they
    C) year, birds
    D) year,

7-3. Adverb Clauses

One-Point Lesson

Adverb Clauses modify the **entire main clause**.
The following are often used conjunctions usually placed in front of the dependent clause according to each described circumstance:

Time-related	when, before, since, until, after, by the time
Reason	because, since
Contrast	although, though, even though
Conditional	if, unless
others	in that, inasmuch as

Keep in mind that if an adverb clause is placed **in front of** the main clause, you must use a **comma(,)** between the clauses. If an adverb clause is placed **after** the main clause, the **comma(,)** is not necessary.

Example 1: When I was young, I used to go to church. (○)
   time-related conjunction, 'when' is used.

Example 2: I am studying English because I want to attend an American college. (○)
   reason-related conjunction, 'because' is used.

Example 3: Although I am overweight I run pretty fast. (×)
   Although I am overweight → Although I am overweight,
   contrasting conjunction, 'although' is used adequately, but a **comma** is missing.

Example 4: If you go, then I'll go. (○)
   conditional conjunction, 'if' is used.

SAT-Style Example

Choose the answer that best replaces the underlined part:

Although the Bengal tiger is the most common tiger subspecies, <u>but it is</u>₁ still considered to be endangered. Over the past century, tiger numbers have fallen dramatically, largely due to habitat losses and large scale poaching. In the regions around Nepal and India, poaching is rampant as there is high demand for tiger skin in the black market. Even though recent efforts to protect the animal have increased, with the WWF collaborating with actor Leonardo DiCaprio to start a campaign called *Save Tigers Now*, <u>yet much has</u>₂ to be done to create support for a sustainable tiger population by 2022.

1. A) NO CHANGE
   B) it is
   C) and it is
   D) since it is

2. A) NO CHANGE
   B) much has
   C) and much has
   D) because much has

Explanation:
The correct answers are (B) and (B).
Usually, the adverb clauses problems test you on the right number of conjunctions; either they have too many or too few. Always remember the equation, 'No. of subjects – No. of conjunctions = 1.'
In the first question, there are 2 subjects in the first sentence and the conjunction 'Although' is given. Therefore, in order to satisfy 2-1 = 1 equation, there should not be any more conjunctions in the underlined part. Therefore, the answer is (B). On a similar note, the second question has 'even though' in the beginning. Since 'yet' is another conjunction, you should delete it and thus pick (B) as your answer. Keep in mind that no matter how long or complex the sentence may be, you need to be able to pinpoint the right clauses and conjunctions to examine the error properly.

Practice Questions

Correct any errors, if present, for the underlined words in the sentence below.

1. <u>By the time the members of the Russian Federation were freed from the yoke of communist oppression,</u> capitalist economies had already begun to flourish all around the globe. <u>No error</u>

2. The company in charge of creating the tests has to prove the reliability of test scores <u>when standardized tests are made mandatory for college admission.</u> <u>No error</u>

3. Even though some archaeologists claim that the Mayan civilization died out due to environmental disasters, <u>however, others describe their dissolution as a result of the plague introduced by Europeans.</u> <u>No error</u>

4. <u>If the committee had given us permission to implement our plans for animal protection</u> we would have eagerly finished the job. <u>No error</u>

5. If the Allied forces had chosen to give in to the Axis powers, the world would have looked very different today. No error

6. Because gas prices continue to rise, then I may buy a bicycle.
    A) NO CHANGE
    B) so I may buy a bicycle.
    C) a bicycle may be bought by me.
    D) I may buy a bicycle.

7. Since 1983 I've completely neglected to pay my taxes.
    A) NO CHANGE
    B) Since 1983,
    C) In 1983
    D) In 1983,

8. I've wasted too much time going out and spending money since my breakdown last year.
    A) NO CHANGE
    B) my breakdown last year.
    C) since, my breakdown last year.
    D) in my breakdown last year.

9. Although Shelly had an impressive record of apprehending the most heinous criminals, but she was not on the list of potential promotion candidates.
    A) NO CHANGE
    B) so she was not on the list of potential promotion candidates.
    C) she was not on the list of potential promotion candidates.
    D) but the list of potential promotion candidates did not have her on it.

10. Since its inception the Red Cross has been servicing war zones, aiding millions of people each year.
    A) NO CHANGE
    B) Since its inception,
    C) At its inception
    D) At its inception,

7-4. Conjunctions vs. Conjunctive Adverbs

One-Point Lesson
Often, the SAT questions you on adverbs that look like conjunctions. These are called **"Conjunctive Adverbs."** Here are some commonly confused conjunctive adverbs:

Result	therefore, thus, consequently, accordingly, thereby, hence
Comparison	likewise, similarly, comparatively
Contrast	however, instead, rather, still, yet, contrarily, nevertheless, nonetheless
Sequence	finally, next, then, lastly, first, second, third
Addition	again, besides, furthermore, indeed, moreover, also

Keep in mind that conjunctive adverbs **are used with conjunctions** or **as adverbs themselves.**

Example 1: I liked the car, <u>however,</u> somebody already bought it. (✕)

however, → but

Because 'however' is not a conjunction, there is no conjunction in the sentence. Therefore, 'but' should be used.

Example 2: I went into the house, <u>then,</u> I showered. (✕)

then, → and OR and then

Conjunctive adverbs are used with conjunctions.

SAT-Style Example

Choose the answer that best replaces the underlined part:

When Robert Galbraith released the crime fiction novel *The Cuckoo's Calling*, it did not receive much attention despite receiving positive reviews. In fact, the book was the winner of the 2013 Los Angeles Times Book Prize in the Mystery/Thriller category. <u>However, it</u>$_1$ was later revealed in 2014 that the author was actually J.K Rowling, the author of the famous *Harry Potter* series, writing under a pseudonym. The book climbed from 4709th to best-selling novel on Amazon, <u>consequently,</u>$_2$ the book is set to be produced as a TV series on the British TV channel BBC.

1. A) NO CHANGE
   B) But, it
   C) Although, it
   D) And, it

2. A) NO CHANGE
   B) finally
   C) therefore
   D) and

Explanation:

The correct answers are (A) and (D).

It is important to note that you cannot have a clause containing only a conjunction. Be careful when distinguishing adverbs from conjunctions.

The first question is an example of using 'however.' However can be a modifier and start a sentence on its own. Therefore, the usage is adequate, and the answer is (A).

In the second question, 'consequently' is an adverb. Therefore, it cannot be used in place of a conjunction. The answer is, therefore, (D) — the only conjunction among the answer choices.

Practice Questions

Correct any errors, if present, for the underlined words in the sentence below.

1. Few people stop to think about the number of inventions that influence their lives everyday, <u>nevertheless,</u> even the smallest tasks involve some piece of human innovation and previous labor. <u>No error</u>

2. Most people tend to accept information that agrees with their preconceptions, <u>although,</u> they are rarely tolerant to challenging ideas. <u>No error</u>

3. Danielle would like to host, <u>nonetheless,</u> she is not able to manage the party. <u>No error</u>

4. Raising chickens in your backyard is a great way to reduce your carbon emissions, <u>accordingly</u> it can contribute to preserving the environment. <u>No error</u>

5. Most people usually consider Mt. Everest the highest point in the world, <u>yet</u> Mt. Chimborazo in Uruguay extends farther into the atmosphere due to the shape of the earth. <u>No error</u>

6. In 1928, pilot Amelia Earhart was the first woman to fly across the Atlantic, <u>moreover,</u> in 1937 she made an unsuccessful attempt to fly around the world.
    A) NO CHANGE
    B) and
    C) so
    D) however

7. As an early inventor, Leonardo Da Vinci explored ideas of parachutes and helicopters, <u>also</u> he encrypted his notes by writing upside down and backwards.
    A) NO CHANGE
    B) however
    C) therefore
    D) and

8. Repeated sonar and satellite imagery has failed to provide evidence of the Loch Ness monster, <u>since such is the case,</u> most respected scientists no longer believe its existence is possible.

    A) NO CHANGE
    B) such is the case,
    C) so
    D) but

9. Bamboo is frequently applied to regions in which there has been massive deforestation, <u>because it grows quickly,</u> developers can address the lack of foliage rapidly.

    A) NO CHANGE
    B) its quick growth is why
    C) because of its quick growth,
    D) and because it grows quickly,

10. Flying fish and squirrels do not technically fly, <u>still</u> they do glide for long distances over the surface of the ocean and amongst trees, respectively.

    A) NO CHANGE
    B) but
    C) instead
    D) however

Chapter Test

Passage 1

Choose the answer that best replaces the underlined part:

While the reading of actual, paper-bound books seems to be on the decline these days, <u>and it is</u>₁ still hard to deny the joy that can come from finding a quiet place to hide and spending a day with nothing but the printed words to keep you company. <u>Although the</u>₂ advantages of the Internet cannot be discredited, but the peace that comes from contemplating a literary work is nearly impossible while connected to the world at large. The next time you get a chance, turn off your Wi-Fi and pick up a book, <u>consequently, you'll</u>₃ feel that you are more relaxed and calm.

1. A) NO CHANGE
   B) however it is
   C) but it is
   D) it is

2. A) NO CHANGE
   B) And the
   C) The
   D) Or the

3. A) NO CHANGE
   B) finally, you'll
   C) and you'll
   D) therefore, you'll

Passage 2

Choose the answer that best replaces the underlined part:

The news <u>full</u>₄ of reports of corrupt governments and organization that persist in subjugating people. Sometimes one might wonder why people don't just fight back and win their freedom. The fact is that organizing of any kind is difficult. For any problem on a national scale, to coordinate activity among a great number of people is hardly feasible for the inexperienced. Also, even if people want change, they may not have the resources to make <u>it happen. Because</u>₅ inadequate planning results in the collapse of many revolutions, many ineffectual or corrupt governments continue despite public unrest.

4. A) NO CHANGE
   B) filled
   C) are full
   D) is full

5. A) NO CHANGE
   B) it happen but
   C) it happen and
   D) it happen because

Passage 3

Choose the answer that best replaces the underlined part:

Driving down the road during the summer, wondering₆ about the best way to keep cool and be environmentally friendly at the same time. Even though the air conditioner is certainly effective, but it₇ also burns a lot of fuel. Alternatively, if you roll down your windows to get a nice breeze, you will also be able to cool off, but how much will it affect your gas mileage? Comparing the two methods actually showing₈ a surprising continuum. At certain speeds, the air conditioner is more efficient; at other speeds, having your windows rolled down is more efficient.

6. A) NO CHANGE
   B) summer, wonders
   C) summer, you could wonder
   D) summer, you wondering

7. A) NO CHANGE
   B) effective, and it
   C) effective, it
   D) effective, but

8. A) NO CHANGE
   B) actually shows
   C) actually having shown
   D) actually show

Passage 4

Choose the answer that best replaces the underlined part:

My best friend thinks she can lift more weight than any other person at her gym, moreover, she₉ has the muscles to prove it. Just last week, she even challenged the big power lifters, who are always hogging the squat machine, to a duel. Because it is dangerous to lift competitively, so the₁₀ gym required both my friend and her competitors to be supervised. They even distributed fliers to advertise to locals to come and watch. Eventually, they₁₁ actually tied by lifting the same amazing amount. I don't think I could ever lift that much myself.

9. A) NO CHANGE
   B) indeed, she
   C) furthermore, she
   D) and she

10. A) NO CHANGE
    B) therefore the
    C) the
    D) consequently, the

11. A) NO CHANGE
    B) And they
    C) So they
    D) When they

Passage 5

Choose the answer that best replaces the underlined part:

One of the most famous and beloved monarchs of England being King Arthur.₁₂ Although it is now certain that neither his advising wizard Merlin nor his magical sword Excalibur ever existed, the₁₃ legend itself may be based on actual events that took place in the time just after the fall of Rome and before the Anglo-Saxon invasion. Some historians suggest that a former Roman general held off a series of invasions therefore₁₄ established a kingdom briefly during this time. This kingdom may have served as the basis for the legend of King Arthur.

12. A) NO CHANGE
    B) be King Arthur.
    C) having been King Arthur.
    D) is King Arthur.

13. A) NO CHANGE
    B) existed the
    C) existed, but
    D) existed and

14. A) NO CHANGE
    B) invasions but
    C) invasions and
    D) invasions hence

8 Tense

One-Point Lesson

Regarding verb tense, the SAT will test you on whether you know when exactly to use each tense form. The following are some signifiers that serve as cues as to which tense form should be used.

Tense Form	Expressions signifying tense
Past Perfect	by + (point in past), subject had + p.p., by the time subject + past tense, subject had p.p.
Simple Past	ago, yesterday, one/last/in/during + (point in past), those days, at that time, until recently
Present Perfect	(ever) since + (point in past), in/during/for + the past/for the last + (duration)

Sometimes, there are no obvious key words that signal what tense form to use. In these cases, it is best to look at what tenses are used in the context. Particularly, the words **when**, **until**, **before**, and **after** are clear indicators to look at the context of the passage.

Let's look at these in more detail with some examples:

Example 1: By the time I rushed back from school, my house <u>burned</u> down to the ground. (✗)

burned → had burned

'By the time' signifies that the verb tense must be in past perfect form. Therefore, 'had burned' should be used.

Example 2: Yesterday, all my troubles <u>have seemed</u> not so far away. (✗)

have seemed → seemed

'Yesterday' signifies that the verb tense must be in simple past form. Therefore, 'seemed' should be used.

Example 3: Ever since Wendy taught me how, I <u>flew</u> kites every Saturday. (✗)

flew → have flown

'Ever since' signifies that the verb tense must be in present perfect form. Therefore, 'have flown' should be used (remember, 'fly' is an irregular verb).

Example 4: Greg's mother gave Greg a box of cookies when he first started high school. She also had kissed him on the cheek. (×)

had kissed → kissed

Pay attention to the context of these sentences. Since a simple past tense is used in the first sentence ('gave'), the same tense should also be used in the second. Therefore, 'kissed' should be used.

Example 5: In the concert, The Who sang 'Doctor Jimmy' and has performed 'Tattoo.' (×)

has performed → performed

Pay attention to the context of the sentence. Since a simple past tense is used ('sang'), the same tense should be used when The Who 'performed' another song.

Example 6: After Mr. Kurts descended into madness and evil, he impales the heads of the savages on the sticks. (×)

impales → impaled

'After' is a clear indicator to pay attention to the context of the sentence. Since a past tense is used ('descended'), the same tense should be used when Mr. Kurts 'impaled' the heads.

SAT-Style Example

Choose the answer that best replaces the underlined part:

One day in the late seventeenth century, a ripe apple had snapped₁ from its delicate stalk and fell on Isaac Newton's head. Furious but inspired, Newton then went on to formulate his groundbreaking theory of gravitation, which revolutionized scientific thinking for centuries to come. The story, however, is only half true. Newton was indeed inspired by an apple falling from a tree, but he was nowhere underneath the tree when this happened. Despite the fact that it never happened, this image prevailed₂ over our imaginations for the last three centuries.

1. A) NO CHANGE
   B) has snapped
   C) snapped
   D) snaps

2. A) NO CHANGE
   B) has prevailed
   C) had prevailed
   D) will prevail

Explanation:
The correct answers are (C) and (B).
For the first question, the expression 'in the late seventeenth century' indicates that simple past tense must be used. A simple past form lacks 'has,' 'have,' or 'had' and, in the case of a regular verb, ends with –ed. Therefore, the answer is (C).
For the second question, 'for the last three centuries' indicates that present perfect tense must be used. A present perfect form always has 'has' or 'have' in front of the past participle verb. Therefore, the answer is (B).

SAT-Style Example

Choose the answer that best replaces the underlined part:

Dominic and Gareth are the best of friends, and like all good friends they <u>argue</u>₁ about the most trivial things. They once even got into a serious fight about whether a dress was black and blue, or white and gold! Like all good friends, though, when they have had some time to blow off some steam, they always <u>embraced</u>₂ each other with open arms.

1. A) NO CHANGE
   B) argued
   C) will argue
   D) have argued

2. A) NO CHANGE
   B) will embrace
   C) had embraced
   D) embrace

Explanation:
The correct answers are (A) and (D).
For the first question, pay attention to 'are.' This sets the tense of the sentence as simple present tense. The only option that is in the simple present tense is 'argue.' Therefore the answer is (A).
For the second question, pay attention to 'have had.' This is in the present perfect tense, and implies that the tense must be in present tense — either present perfect or simple present. The only option that is in the present tense is 'embrace.' Therefore, the answer is (D).

Practice Questions

1. Now that Abby <u>trained</u> for three months, she feels somewhat comfortable about running the marathon in support of cancer research. <u>No error</u>

2. Iowa is an important center of Transcendentalism, mostly because practitioners there <u>welcomed</u> potential devotees from any background to come and learn about the beliefs expressed there. <u>No error</u>

3. From 331 BC until 641 AD, Alexandria, still a remarkable city, was the capital of Egypt; however, it <u>has been conquered</u> by Muslims and replaced as capital by 642 AD. <u>No error</u>

4. Before air conditioning became widespread in the mid-20th century, the best way to cool off during summer months <u>has been</u> sitting outside on porches. <u>No error</u>

5. For the past 10 years, the winery <u>had been producing</u> quality champagne esteemed by connoisseurs and the public alike. <u>No error</u>

6. Before our trip to Vietnam, Noel has never eaten rice noodle. Now he can't get enough of it.
    A) NO CHANGE
    B) had never eaten
    C) was never eaten by
    D) was never eating

7. Psy recently was releasing a new album, '7th cider'.
    A) NO CHANGE
    B) was released by
    C) is releasing
    D) released

8. Despite dropping out of college and being removed from the company he helped found, Steve Jobs went on to become CEO of Apple and one of the world's greatest inventors. His most famous invention has been the iPhone, the most widely used smartphone in the present US.
    A) NO CHANGE
    B) were
    C) is
    D) would be

9. A monument in Yonsei University presents an engraving of a poem by Yun Dong-ju; students visit here to pay their respects to the now deceased independence fighter.
    A) NO CHANGE
    B) was presenting
    C) was presented by
    D) would be presenting

10. Despite the rumors, the Korean girl group Orange Caramel is not owning a caramel shop.
    A) NO CHANGE
    B) is not owned by
    C) does not own
    D) is not owning

Chapter Test

Passage 1

Choose the answer that best replaces the underlined part:

Sometime in the Ming dynasty, the seas <u>beared</u>₁ a single clam. Many years later, scientists picked up the clam from the Icelandic coasts in 2006. After they counted the annual growth lines on the clam's shell, they <u>have discovered</u>₂ that it had lived for 405 years! More accurate assessment later revealed that the clam was, in fact, 507 years old. By the time the scientists realized they had just split open the oldest recorded animal in the world, however, the clam <u>had already died</u>₃. The famous clam is now known as Ming, named after the dynasty that was in power when the clam came into existence.

1. A) NO CHANGE
   B) have beared
   C) bore
   D) have bore

2. A) NO CHANGE
   B) discover
   C) had discovered
   D) discovered

3. A) NO CHANGE
   B) already died
   C) will have already died
   D) had already deaded

Passage 2

Choose the answer that best replaces the underlined part:

Fall began like it always did. Once the corn <u>had rose</u>₄ about two meters, Father was ready to send us out to begin the harvest of this year's crop. We had all of our equipment ready, and the machineries <u>will all be</u>₅ oiled and fueled. There was no school for a week to ensure that every family in the community had the help they needed. What I wasn't ready for was the horrible case of scarlet fever that I came down with just a day before we were ready to begin. In the past eleven years of my life I <u>have never suffered</u>₆ so terribly, as my fever reached ninety-nine degrees. Father was going to have to hire part time labor, and that meant I would have to wear the same clothes for another year.

4. A) NO CHANGE
   B) had risen
   C) had raised
   D) had rise

5. A) NO CHANGE
   B) are all
   C) were all
   D) has all been

6. A) NO CHANGE
   B) never suffered
   C) never will have suffered
   D) never will suffer

100 | Paul's SAT Writing

Passage 3

Choose the answer that best replaces the underlined part:

Prevention is always better than cure. Such an adage is especially true for cancer, the infamous disease that kills millions annually. Before cancer <u>accelerated</u>₇ into its deadly advanced stages, it starts as a much smaller tumor that has yet to infect other tissues. This stage of cancer is known as Stage 0, and the tumor is easy for doctors to surgically remove. Don't put off routine check-ups or ignore monthly appointments. There have been many situations in which by the time a doctor diagnosed cancer, the tumor <u>has already began</u>₈ its terrible rampage.

7. A) NO CHANGE
   B) accelerates
   C) will accelerate
   D) had accelerated

8. A) NO CHANGE
   B) already began
   C) has already begun
   D) had already begun

Passage 4

Choose the answer that best replaces the underlined part:

Words have many interesting origins. In England in the 16th century, Shakespeare <u>has invented</u>₉ many of them, some of which are used in the following sentence: Reading Shakespeare may be an "eyesore," but when you learn his "new-fangled" words, you <u>will walk</u>₁₀ with a "swagger"! Some find it difficult to believe that one person coined such a great number of neologisms. Another commonly used word was named after the scientist Luigi Galvani, who discovered that frog legs moved when he passed electricity through them. Since then the term "galvanize" <u>has took</u>₁₁ the meaning of "to stimulate into action".

9. A) NO CHANGE
   B) had invented
   C) will invent
   D) invented

10. A) NO CHANGE
    B) walked
    C) have walked
    D) had walked

11. A) NO CHANGE
    B) had took
    C) takes
    D) has taken

Passage 5

Choose the answer that best replaces the underlined part:

Everyone has his or her own greatest fear, ranging from heights to tiny little ants. Fears usually reflect a genetic predisposition to avoid dangerous animals, situations, or objects. My greatest fear is, however, rather irrational – I have no qualms with dark alleyways or bungee jumping, but lifeless dolls and puppets give$_{12}$ me the chills. Ever since I could remember, I have had$_{13}$ awful nightmares about glass-eyed, man-sized dolls coming to life and forcing me into their mouths.

12. A) NO CHANGE
    B) gave
    C) have given
    D) will give

13. A) NO CHANGE
    B) had had
    C) have
    D) had

Part II

Expression of Ideas

9 Usage

9-1. Diction

One-Point Lesson

The following is a list of confusing **diction**.

Diction	Explanation	Example
Than vs. Then	Than – a conjunction used to introduce an unequal comparison Then – at that time, immediately or soon after	I like bananas more **than** apples. I liked apples **then**, but I like bananas now.
Whose vs. Who's	Whose – possessive case of "who" Who's – contraction of "who is" or "who has"	**Whose** ball is this? **Who's** got my ball?
's vs. –ies / -s	's – usually indicates possession of something -ies – usually indicates a plural form	Our family**'s** dinner with my fiancé**'s** family went smoothly. The two famil**ies** got along just fine.
Could / Would / Should / Must / Might Have vs. Of	ALWAYS use "have". There is no such expression as "could / would / should / must / might of"	We should **have** gone there. (○) We should **of** gone there. (✗)
There vs. They're vs. Their	There – in or at that place They're – contraction of "they are" Their – possessive case of "they"	I will have lunch over **there**. **They're** serving tacos today. **Their** tacos are delicious.
Too vs. To	Too – in addition, to an excessive extent To – preposition used to direct to a point or place	I want **to** be there, **too**, but the traveling time is **too** long for me.
Lay vs. Lie	Lay (verb transitive) – to put or place something Lie (verb intransitive) – to be in or assume a horizontal position Present / Past / Past Participle Lay / Laid / Laid Lie / Lay / Lain	I **lay** myself on the bed. I **laid** myself on the bed. I **have laid** myself on the bed. I **lie** on the bed. I **lay** on the bed. I **have lain** on the bed.

Raise vs. Rise	Raise (verb transitive) – Lift or move something to a higher position or level Rise (verb intransitive) – move from a lower position to a higher one Present / Past / Past Participle Raise / Raised / Raised Rise / Rose / Risen	I **raise** my hand. I **raised** my hand. I **have raised** my hand. I **rise** from my chair. I **rose** from my chair. I have **risen** from my chair.
Between vs. Among	Between – comparing two objects Among – more than two objects	**Between** bananas and apples, I like bananas more, but **among** all fruit, I like watermelons the most.
Wait vs. Await	Wait – used with preposition 'for' Await – does not require preposition	I **wait for** the school bus. I **await** your arrival.

9-2. Precision and Concision

One-Point Lesson

The SAT will test you not on especially difficult words, but words that are similar in meaning. Although these words are synonyms, not all synonyms can replace each other. Some words may be **synonyms** but have different **connotations**. In other words, the words may have similar meanings but are used in different situations. Below is a list of synonyms that are used in different situations or contexts.

#				
1	**vacate** *verb* to leave; go away	**evacuate** *verb* to remove from a place of danger to a safer place	**depart** *verb* to leave, especially in order to start a journey	**retire** *verb* to leave one's job and cease to work
2	**outdo** *verb* to do better than something or someone	**defeat** *verb* to win a victory over in a war	**outperform** *verb* to perform better than	**outweigh** *verb* to exceed in value, importance, influence
3	**satiate** *verb* to satisfy to the full	**fulfill** *verb* to develop the full potential of	**complacent** *adjective* pleased, especially with oneself	**sufficient** *adjective* adequate for the purpose
4	**devour** *verb* to swallow or eat up	**dispatch** *verb* to send off or away with speed	**overindulge on** *verb* have too much of something enjoyable	**dispose of** *verb* to get rid of; discard
5	**austere** *adjective* severe in manner or appearance; uncompromising	**egregious** *adjective* extraordinary in some bad way	**unmitigated** *adjective* not softened or lessened	**stark** *adjective* obvious or complete in appearance or outline
6	**tight** *adjective* fixed, fastened, or closed firmly; hard to move	**firm** *adjective* not likely to change; not soft or yielding when pressed	**stiff** *adjective* difficult to bend or flex	**taut** *adjective* emotionally or mentally strained or tense
7	**decree** *verb* to officially order something that has the force of law	**commission** *verb* to order to do or produce something	**force** *verb* to make a way through or into by physical strength	**license** *verb* to permit to do something
8	**confide** *verb* to tell in assurance of secrecy	**promulgate** *verb* to make known by open declaration	**impart** *verb* to tell; to give	**unveil** *verb* to reveal or disclose by or as if by removing a veil or covering
9	**emphatic** *adjective* very impressive or significant; striking	**paramount** *adjective* above others in rank or authority	**eminent** *adjective* high in station, rank; distinguished	**important** *adjective* of much or great significance or consequence
10	**tolerate** *verb* to allow the existence	**pursue** *verb* to follow close upon	**persist** *verb* to continue firmly	**keep going** *verb* continue uninterrupted
11	**crystalline** *adjective* of or like crystal	**clear** *adjective* free from any doubt	**limpid** *adjective* completely calm	**sheer** *adjective* unmixed with anything else
12	**point** *noun* a mark made with the sharp end of something	**position** *noun* condition with reference to place	**location** a place of settlement, activity, or residence	**orientation** *noun* one's position to a specific place or object.
13	**challenge** *noun* difficulty in a job or undertaking	**impediment** *noun* something that slows down one's progress	**obstruction** *noun* something that blocks a passage	**opposition** *noun* strong disagreement

14	**well-connected** *adjective* having friends who are important or powerful	**important** *adjective* of great significance	**prestigious** *adjective* very much respected and admired	**weighty** *adjective* heavy
15	**acuteness** *noun* sharp or penetrating in intellect	**knack** *noun* a clever way of doing something	**prowess** *noun* exceptional or superior ability, skill, or strength	**astuteness** *noun* cleverness or skillfulness
16	**scuffle** *noun* an act or sound of moving in a hurried, confused, or shuffling manner	**melee** *noun* a confused crowd of people	**struggle** *noun* a determined effort under difficulties	**bout** *noun* a short period of intense activity of a specified kind
17	**perpetuates** *verb* to make something last for long period of time	**stores** *verb* to accumulate for future use	**preserves** *verb* to maintain and reserve for continued survival	**stashes** *verb* to put away something, usually in a secret place, for future use
18	**navigate** *verb* to direct on its course	**convey** *verb* to take or carry from one place to another	**voyage** *verb* to make a travel or journey	**maneuver** *verb* to change the position of a vehicle
19	**harvest** *verb* to win, acquire or gain from a result of any past act	**cultivate** *verb* to develop or improve by care	**tend** *verb* to pay attention, to apply oneself to the care of	**burgeon** *verb* to grow or develop quickly (usually plant
20	**hurl** *verb* to throw or cast down	**spur** *verb* to strike or to press forward	**heckle** *verb* to harass a public speaker or performer with rude questions	**launch** *verb* to to send forth or release a weapon
21	**gamble** *verb* to play at any game of chance for money or other stakes	**scatter** *verb* to throw loosely about	**squander** *verb* to spend or use wastefully	**misplace** *verb* to put in a wrong place
22	**submerge** *verb* to put or sink below the surface of water	**drown** *verb* to die under water of suffocation	**engulf** *verb* to swallow up in	**sheathe** *verb* to cover with a protective layer
23	**communal** *adjective* used or shared in common by everyone in a group	**congruous** *adjective* appropriate or fitting	**conjoint** *adjective* joined together	**coincident** *adjective* happening at the same time
24	**young** *adjective* not old	**naive** *adjective* showing a lack of experience	**undeveloped** *adjective* not developed	**callow** *adjective* immature or inexperienced
25	**pure** *adjective* free from anything of a different	**spotless** *adjective* immaculately clean	**stainless** *adjective* having no stain	**antiseptic** *adjective* free from germs and other microorganisms
26	**silhouette** *noun* a dark image outlined against a lighter background	**shadow** *noun* a dark shape on a surface that is made when something stands between a light and the surface	**likeness** *noun* a representation, picture, or image, especially a portrait	**lineament** *noun* a feature of a face, body, or figure
27	**innocuous** *adjective* harmless	**weak** *adjective* lacking in bodily strength	**sapless** *adjective* lacking vitality or spirit	**insipid** *adjective* without distinctive, interesting qualities
28	**controversial** *adjective* causing disagreement or discussion with strong opposing viewpoints	**arguable** *adjective* susceptible to being supported by convincing or persuasive argument	**disputable** *adjective* not certain	**debatable** *adjective* open to question
29	**unfinished** *adjective* lacking some special finish, incomplete	**inconclusive** *adjective* without final results or outcome	**deficient** -(*adjective* lacking some element or characteristic	**unfruitful** *adjective* not producing good or helpful results

30	**serviceable** *adjective* capable of or being of service; useful	**empirical** *adjective* provable or verifiable by experience or experiment	**experimental** *adjective* based on or derived from experience	**practical** *adjective* suitable for the situation in which something is used
31	**dot** *noun* a small spot on a surface	**variable** *noun* a quantity or function that may assume any given value or set of values	**coordinate** *noun* any of the magnitudes that serve to define the position of a point, line by reference to a fixed figure.	**quantity** *noun* an exact or specified amount or measure
32	**falsely** *adverb* not true or correct; erroneous	**virtually** *adverb* by means of virtual reality	**implicitly** *adverb* in a way that is not directly expressed	**computationally** *adverb* in a way that uses or relates to computers
33	**unpredictable** *adjective* not able to be predicted	**doubtful** *adjective* ambiguous	**fluctuating** *adjective* to change continually	**whimsical** *adjective* subject to erratic behavior
34	**perdurable** *adjective* very durable	**perpetual** *adjective* continuing forever	**rolling** *adjective* moving along a surface	**interminable** *adjective* continuing for a very long time wishing that it was shorter or would stop
35	**concentrate** *verb* to put or bring into a single place	**stockpile** *verb* to accumulate for future use	**accumulate** *verb* to gather into a mass, steadily increasing	**amalgamate** *verb* to mix or merge so as to make a combination
36	**impulsive** *adjective* acting without being aware of its consequence	**makeshift** *adjective* temporarily replacing something because of availability of a service or product.	**impromptu** *adjective* made or done without previous preparation	**unscripted** *adjective* not written at an earlier time
37	**reclusive** *adjective* shut off or apart from the world	**sequestered** *adjective* to kept apart from others	**restricted** *adjective* limited to or admitting only members of a particular group or class	**sheltered** *adjective* protected or shielded from disasters
38	**vulnerable** *adjective* open to assault; difficult to defend	**malignant** *adjective* feeling or showing ill will or hatred	**susceptible** *adjective* accessible or liable to some influence	**treacherous** *adjective* dangerous
39	**rupture** *verb* to make a crack or break in something	**divide** *verb* to separate (something into two or more parts or pieces	**split** *verb* to break apart or into pieces especially along a straight line	**fracture** *verb* to cause or to suffer from a break in bone
40	**maintain** *verb* cause or enable a condition or situation to continue	**bolster** *verb* to support with a pillow or cushion	**endure** *verb* to bear with patience; tolerate	**support** *verb* to bear or hold up; serve as a foundation for
41	**twins** *adjective* being two persons or things closely related to or closely resembling each other	**Equivalent** *adjective* equal in value	**tantamount** *adjective* equal in value, force or effect	**indistinguishable** *adjective* not able to be identified as different or distinct
42	**anger** *verb* fill with anger	**incense** *verb* to inflame with wrath; make angry	**shock** *verb* to strike against violently	**provoke** *verb* to give rise to
43	**fame** *verb* to have or spread the renown of; to make famous	**tout** *verb* to describe or advertise boastfully	**renowned** *adjective* honored or distinguished	**appreciate** *verb* to be grateful or thankful for
44	**ordinance** *noun* an authoritative rule or law	**treaty** *noun* a formal document embodying such an international agreement	**proclamation** *noun* a public and official announcement	**announcement** *noun* public or formal notice

#				
45	**motivate** *verb* cause someone to have interest in or enthusiasm for something	**animate** *verb* bring to life	**energize** *verb* give vitality and enthusiasm to	**instigate** *verb* incite someone to do something, especially something bad
46	**mastery** *noun* expert skill or knowledge	**suction** *noun* the act, process, or condition of sucking	**leverage** *noun* power or ability to act or to influence people, events, decisions	**capacity** *noun* the ability to receive or contain
47	**Truncate** *verb* to shorten by cutting off; cut short	**shear** *verb* to remove by or as if by cutting with a sharp instrument	**curtail** *verb* reduce or cut off a part of	**diminish** *verb* to make or cause to seem smaller
48	**inventory** *verb* to make a complete list of	**enumerate** *verb* to mention one by one	**recite** *verb* to repeat aloud from memory before an audience	**compute** *verb* to calculate
49	**ornery** *adjective* ugly and unpleasant in temper	**unrepentant** *adjective* not feeling regret or sorrow	**taxing** *adjective* requiring a lot of effort	**adamant** *adjective* too hard to cut, break, or pierce
50	**permeate** *verb* to pass into or through every part of	**saturate** *verb* to soak thoroughly or completely	**infiltrate** *verb* to filter into or through	**shroud** *verb* to wrap or cloth for burial
51	**excuse** *verb* to regard or judge with forgiveness	**expel** *verb* to drive or force out	**dismiss** *verb* treat as unworthy of serious consideration	**discharge** *verb* to tell someone officially that he/she can or must leave
52	**articulated** *adjective* having or showing the ability to speak fluently and coherently	**decipherable** *adjective* convert a coded signal into normal language	**meaningful** *adjective* important, or worthwhile	**distinct** *adjective* different in nature from something else of a similar type
53	**imperative** *adjective* of vital importance; crucial	**inevitable** *adjective* certain to happen; unavoidable	**momentous** *adjective* of great importance or significance, especially in having a bearing on future events	**insistent** *adjective* demanding something; not allowing refusal
54	**questioning** *adjective* ask questions	**analytical** *adjective* relating to or using analysis or logical reasoning	**reasonable** *adjective* having sound judgement; fair and sensible	**detailed** *adjective* having many details or facts
55	**inconclusive** *adjective* not leading to a firm conclusion or result	**uncertain** *adjective* not able to be relied on; not known for definite	**ambiguous** *adjective* open to more than one interpretation	**unsettled** *adjective* lacking order or stability
56	**material** *adjective* physical rather than spiritual or intellectual	**corporeal** *adjective* having, consisting of, or relating to a physical material body	**mortal** *adjective* certain to die	**living** *adjective* currently active or being used
57	**carry** *verb* to have something as a part, quality, or result	**promote** *verb* to encourage or support something, or to help something become successful	**uphold** *verb* to defend or maintain a principle or law	**enjoy** *verb* to have the benefit of something
58	**optimize** *verb* to make something as good as possible	**select** *verb* to choose a small number of things, or to choose by making careful decisions	**elevate** *verb* to give someone a higher or more important position	**elect** *verb* to decide on or choose, esp. by voting
59	**diligently** *adverb* carefully and using a lot of effort	**emphatically** *adverb* done or said in a strong way and without any doubt	**stringently** *adverb* having a very severe effect, or being extremely limiting	**dispassionately** *adverb* able to think clearly or make good decisions because not influenced by emotions

60	**cruel** *adjective* extremely unkind and unpleasant and causing pain intentionally	**hurtful** *adjective* causing emotional pain	**venomous** *adjective* poisonous; usually used for secretions from living animals	**toxic** *adjective* poisonous; usually used for wastes, chemicals

Example 1: Jerry, however, <u>evacuated</u> from the corrupt tradition by treating his subordinates with kindness instead of abuse and violence which his superiors treated him with.

    A) NO CHANGE
    B) vacated
    C) departed
    D) retired

Explanation:
The correct answer is (C).

evacuate: escape due to an emergency
(ex. evacuate the building due to an earthquake)

vacate: empty a space
(ex. vacate the room while the workers clean it)

retire: leave a job position or responsibility
(ex. retire from the position of President)

depart: leave; diverge from (something expected)

A tradition is neither an emergency, a space, or a responsibility. However, it is by definition something people are used to. Therefore, 'depart' is the correct verb to use with 'tradition.'

Example 2: Given the trouble I had while wearing glasses, the benefits of the LASEK surgery seems to vastly <u>outdo</u> its possible drawbacks.

    A) NO CHANGE
    B) outperform
    C) defeat
    D) outweigh

Explanation:

The correct answer is (D).

outdo: (A outdo B) A do better than B; A is more successful than B
(ex. Jake outdid Ken in the math test)

outperform: (A outperform B) A perform better than B; A is more successful than B
(ex. Android outperformed iPhone in the world market)

defeat: (A defeat B) A conquer B, A fight with B and win
(ex. Batman defeated Superman in the battle)

outweigh: (A outweigh B) there is more of A than B; A is more important than B

Benefits cannot do or perform better than drawbacks. Neither can they fight with drawbacks and win. You can only describe something as having more benefits than drawbacks. Therefore, 'outweigh' is the correct verb to use with 'benefits' and 'drawbacks.'

Practice Questions

1. Organic food, unlike fast food, contains nutrients most needed by the human body and can help people stay <u>satiated</u> for a longer span of time.
    A) NO CHANGE
    B) fulfilled
    C) complacent
    D) sufficient

2. Covering the surface of slices of apples with salt water can keep them <u>tight</u> and bright yellow for weeks.
    A) NO CHANGE
    B) firm
    C) stiff
    D) taut

3. Even if a class doesn't seem to be directly linked to your major, it may still help you develop <u>emphatic</u> skills for use later in life. For example, by taking a debate class, a student majoring in physics can learn to give better speeches regarding his or her research.
    A) NO CHANGE
    B) paramount
    C) eminent
    D) important

4. Even though she had called the pest control agency numerous times, the termite problems still <u>keep going</u>. Her husband thinks it might be a good idea to move.

   A) NO CHANGE
   B) tolerate
   C) persist
   D) pursue

5. Carmen couldn't believe that Nina was actually surprised at how the movie turned out. The protagonist's intention was <u>sheer</u> from the start.

   A) NO CHANGE
   B) limpid
   C) crystalline
   D) clear

6. Encouraged by the success of the Krusty Krab restaurant, Mr. Krabs decided to open a second joint at a new <u>position.</u>

   A) NO CHANGE
   B) location.
   C) orientation.
   D) point.

7. Batman had vowed never to kill anyone in his act of exacting justice, but it was a <u>challenge</u> to stick to that rule when the Joker had killed his second Robin and crippled Batgirl.

   A) NO CHANGE
   B) an obstruction
   C) a impediment
   D) a opposition

8. It may be difficult to get into a habit of, but exercising daily can have <u>weighty</u> benefits for your health.

   A) NO CHANGE
   B) important
   C) prestigious
   D) well-connected

9. Environmentalists and zoologists are shocked by news that continued habitat destruction and the consequent loss of food source have caused a mother polar bear to <u>devour</u> its cub out of hunger.

   A) NO CHANGE
   B) dispatch
   C) overindulge on
   D) dispose of

10. My school timetable filled with math and science classes stands in <u>austere</u> contrast to my brother's with only gym and theater art classes.

    A) NO CHANGE
    B) egregious
    C) unmitigated
    D) stark

9-3. Frequently Confused Words

One-Point Lesson

Some words may look or sound similar but have completely different meanings. Hence, they are frequently confused words.

#				
1	**loose** *verb* free from bonds or restraint	**loss** *noun* something that is lost	**lose** *verb* to come to be without something in one's possession	
2	**corps** *noun* a military unit of ground combat force	**chore** *noun* a small or odd job; routine task	**core** *noun* the central part of a fleshy fruit, containing seeds	**court** *noun* a place where justice is administered
3	**pore** *verb* to read or study with steady attention	**pour** *verb* to make a liquid flow from or into a container		
4	**boar** *noun* a type of wild pig	**bore** *noun* a person or a situation that is boring		
5	**whether** *conjunction* used to talk about a choice between two or more possibilities	**wither** *verb* to lose the freshness of youth, as from age	**weather** *noun* the temperature or conditions outside	**when** *conjunction* at what time
6	**compliment** *noun* an expression of praise, commendation or admiration	**completion** *noun* the time when something that you are doing or making is finished	**complement** *noun* something that completes or makes perfect	**compel** *verb* to force someone to do something
7	**precede** *verb* to go or come before	**proceed** *verb* to move or go forward or onward	**cede** *verb* to allow someone else to have or own something	
8	**die** *verb* to stop living	**dye** *verb* to change the color of something	**dry** *verb* to free from moisture	
9	**rein** *verb* to check or guide by exerting pressure on a bridle bit by means of the rein	**reign** *verb* to possess or exercise sovereign power or authority	**rain** *noun* precipitation that falls from the cloud	**wane** *verb* to decrease in strength
10	**illicit** *adjective* not legally permitted or authorized	**elicit** *verb* to draw or bring out or forth	**elucidate** *verb* to make lucid or clear	**exude** *verb* to come out gradually in drops
11	**envelop** *verb* to wrap up in or as in a covering	**envelope** *noun* a flat paper container for a letter or thin package	**develop** *verb* to change and become better	**redevelop** *verb* to replace the buildings in an area with new ones
12	**except** *preposition* not including a particular fact, thing, or person	**accept** *verb* to take something that someone offers you	**expect** *verb* to look forward to	**intercept** *verb* to cut off from an intended destination
13	**oral** *adjective* uttered by the mouth	**orally** *adverb* expressed in speech, not writing	**aura** *noun* a feeling or character that a person or place seems to have	**aural** *adjective* relating to hearing
14	**patience** *noun* the ability to stay calm and not get upset	**patient** *noun* someone who is being treated by a doctor	**patent** *noun* the official legal right to make or sell an invention for a particular number of years	**patina** *noun* a thin surface layer develops on something because of use, age, or chemical action

#				
15	**sight** *noun* the ability to use your eyes to see	**site** *noun* the position or location of a town, building, etc	**side** *noun* position to the left of right	**cite** *verb* to quote, especially as an authority
16	**effect** *noun* a change or result that is caused by something	**affect** *verb* to cause a change in someone or something	**infect** *(verb)* to give someone a disease	**defect** *noun* a shortcoming, fault, or imperfection
17	**insure** *verb* to guarantee against loss or harm	**ensure** *verb* to secure or guarantee	**sure** *adjective* free from doubt as to the reliability, character, action, etc	**secure** *adjective* free from or not exposed to danger or harm
18	**discrete** *adjective* having a clear independent shape or form	**secrete** *verb* to produce and release a liquid	**concrete** *adjective* constituting an actual thing or instance	**discreet** *adjective* careful not to cause embarrassment or attract too much attention
19	**stationery** *noun* things that you use for writing, such as pen and paper	**stagnant** *adjective* not flowing or running	**sanctuary** *noun* the most holy part of a religious building	**stationary** *adjective* not moving
20	**mettle** *noun* courage and fortitude	**medal** *noun* a piece of metal given as a prize in a competition	**metal** *noun* a hard, shiny material such as iron, gold or silver	**meddle** *verb* to change things that are not your responsibility
21	**wonder** *verb* to think or speculate curiously	**wander** *verb* to walk slowly around a place without any purpose		
22	**accent** *noun* the way that someone speaks, showing where they come from	**assent** *noun* agreement or approval	**ascent** *noun* a movement or climb up something	**essence** *noun* the basic or most important idea or quality of something
23	**immoral** *adjective* not correct, honest, or good	**amoral** *adjective* without moral principles	**memorial** *noun* something designed to preserve the memory of a person, event, etc	**immortal** *adjective* living or lasting forever
24	**thorough** *adjective* careful and covering every detail	**threw** past tense of throw	**through** *preposition* from one end or side of something to the other	**though** *conjunction* used before a fact or opinion that makes the other part of the sentence surprising
25	**lay** *verb* to put something down somewhere	**allay** *verb* to put to rest	**lying** present participle of lie	**ally** *verb* to unite formally
26	**ensure** *verb* to secure or guarantee	**reassure** *verb* to say something to stop someone from worrying	**assure** *verb* to declare earnestly to	**posture** *noun* the relative disposition of the parts of something
27	**principal** *adjective* main, or most important	**principate** *noun* supreme power or office	**principality** *noun* a country ruled by a prince	**principle** *noun* a belief about how you should behave
28	**complementary** *adjective* useful or attractive together	**alimentary** *adjective* concerned with the function of nutrition	**complimentary** *adjective* praising or expressing admiration for someone	**supplementary** *adjective* added to something else in order to improve it or complete it
29	**allude** *verb* to refer casually or indirectly	**elude** *verb* to avoid or escape by speed	**exclude** *verb* to not include something	**preclude** to prevent something or make it impossible
30	**conscious** *adjective* awake and able to think and notice things	**cornichon** *noun* a black vinifera grape grown for table use	**conscience** *noun* the inner sense of what is right or wrong in one's conduct or motives	

#				
31	**succeed** verb to accomplish what is attempted or intended	**accede** verb to give consent, approval, or adherence	**exceed** verb to be more than a particular number or amount	**secede** verb to withdraw formally from an alliance, federation, or association
32	**indigenous** adjective originating in and characteristic of a particular region or country	**indigent** adjective lacking food, clothing, and other necessities of life because of poverty	**indignant** adjective angry because of something that is wrong or not fair	**indigo** noun a bluish-purple color
33	**apprehend** verb arrest someone who has not obeyed the law	**appreciate** verb to be grateful or thankful for		
34	**extant** adjective still existing	**exile** noun a situation in which someone has to leave their home and live in another country, often for political reasons	**extent** noun the size or importance of something	**exigent** adjective needing urgent attention
35	**lectern** noun a reading desk in a church on which the Bible rests	**letter** noun a written or printed communication addressed to a person	**lector** noun a lecturer in a college or university	**lecture** noun a talk to a group of people about a subject
36	**allusion** noun a passing or casual reference	**illusion** noun something that is not really what it seems to be	**delusion** noun belief in something that is not true	**collusion** noun agreement between people to act together secretly
37	**advise** verb to give counsel to	**advice** noun a recommendation offered as a guide to action	**advance** noun a forward movement	**advertise** verb to announce a product in some public medium of communication
38	**eminence** noun the state of being famous	**imminence** noun the state of being likely to occur at any moment	**innocence** noun the state of being free from moral wrong	**immanence** noun the state of existing in something as a permanent
39	**immanent** adjective remaining within	**eminent** adjective high in rank; famous	**imminent** adjective likely to occur at any moment	**innominate** adjective without a name
40	**ingenuous** adjective honest and sincere	**ingenious** adjective very clever and involving new ideas	**igneous** adjective produced under conditions involving intense heat	**ingenue** noun the part of innocent girl, especially as played in films and plays
41	**capitol** noun a building occupied by a state legislature	**capitulation** noun an acceptance of military defeat	**capital** noun money used in business	**caption** noun a title or explanation for a picture
42	**prescribe** verb to order treatment for someone	**proscribe** verb to not allow something	**inscribe** verb to write words in a book or carve them on an object	**describe** verb to tell or depict in written or spoken words
43	**afflict** verb to make someone suffer physically or mentally	**inflect** verb to slightly influence	**inflict** verb to force someone or something to experience something unpleasant	**affect** verb to cause a change in someone or something
44	**apprise** verb to give notice to	**excise** noun an internal tax or duty on certain commodities within the country	**apprize** appraise	**appraise** verb to examine something in order to judge their qualities
45	**personal** adjective belonging to a particular person	**personnel** noun a body of persons employed in an organization or place of work	**personality** noun the qualities that make one person different from another	**personally** adverb done by you and not someone else
46	**illicit** adjective not legally permitted or authorized	**tacit** adjective understood without being expressed directly	**elicit** verb to get something, especially information or reaction	**implicit** adjective implied, rather than expressly stated

47	**inflation** *noun* a continuing rise in prices caused by an increase in the money supply and demand for goods	**influx** *noun* the fact of a large number of people or things arriving at the same time		
48	**access** *noun* the right or opportunity to use or look at something	**excess** *noun* an amount or action that is more than acceptable, expected, or reasonable	**recess** *noun* a period of time in which an organized activity such as study or work is temporarily stopped	**success** *noun* the achieving of the results wanted or hoped for

Example 1: Teenagers find it hard to <u>except</u> that their parents are usually wiser than them.

    A) NO CHANGE

    B) accept

    C) expect

    D) intercept

Explanation:

The correct answer is (B).

except: not including; other than

(ex. everyone except me was invited to the party)

expect: believe something will happen

(ex. I expected it to rain tomorrow but it did not)

intercept: stop something from getting from one place to another

(ex. the Americans secretly intercepted German codes during the war)

accept: agree; admit yes to

Example 2: Clay and Lauren were <u>discrete</u> about their actual relationship at work.

    A) NO CHANGE

    B) disagree

    C) concrete

    D) discreet

Explanation:

discrete: separate from each other
(ex. when trying to achieve a goal, try to break it down into discrete steps)

disagree: say no to; not accepting as true
(ex. I disagree with the idea that cats are better pets than dogs)

concrete: definite and specific
(ex. the detective wants concrete evidence instead of just guesses)

discreet: hiding something from others

Practice Questions

1. British Royal Guards can remain <u>stationery</u> for hours before switching post with the next officer.
    A) NO CHANGE
    B) stagnant
    C) sanctuary
    D) stationary

2. When my blind date refused to turn her seat over to the elderly on the bus, I ended the date right th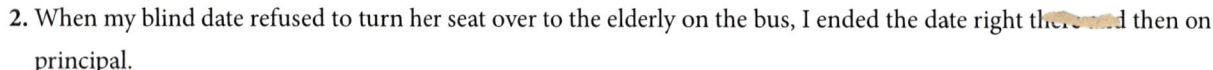d then on <u>principal</u>.
    A) NO CHANGE
    B) principate
    C) principality
    D) principle

3. "I'm telling you again that I did not <u>loss</u> my wallet on the train!" Kathy shouted.
    A) NO CHANGE
    B) lose
    C) loosen
    D) loose

4. Despite the advance in technology, scientists still don't know what exactly resides in the <u>chore</u> of our planet Earth.
    A) NO CHANGE
    B) court
    C) core
    D) corps

5. Hannah was furious that her boyfriend had poured too much water for her plant and caused it to die.
    A) NO CHANGE
    B) had pored
    C) have poured
    D) have pored

6. When you tell the same story over and over again, even if it is very unique and interesting, it becomes a bit of a boer.
    A) NO CHANGE
    B) bohr.
    C) boar.
    D) bore.

7. It was time for Anthony to decide: weather to marry the girl his parents had chosen for him or run away and go after his true love.
    A) NO CHANGE
    B) when
    C) wither
    D) whether

8. To everyone's surprise, chili sauce turned out to be a good compliment to crackers.
    A) NO CHANGE
    B) comment
    C) completion
    D) complement

9. With the meeting in a state of chaos, the delegate didn't know whether to precede with her speech.
    A) NO CHANGE
    B) proceeds
    C) proceed
    D) cede

10. With just one week left until he enters the army training center, Park decided to die his hair pink.
    A) NO CHANGE
    B) dye
    C) dice
    D) dry

Chapter Test

Passage 1

Choose the answer that best replaces the underlined part:

From pyramids to hieroglyphs, ancient Egyptians created many wonders of the ancient world. Among them, the sphinx is <u>debatably</u>₁ one of the most well-known — we are all familiar with the great lionlike sentinels accompanying Egyptian pyramids. <u>All of</u>₂ them, the largest and most famous is the Sphinx of Giza, with its <u>location</u>₃ right next to the Great Pyramids of Giza.

The exact names <u>they're</u>₄ builders had given them is still unknown, but scholars believe that the original names would have been related to the sun deity "Sekhmet." Egyptians often linked their leaders, "pharaohs," with the Sun God "Ra." Sekhmet was the daughter of Ra according to Egyptian myth, making it <u>sheer</u>₅ how the ancient Egyptians identified their leader with the Sun God. It would have made sense to them to believe that the Sun God's daughter would be the one to guard his proxy.

The Egyptians <u>stiffly</u>₆ believed in resurrection, and that sphinxes acted as protectors of the pyramids. They believed that sphinxes would keep the tomb of the Sun God <u>sheltered</u>₇ until the Sun God finally <u>raised</u>₈ from the dead to <u>rein</u>₉ once more.

1. A) NO CHANGE
   B) arguably
   C) disputably
   D) controversially

2. A) NO CHANGE
   B) Between
   C) With
   D) Among

3. A) NO CHANGE
   B) position
   C) orientation
   D) point

4. A) NO CHANGE
   B) there
   C) their
   D) they are

5. A) NO CHANGE
   B) crystalline
   C) clear
   D) limpid

6. A) NO CHANGE
   B) tautly
   C) tightly
   D) firmly

7. A) NO CHANGE
   B) sequestered
   C) restricted
   D) reclusive

8. A) NO CHANGE
   B) raisen
   C) rose
   D) risen

9. A) NO CHANGE
   B) reign
   C) rain
   D) wane

Passage 2

Choose the answer that best replaces the underlined part:

During the Second World War, the Germans possessed a strong aerial arsenal that facilitated the German accent₁₀ into the ranks of the major powers. "Luftwaffe" was the name of the German air force, and the name alone was enough to engender fear in the minds of those who lived then₁₁.

The Luftwaffe's main tactic was quite simple but very lethal. The fighters flew in a formation called "the Schwarm," in which 2 pairs of aircraft — a leader flight completed₁₂ by a wingman in each pair — operated as one team. It allowed them to create the delusion₁₃ that only one pair of fighters was approaching, when actually they moved in two pairs — a huge strategic advantage when engaging the enemy. Though₁₄ this tactic, Germany was able to achieve air superiority and eventually air supremacy.

Once the danger of Germany became eminent₁₅, the British Royal Air Force (RAF) started to expand vastly. RAF began to bomb Germany back, with its newest squadrons equipped with radar to posture₁₆ more accurate communication. Luftwaffe fought back with reorganized flights called "night fighters," which had been modified to equip Lichtenstein radars and enabled them to adapt to nighttime battles. With both sides using the latest radar technology, the war seemed to last forever.

The brutal war soon came to an end, with the Axis powers ultimately defeated₁₇. Ironically, the aerial tactics utilized by Luftwaffe and RAF became the basis for modern air force tactics.

10. A) NO CHANGE
    B) ascent
    C) assent
    D) essence

11. A) NO CHANGE
    B) than
    C) when
    D) there

12. A) NO CHANGE
    B) complimented
    C) complemented
    D) compelled

13. A) NO CHANGE
    B) illusion
    C) allusion
    D) collusion

14. A) NO CHANGE
    B) Thorough
    C) Threw
    D) Through

15. A) NO CHANGE
    B) imminent
    C) immanent
    D) innominate

16. A) NO CHANGE
    B) insure
    C) ensure
    D) reassure

17. A) NO CHANGE
    B) outdone
    C) outperformed
    D) relinquished

Passage 3

Choose the answer that best replaces the underlined part:

Whose₁₈ to blame for the heavy air pollution in the State of California? In the US, there constantly has been an unresolved struggle₁₉ to solve the problem of air pollution. Long has the once-clean air of California been eloped₂₀ in dust clouds and smog.

Since the 1960's, the US Congress has enacted several laws — namely "Clean Air Acts" — too₂₁ strengthen the regulation of air pollution. These bills set limits on the stockpiling₂₂ of pollutants allowed in the air and provided guidelines to limit recessive₂₃ consumption of fuels that affect₂₄ air pollution. However, it rests uncertain whether these efforts have yielded enough results to create an actual impact.

Despite all the efforts to reduce air pollution, the residents of California still argue that these efforts have largely been unfinished₂₅ — they are still exposed to highly toxic material in the air. They are indeed correct, with Los Angeles having the most contaminated air in the whole country. Chemicals from engines, motor vehicles and industries are still driving up the pollutant levels, yet nothing empirical₂₆ is being done to alleviate the health consequences. Even the Environmental Protection Agency (EPA) has issued several warnings about the health threats. It is momentous₂₇ that the state addresses these issues, which may have far-reaching consequences for citizens.

18. A) NO CHANGE
    B) Who's
    C) Who
    D) Whom

19. A) NO CHANGE
    B) scuttle
    C) melee
    D) bout

20. A) NO CHANGE
    B) developed
    C) redeveloped
    D) enveloped

21. A) NO CHANGE
    B) to
    C) through
    D) two

22. A) NO CHANGE
    B) concentration
    C) accumulation
    D) amalgamation

23. A) NO CHANGE
    B) accessive
    C) excessive
    D) successive

24. A) NO CHANGE
    B) effect
    C) infect
    D) defect

25. A) NO CHANGE
    B) deficient
    C) unfruitful
    D) inconclusive

26. A) NO CHANGE
    B) experimental
    C) serviceable
    D) practical

27. A) NO CHANGE
    B) imperative
    C) inevitable
    D) insistent

10 Style, Tone and Syntax

10-1. Style and Tone

One-Point Lesson

Style refers to the way something is written. In order to achieve a particular style, the writer may use the following:

1) Sentence structure
   - Pattern of repeating words
   - Pattern of repeating structures

Example: You must speak with earnestness, dream with passion, and <u>act courageously</u> (✕).

act courageously → act with courage

2) Literary techniques
   - Irony
   - Understatement
   - Overstatement/hyperbole

Example 1: <u>Today wasn't too bad</u> — I tripped and sprained my ankle on my way to school, forgot to bring my math assignment, and accidentally threw away 50 dollars.

'Today wasn't too bad' is an example of understatement.

Example 2 : His voice <u>thundered like a storm.</u>

Human voice cannot literally 'thunder like a storm.' This is an overstatement.

Tone refers to the writer's attitude.
Most common examples
- Humorous vs. serious
- Passionate vs. detached
- Casual vs. formal

Tone is often conveyed through the writer's **Diction** (=word choice).

Example 1

Formal	Casual
The guests were *not pleased with* the menu	The guests *didn't like* the menu

Diction may also convey positive or negative connotations.

Example 2

Positive	Negative
Stephen has an *inquisitive* mind.	Stephen is a *nosy* child.

SAT-Style Example

1. The author wants to use understatement as a rhetorical style. Which choice best accomplishes this goal?

   I would say that the meal <u>was simply horrible</u>₁. To begin with, the onion soup was served cold; then the rice for the main dish wasn't even cooked properly; and as for the dessert, I found a strand of grey hair in my parfait.

   1. A) NO CHANGE
   B) was absolutely delightful
   C) did not quite live up to my expectations
   D) was the worst thing I've ever tasted in my life

2. For the sake of rhetorical effect, the writer wants to maintain the pattern of using words with contrasting definitions. Which choice best accomplishes this goal?

   We should always bear in mind that the difference between Asian and American culture is not nearly as simple as conformity versus uniqueness, community versus individual, or <u>tradition versus conservation</u>₂.

   2. A) NO CHANGE
   B) tradition and conservation
   C) preservation versus conservation
   D) tradition versus innovation

3. Choose the answer that best expresses enthusiasm consistent with the tone of an informative essay.

   1492 was a year of immense historical importance; it witnessed several major global events which led to the world as we know it. Perhaps the most well-known fact is the discovery of the New World by Christopher Columbus. However, <u>it is also important to note</u>₃ the events that happened before — and led to — Columbus's voyage. To begin with, there is the Fall of Granada which took place in January 1492.

   3. A) NO CHANGE
   B) you should also know
   C) we must remember
   D) it is recommended to note

Explanation:

The correct answers are (C), (D), and (A).

1. The original sentence conveys its meaning in a literal way without any rhetorical effect. Since the question is asking for an understatement, choice (A) can be ruled out. Choice (B) is verbal irony, which says the exact opposite of what the writer actually means. Choice (D) is an example of overstatement, not understatement. Therefore, choice (C) is the answer.

2. In order to maintain the pattern of the sentence, make sure that the last 3 phrases of the sentence are identical in structure. The first two phrases ('conformity versus uniqueness, community versus individual') show that a pair of opposite words is used in each phrase. Thus, the third phrase should be 'tradition versus innovation.' Therefore, choice (D) is the answer.

3. Note that this paragraph is written in an objective tone and its purpose is to convey information. Thus, choices (B) and (C) can be immediately ruled out since they deviate from the passage's academic nature by using the pronouns 'you' and 'we.' Choice (D) is grammatically correct, but it presents an awkward and unnecessary wording. Therefore, choice (A) is the answer.

Practice Questions

1. The author wants to use understatement as a rhetorical style. Which choice best accomplishes this goal?

I have an interview tomorrow for a company I've been preparing for my entire college life and my ex-boyfriend is applying for it too. Yeah, you could say I'm feeling hysterical!

   A) NO CHANGE
   B) I'm feeling so comfortable!
   C) Yeah, you could say I'm a little tense!
   D) I've never been more agitated in my life!

2. The author wants to use overstatement in order to emphasize the speaker's hunger. Which choice best accomplishes this goal?

I haven't had anything to eat since I got up. I'm so hungry I could eat a three-course meal!

   A) NO CHANGE
   B) don't think I can eat anything!
   C) won't be able to eat for hours!
   D) could eat an entire brontosaurus!

3. Which choice best expresses enthusiasm consistent with the tone of a formal award acceptance speech?

I <u>am excited to accept</u> this award for the best actor. I am glad the audience enjoyed my performance as Mr. Jonas. He was a very interesting character to portray and I thoroughly enjoyed my time living as him. I would like to thank director Darrel Thornton for casting me and all the staffs for tirelessly working to make this movie possible. I would also like to thank my friends and family who never fail to inspire and help me. I look forward to seeing you all again in my next work.

    A) NO CHANGE

    B) am accepting

    C) am required to accept

    D) am all hearts and butterflies to accept

4. In order to emphasize the contrast between a diet and his preference, the author wants to use two adjectives that are derived from the same root word. Which choice best accomplishes this goal?

Diet seems to be on everyone's mind these days. But life is too short for me to not eat the food I enjoy. When other are having their <u>nutritious diet, I prefer an unhealthy</u> assortment of hamburgers, beef jerky, and ice cream sundaes.

    A) NO CHANGE

    B) balanced diet, I prefer a toxic

    C) healthy diet, I prefer a disgusting

    D) healthy diet, I prefer an unhealthy

5. When drunk, Don gets into a habit of throwing things, punching things, and breaking things. <u>He also kicks things.</u>

    A) NO CHANGE

    B) He also starts kicking things.

    C) He also starts to kick things.

    D) Kicking is also a habit he develops.

10-2. Redundancy

One-Point Lesson

Redundancy happens when the same idea is **unnecessarily** repeated within a sentence or paragraph using synonyms or slightly different wording. If there are any redundant words or phrases in the underlined part, always pick the answer that omits the redundancy.

Keep in mind that redundancy can also occur in **quotation marks**. If the writer uses quotation marks around a word to signal that he/she is using the word in an *ironic sense*, it is redundant for the sentence to spell out the ironic meaning.

Example 1: The loud car emitted a deafening roar as it sped along the road (×)

    The car emitted a deafening roar

    'loud' and 'deafening' are redundant. Take out one of the words.

Example 2: The so-called "feast", which was not actually a feast, was not enough to satisfy the guests (×)

    The so-called "feast" was not enough to satisfy the guests.

    the use of 'so called' and the quotation marks around 'feast' already signal that this is not actually a feast.

SAT-Style Example

Choose the answer that best replaces the underlined part:

On February 9th 2014, visitors of Copenhagen Zoo at the giraffe house witnessed a shocking event. In front of a crowd of watching spectators₁, a 2-year old giraffe was fed its favorite meal of rye bread by a zookeeper and promptly shot in the head with a rifle. Afterwards the lifeless giraffe₂, was dissected in public, accompanied by detailed explanations from a zoo official. Chunks of its meat were carried away and fed to the lions at the zoo. This public killing has sparked outrage around the world, and many protestors have accused the zoo of staging a cruel publicity stunt.

1. A) NO CHANGE
   B) a watching audience
   C) a crowd of spectators
   D) spectators, who watched the event

2. A) NO CHANGE
   B) the giraffe's dead carcass
   C) the dead giraffe's carcass
   D) the giraffe's dead and lifeless body

Explanation:

The correct answers are (C) and (A).

You must decide whether there are any redundant words or phrases in the underlined part.

In the first question, the word 'spectator' already means 'someone who observes, or watches, an event', and is therefore redundant with the word 'watching'. The correct answer (C) eliminates this redundancy.

In the second question, the original sentence does not contain any redundancies, while the other answers feature redundant words such as 'dead', 'carcass', and 'lifeless'. Therefore, the answer is (A).

Practice Questions

Make changes, if necessary, to the underlined phrase in order to eliminate redundancy.

1. In the 1970s, street crime in major cities, especially <u>the kind similar to</u> the New York neighborhoods, became an increasingly more pressing issue to municipal politicians across the country. <u>No error</u>

2. The Arbor Day Foundation has been encouraging the development of tree populations in the US since 1872, <u>annually planting almost 10 million trees each year.</u> <u>No error</u>

3. New Orleans is <u>famous for its well-known jazz artists</u>, whose talent set the grounds for a burgeoning new genre. <u>No error</u>

4. Many of the journalist's articles, which were <u>rapturously enjoyed</u> by readers and fellow pundits alike, focused on an important issue - fossil fuel depletion. <u>No error</u>

5. For years thought of a <u>distant, remote place</u> where one moved to escape the city, the outer boroughs of New York City have been attracting young entrepreneurs in recent years. <u>No error</u>

6. When for the first time the United States imported more oil than it exported, Americans should have realized that an energy crisis may soon <u>happen imminently in the future.</u>
   A) NO CHANGE
   B) happen.
   C) imminently happen.
   D) possibly happen.

7. Catherine the Great could not further her quest for the Russian throne until she could call upon an advisor who commanded stronger <u>forces greater than hers.</u>
   A) NO CHANGE
   B) forces than hers.
   C) forces with more power than hers.
   D) than her.

8. Russia in the mid-20th century was a dictatorship <u>ruled by tyrant Josef Stalin</u>, where dissenters would be purged through trials as enemies of the state.
   A) NO CHANGE
   B) ruled by a tyrant
   C) ruled solely by Josef Stalin
   D) ruled by Josef Stalin

9. A recent discovery is the finding that willpower is a finite resource, and that focusing too much on correcting one's weakness may weaken one's resolve in other areas.
    A) NO CHANGE
    B) is the uncovering of the fact that
    C) lately made is that
    D) is that

10. Fran simultaneously did the dishes and watched TV at the same time because she thought that the TV allowed her to relax while she worked.
    A) NO CHANGE
    B) while watching TV
    C) watched TV
    D) watched TV for leisure

10-3. Wordiness

One-Point Lesson
A wordy sentence uses **complicated syntax** and an **excess of modifying phrases** to convey a simple idea. It can also include ideas that are **irrelevant to the main point** of the sentence. To answer these types of questions, choose the answer that represents the main idea of the underlined part in the *most straightforward way* possible.

Tip: redundant vs. wordy
- *redundant* sentence: The encyclopedia was written for learned scholars.
- *wordy* sentence: The encyclopedia might have originated in the 18th century though nobody is sure, being written for scholars at the time.

Example: The bird eaten by the alligator was delicious to the reptile, as it was its second meal of the day, while the first might have been a snake. (×)

The alligator had a delicious bird for lunch.

the original sentence is confusing because the subject is unclear, and includes irrelevant information at the end.

SAT-Style Example

Choose the answer that best replaces the underlined part:

In the past, diamonds were fairly rare gems, as they had to be panned by people for them in riverbeds that made it a difficult process that likely took a long time$_1$. Then one day in the late 1800s, a material later dubbed "Kimberlite" was found in a South African city of Kimberley. Prospectors realized that they could extract diamonds out of Kimberlite. They found so much Kimberlite that the price of diamonds fell to about $5 per carat. A businessman and diamond magnate named Cecil John Rhodes, came up with the plan to restrict diamond supply in order to retain their scarcity. All of the owners of the South African diamond mines agreed to form a cartel, which later became De Beers Mining Company. Thanks to Rhodes' strategy, along with genius marketing from an advertising firm that also created slogans for AT&T$_2$, diamonds are believed to be rare and expensive jewels to this day.

1. A) NO CHANGE
   B) as people had to pan for them, in difficult riverbeds for a long time
   C) because people had to pan for them in riverbeds, which was a difficult and long process
   D) DELETE the underlined portion and end the sentence with a period.

2. A) NO CHANGE
   B) which was actually a product of genius marketing by an advertising firm
   C) combined with genius marketing
   D) especially after the advertising firm that De Beers hired

Explanation:

The correct answers are (C) and (C).

In the first question, the main idea of the sentence is best expressed by answer choice (C). Deleting the portion altogether would leave out a significant part of the sentence.

In the second question, the information about the advertising firm is irrelevant to the passage. Therefore the best answer that eliminates wordiness is (C).

Practice Questions

1. For <u>as many as twenty years and more</u> Joseph Conrad lived the life of a sailor.
    A) NO CHANGE
    B) more than twenty years
    C) the length of over twenty year
    D) twenty years and additional years after

2. Contemporary celebrities may attract notice by employing social media; however, <u>there is still worth in traditional hard work and talent</u> by encouraging fans to spread their fame by word of mouth.
    A) NO CHANGE
    B) the value of traditional hard work and talent is still found
    C) hard work and talent are still valuable
    D) hard work and traditional work and their value can be shown by

3. Many cooks are afraid to make new or exotic dishes in their kitchens, <u>it is because they are unfamiliar with the ingredients and are wary of them as a result</u>.
    A) NO CHANGE
    B) due to the lack of familiarity with the ingredients and the wariness of them that result from it
    C) the result of the cooks' unfamiliarity and wariness of the ingredients
    D) because they are unfamiliar with and wary of the ingredients

4. <u>At the same time when she demonstrated her final attempt to master juggling</u>, Janice was amused by the attention her classmates were giving her.
    A) NO CHANGE
    B) When she tried again and for the last time to become master at the art of juggling
    C) When she demonstrated her final attempt to master juggling
    D) In her final demonstration to the class, in which she was trying to master juggling

5. Quincy protected his job during the last round of firings <u>with his identifying a vital task in the company that no one but he himself could handle</u>.

    A) NO CHANGE

    B) by identifying a vital task in the company that only he could handle

    C) by finding a way to identify a vital task inside the company that could be handled by only him and him alone

    D) by doing the following: identifying a task so vital but can only be handled by him

6. <u>Stephen King is the renowned author of *The Shining*. He recently</u> unveiled his plans for a sequel named *Doctor Sleep*.

Which choice most effectively combines the two sentences at the underlined portion?

    A) Stephen King is the renowned author of *The Shining*; he recently

    B) As the renowned author of *The Shining*, Stephen made a recent announcement: he

    C) In a recent announcement, Stephen King, renowned author of *The Shining*,

    D) Stephen King, renowned author of *The Shining*, recently

7. Yesterday, Puck suddenly yelled "Super Bubba Bomba!" at the top his lungs and ran out of the <u>classroom. The reasons why he did this remain untold by him.</u>

Which choice most effectively combines the two sentences at the underlined portion?

    A) classroom; the reasoning behind this outburst is untold by him.

    B) classroom; consequently, the reasons behind this outburst are untold by him.

    C) classroom, but he would not say why he did this.

    D) classroom; however, the reasons behind this outburst remain untold by him.

8. Glenda has been on a diet for three months now and has significantly lost <u>weight. This weight loss has led to an unfortunate situation:</u> none of her old clothes will fit.

Which choice most effectively combines the two sentences at the underlined portion?

    A) weight, and this weight loss had led to an unfortunate situation, because

    B) weight, resulting in an unfortunate situation:

    C) weight; this weight loss has led to an unfortunate situation:

    D) weight, and has led to an unfortunate situation, because

9. <u>Fans were thrilled by the news of an autograph event featuring all the casts of the popular TV show "Reply 1988". Hundreds of excited viewers</u> queued up at the event location hours in advance.

Which choice most effectively combines the two sentences at the underlined portion?
- A) Fans were thrilled by the news of an autograph event featuring all the casts of the popular TV show "Reply 1988"; in fact, these fans were so thrilled that they
- B) In order to ensure their gain of autographs from the casts of the popular TV show "Reply 1988", hundreds of excited viewers
- C) Fans were so thrilled by the news of an autograph event featuring all the casts of the popular TV show "Reply 1988" that they
- D) Fans of the TV show "Reply 1988", thrilled by the news of an autograph event featuring all the casts, numbered in hundreds and

10. <u>Emperor Claudius was a Gallic transplant to the city. He</u> always felt out of place in the courts of Rome.

Which choice most effectively combines the two sentences at the underlined portion?
- A) Emperor Claudius, being that he was a Gallic transplant to the city,
- B) Emperor Claudius, a Gallic transplant to the city,
- C) Emperor Claudius was a Gallic transplant to the city; so he
- D) A Gallic transplant to the city, Claudius, Emperor of Rome,

10-4. Voice

One-Point Lesson

There are two voices in the English language: active and passive.

Active voice: Subject *does* the action of the verb
    ex) I threw the ball to my dog. (Subject: I/ Verb: threw)

Passive voice: Subject *receives* the action of the verb— normally the role of the direct object
    ex) The ball was thrown by me to my dog (Subject: The ball/ Verb: was thrown)

Except for a few special cases, ACTIVE voice is better than PASSIVE voice. If a passive voice is used in the underlined part, choose the answer that corrects the voice to an active one **especially** if the subject in this case is a person.

Example: A test was taken by Gary. (×)
    Gary took a test.
    The sentence should be corrected to an active voice. Gary is the one who *does* the action of the verb (take), so he should be the subject.

SAT-Style Example

Choose the answer that best replaces the underlined part:

Ancient Greek philosopher Epicurus believed that the human body and mind were both made of material elements, and based his philosophy of happiness upon this belief. He said that <u>happiness can only be gotten by you through things that are</u>₁ directly under your control. Happiness comes at fulfilling your body's most basic needs, such as hunger, thirst, and cold. You must also not procrastinate, because you cannot control the future, only the present. Putting things off for "the right time", when you don't know what might happen in the future, is a waste of life. <u>Your happiness will be taken away by meddling in the business of others, or forcing yourself to do something beyond your power</u>₂. Lastly, pleasure and wisdom, well-being, and justice go hand in hand; a man whose life lacked any of those elements will never be able to be truly happy.

1. A) NO CHANGE
   B) happiness can only be achieved through things that are
   C) happiness is only the things
   D) you can only achieve happiness through things that are

2. A) NO CHANGE
   B) Meddling in the business of others, or forcing yourself to do something beyond your power, will take away your happiness
   C) Meddle in the business of others, or force yourself to do something beyond your power, and you will be less happy
   D) Your happiness will be less if you meddle in the business of others, or force yourself to do something beyond your power

Explanation:

The correct answers are (D) and (B).

In the first question, the sentence's verb in its base form is 'get'. The subject that *does* this verb is 'you'. Therefore the correct answer that uses 'you' as the subject is (D).

It is a little harder to locate the subject of the second question, but let's start by finding the verb. The verb in its base form is 'take (away)'. The subject is 'meddling in the business of others' or 'forcing yourself to do something beyond your power'. The answer that correctly uses the active voice is (B).

Practice Questions

Change the underlined phrase into a different voice (active/passive) if necessary.

1. All over the country, <u>lawmakers are brought together from opposing sides of issues by The Bipartisan Policy Center.</u> <u>No error</u>

2. In Tsarist Russia, economic stagnation and a series of failed military adventures made many citizens furious, and a <u>communist uprising was begun.</u> <u>No error</u>

3. The seven volumes of In Search of Lost Time by Marcel Proust <u>are begun as</u> a narrator bites into a small cookie and leads to the longest novel in world literature. <u>No error</u>

4. John Sullivan, the first boxer that <u>they recognized as</u> heavyweight champion of the world, began his training in a barn as a youth. <u>No error</u>

5. Despite the fact that the restaurant is always fully booked at night, <u>we are always held responsible by the owners</u> for that day's income if it is not high enough the next morning. <u>No error</u>

6. Signs of life on distant planets, <u>is believed by astronomers to be soon found, thanks</u> to advances in imaging software and telescope capabilities.
    A) NO CHANGE
    B) astronomers believe, will soon be found, thanks
    C) will soon be found is what astronomer believe, thanks
    D) which astronomers believe will soon be found, thanks

7. The plans for the Superconducting Supercollider were completely finished and it was well underway; however, further funding <u>was not able to be secured through</u> Congress.
    A) NO CHANGE
    B) was not secured by the ability of
    C) and its security was not gained by
    D) was not secured with the ability of

8. In the 1920s itinerant workers were known to leave codes on the gateposts of homes, and later travelers were assisted by this by warning them of benefits and dangers.

   A) NO CHANGE
   B) travelers were later assisted by this
   C) later this assisted travelers
   D) travelers were later assisted

9. Because pot-bellied pigs can learn many tricks, pot-bellied pigs are being purchased by some people as house pets.

   A) NO CHANGE
   B) some people are purchasing pot-bellied pigs
   C) being purchased by some people are pot-bellied pigs
   D) pigs with pot-bellies are being purchased by some people

10. Most people tend to accept information that agrees with their preconceptions, and it is rare for tolerance to be shown to challenging ideas.

    A) NO CHANGE
    B) for tolerance to be shown by them regarding
    C) for their tolerance to be shown to
    D) for them to show tolerance to

10-5. Register

One-Point Lesson

Register is the type of language that a writer would use in an essay with a certain purpose and/or tone. When answering a Register question, think about **what kind of register** is used in *the rest of the passage*, and choose the answer that best matches that register.

Tip: "stuff", "things", and slang/nonstandard words usually signal that the answer choice is wrong UNLESS the rest of the passage is written in the same way.

Example: When starting an ant farm, one should always wear a pair of gloves because <u>my bro told me ants are poisonous or something</u>. (✗)
some ants are poisonous
The underlined part is too casual and uses a nonstandard word ('bro'). To match the register of the rest of the sentence, it should be corrected to a more formal tone.

SAT-Style Example

Choose the answer that best replaces the underlined part:

Pantone LLC is a company best known for the Pantone Matching System, the standard for matching colors widely used by the graphic arts community. Each year the company declares a "Color of the Year", which <u>I guess you could say</u>₁ connects with the spirit of the times. This color is chosen by a few representatives from color standards' groups around the world, and influences various fields such as fashion design, makeup, and florists in preparing their <u>thing,</u>₂ for the following year. For example, in 2012 the Color of the Year, Tangerine Tango (a rich burnt orange), was used in Sephora's nail polish, eye shadow, lip gloss, and eyeliner.

1. A) NO CHANGE
   B) I guess
   C) purportedly
   D) may or may not

2. A) NO CHANGE
   B) products
   C) habiliments
   D) junk and stuff

Explanation:
The correct answers are (C) and (B).
For both questions, the register of the original sentence is too casual compared to the generally informative and formal tone of passage. The answers that best match the register of the passage is (C) and (B). (A), (B) and (D), and (A) and (D) are too casual, while (C) 'habiliments' is too formal.

Practice Questions

1. W.A. Mozart is widely considered to be one of the _____ composers of all time, even though his period of composition was relatively short.
   A) greatest
   B) most awesome
   C) most stupendous

2. Attempts at filming the Twilight series caused _____ from purists, who expect Hollywood to follow the original source material page by page.
   A) ireful resistance
   B) angry backlash
   C) bad reactions

3. One conference attendee claimed that thanks to biological modification, soon all of recorded knowledge would be available _____.
   A) in a jiffy
   B) in the blink of an eye
   C) at once

4. An analyst who proves that an assumption is incorrect can then try to _____ a correct one using the collected data.
   A) formulate
   B) make up
   C) cook up

5. During a week-long retreat, _____ who are bitter rivals in the halls of Congress enjoy a dinner together, share a cup of coffee, and discuss the issues they have in common.
   A) people doing legal stuff
   B) rule making persons
   C) lawmakers

6. You _____ increased crime rates when prisoners are released after short periods.
   A) get fears of
   B) get scared of
   C) become concerned about

7. Some consider you unsuccessful if you are making less than 50,000 dollars a year. But what if you do not care about making money? _____, when was money decided as the only important measure of accomplishment?

    A) And another thing

    B) And also

    C) And something else

8. Throughout the world, _____ wrote confusing books trying to explain what their experiments meant.

    A) intelligent men

    B) smart guys

    C) savvy chaps

9. _____ Americans have followed the tale of the Revolution, the Continental Congress, and the beginnings of the nation.

    A) A zillion

    B) Countless

    C) Loads of

10. He tells one of his many jokes, _____, and then my mood seems to lift effortlessly.

    A) does a real funny voice

    B) executes a droll piece of mimicry

    C) makes a hilarious impression

Chapter Test

Passage 1

Choose the answer that best replaces the underlined part:

Sherlock Holmes — Sir Arthur Conan Doyle's creation and main character of his numerous detective novels and short stories— is a household name all around the world. A name less well-known is Joseph Bell, the person from the same era as Charles Dickens and Conan Doyle that the beloved fictional character was based on$_1$. Bell was a Scottish surgeon and lecturer at the medical school of the University of Edinburgh in the 19th century. Like Holmes, he emphasized the importance of making close observations on a subject and deducing logical conclusions from physical evidence. His techniques became the basis for forensic science — the scientific method of collecting, gathering, and examining$_2$ information about the past for use in the court of law.

1. A) NO CHANGE
   B) Bell, on whom the beloved fictional character was based
   C) Bell, who made the beloved fictional character who he is
   D) Bell, who was the background force of inspiration for the beloved fictional character

2. A) NO CHANGE
   B) gathering and examining
   C) the collection and examination of
   D) collecting, gathering, and analyzing

Passage 2

Choose the answer that best replaces the underlined part:

One of my favorite Impressionist paintings is *Two Dancers at* Rest, or *Dancers in Blue* by Edgar Degas. It features two dancers in blue dresses stretching their legs and chatting casually, possibly between performances on stage or during a break from rehearsals. I like this painting because₃ it portrays the dancers in a relaxed mood. One of the dancers is leaning on her elbow while smiling, on her other side the other dancer holding her foot with one hand,₄ perhaps examining it for blisters. The calm peacefulness that the dancers share is well reflected through the color palette of the painting: the soft but vibrant blue of their dresses, the earthy but bright yellow of their background, the snug and fiery₅ red of their hair. The atmosphere of this painting is quite different from the polished perfection exuded by his other "Dancer" paintings, which show₆ performing dancers and tense anticipation of those about to go on stage.

3. A) NO CHANGE
   B) One of its artistic merits that goes undisputed by professionals is that
   C) This painting is really cool because
   D) DELETE the underlined part

4. A) NO CHANGE
   B) elbow, smiling, and the other is holding her foot with one hand,
   C) elbow and smiles, while the dancer on the other side holds her foot and
   D) elbow and visibly smiling, while the other dancer is holding her foot with one hand and

5. Which choice best maintains the intent and pattern of the sentence?
   A) NO CHANGE
   B) snug but fiery
   C) fiery and snug
   D) fiery but snug

6. A) NO CHANGE
   B) the perfectly polished atmosphere of the other "Dancer" paintings, also by Degas, who drew
   C) the atmosphere of his other "Dancer" paintings, which feature the polished perfection of
   D) the atmosphere exuding of polished perfection, visible in his other "Dancer" paintings, through

Passage 3

Choose the answer that best replaces the underlined part:

People usually think that children are illogical thinkers₇, and therefore easy to fool with magic tricks. However, contrary to popular belief, there are several reasons why children are actually pretty good at guessing a magician's secrets. First, children do not fall for misdirection because they shift their focus constantly. Children will pay attention to everything on stage, and not just to what the magician wants them to. A magician has a bumpy ride tricking kids to look at₈, say, the wand in his right hand while he secretly switches the card with his left. Also, children are better at thinking outside the box than adults. They can come up with wild theories about how the magician pulled off a certain move— but these theories are "wild" only to adults because they are beyond the boundaries of what they can imagine₉.

7. A) NO CHANGE
   B) are not very logical
   C) are illogical
   D) think illogically

8. Which choice is most consistent with the casual but formal tone established throughout the rest of the paragraph?
   A) NO CHANGE
   B) This makes it difficult for the magician to guide a children audience's attention to
   C) A magician will grimace and groan getting kids to look at
   D) This can make life real hard for magicians trying to trick kids into looking at

9. A) NO CHANGE
   B) what adults can imagine
   C) the boundaries of what adults can imagine
   D) adult imagination boundaries

Passage 4

Choose the answer that best replaces the underlined part:

The ancient origins of golf are <u>not really clear to me, as it could be like</u>₁₀ the Roman game of *paganica* from the 1ˢᵗ century BC, or the Chinese *chuiwan* played between the 8ᵗʰ and 14ᵗʰ centuries. Modern golf, on the other hand, can be traced back to Scotland during the High Middle Ages (900 – 1300 AD). Golf courses and clubs, as well as the written rules and the <u>18 hole course, were originated in the country</u>₁₁. The earliest written record that mentions golf is James II's banning of the game in 1457; this ban was lifted by James IV (grandson of James II) in 1502. Many golfers consider the Old Course at the Scottish town of St. Andrews a site of pilgrimage, for it is <u>where the sport was first played in the 1400s, as well as where</u>₁₂ the 18 hole course was established.

10. A) NO CHANGE
    B) pretty shady in my opinion, because it could be
    C) heavily debated, as scholars speculate it to be
    D) DELETE the underlined part

11. A) NO CHANGE
    B) 18 hole course, originated there
    C) 18 hole course came to be in the country of Scotland
    D) course of 18 holes comes from this country

12. A) NO CHANGE
    B) the place of the first game of playing golf in the 1400s, and also the site of where
    C) the site of the first game of golf and where
    D) here that the sport was first played in the 1400s and where

Passage 5

Choose the answer that best replaces the underlined part:

Recent studies showed that exercise habits can shape adult bodies and brains regardless of DNA or environment. Researchers at the University of Jyvaskyla and other institutions in Finland wanted to see whether working out could be the direct cause of changes in the human body, unrelated to the person's genetics or the way he or she was raised. They examined 10 pairs of male <u>identical twins, with the exact same genetic material</u>$_{13}$, in their twenties, one of whom regularly exercised while the other did not; their workout routines had diverged within the past three years, but their diets were still similar. The researchers measured each man's endurance capacity, body composition and insulin sensitivity, and also <u>his brain was scanned</u>$_{14}$. They found that the twin who exercised regularly was not only healthier (higher endurance capacity, less body fat, and less metabolic problems), but also had more gray matter in their brains, especially in areas that involve motor control and coordination. This led the researchers to <u>reasonably come to a conclusion that genetics and environment do not have to dictate</u>$_{15}$ a person's workout habits. Even if our genes and our upbringing urge us to slump on the couch, we can overcome those impulses and improve our bodies and brains.

13. A) NO CHANGE
    B) identical twins, who carry the same DNA,
    C) twins who have identical genetic material
    D) identical twins

14. A) NO CHANGE
    B) had a brain scan
    C) their brains were scanned
    D) scanned his brain

15. A) NO CHANGE
    B) say that nothing, including genetics and environment, influences
    C) conclude that genetics and environment do not affect
    D) guess that there are factors other than genetics and environment that have a hold over

11 Insertion/Deletion/Replacement/Content Order

One-Point Lesson

The good thing about SAT Writing passages is that in general, the *content* itself is pretty easy and straightforward. So then the key to this section is to accurately understand the *flow* of a passage – how its structure allows for the buildup, elaboration, and recap of the main idea.

Let's look at an example paragraph below:

> **[1]** The State Hermitage Museum in St. Petersburg, one of Russia's greatest art museums, has long had a productive partnership with a much loved animal: the cat. **[2]** For centuries, cats have guarded this famous museum, ridding it of mice, rats, and other rodents that could damage the art, not to mention scare off visitors. **[3]** Peter the Great introduced the first cat to the Hermitage in the early eighteenth century. **[4]** Continuing the tradition, Peter's daughter Elizaveta introduced the best and strongest cats in Russia to the Hermitage. **[5]** Later Catherine the Great declared the cats to be official guardians of the galleries. **[6]** Today, the museum holds a yearly festival honoring these faithful cats.

The paragraph starts off with a brief introduction **[1]** to the topic (=cats in the Hermitage Museum), giving us a glimpse of what the passage is about. Then, **[2]** is a general statement that explains the significance of the topic, followed by three sentences – **[3]**, **[4]**, and **[5]** – which serve as historical detail. Lastly, a conclusion **[6]** re-emphasizes the main idea: the relationship between the State Hermitage Museum and its cats.

This structure should sound familiar, because it basically is: Introduction/Hook + Main Idea + Supporting Detail + Conclusion! When solving **content ordering problems**, all you need to do is break down the passage into its parts like above and determine if the sentence belongs to its rightful place.

Now let's look at an example **content ordering problem**:

ex) To make this paragraph most logical, sentence 4 should be placed
A) Where it is now.
B) after sentence 2
C) after sentence 5.
D) after sentence 6.

Remember that sentences 3, 4, and 5 are details that support the main idea, so they should be placed between the main idea [2] and conclusion [6]. This immediately eliminates (D). Now look at the context of the three sentences as shown in the original passage – [3] is about Peter the Great, [4] is about his daughter, and [5] is about somebody else who came later. These facts are lined up in chronological order, and they are correctly placed. (B) and (C) are wrong because they disrupt this logical sequence. Thus, the answer is (A).

For **insertion/deletion problems,** a clear understanding of the passage's main idea is crucial. Let's look at an example:

> ex) [2] At this point, the writer is considering adding the following sentence.
>
> This is not surprising when one considers the fact that cat domestication has a long history, dating as far back as 12,000 years ago in the ancient Near East.
>
> Should the writer make this addition here?
> A) Yes, because it supplies quantitative data that will be examined in the rest of the paragraph.
> B) Yes, because it explains the nature of the relationship between cats and the State Hermitage Museum.
> C) No, because it undermines the passage's claim about the popularity of cats in St. Petersburg.
> D) No, because is blurs the passage's focus by introducing a fact that has no direct relevance to it.

Look at the sentence given – it gives information regarding the history of cat domestication. However, bear in mind that the purpose of the passage is to explain why cats have been important to State Hermitage Museum, not how long cats have been domesticated. Thus, the sentence does NOT belong to the passage because it holds irrelevant information. The correct answer is (D).

Replacement problems are similar to sentence ordering problems in that they require a clear understanding of the passage's organization. You will have to replace or maintain an underlined text to provide the best introduction, conclusion, or transition that effectively connects information and ideas. Let's go back to the previous example paragraph.

> The State Hermitage Museum in St. Petersburg, one of Russia's greatest art museums, <u>is always full of art lover from all around the world.</u> For centuries, cats have guarded this famous museum, ridding it of mice, rats, and other rodents that could damage the art, not to mention scare off visitors. Peter the Great introduced the first cat to the Hermitage in the early eighteenth century. Continuing the tradition, Peter's daughter Elizaveta introduced the best and strongest cats in Russia to the Hermitage. Later Catherine the Great declared the cats to be official guardians of the galleries. Today, the museum holds a yearly festival honoring these faithful cats.

The paragraph remains unchanged except for one difference: the introduction. If you have not already noticed, this affects the flow of the passage significantly.

Now let's look at an example of **replacement problem**:

> ex) Which choice provides the most appropriate introduction to the paragraph?
> A) NO CHANGE
> B) hosts a collection of treasured art pieces that cannot be seen anywhere else.
> C) has long had a productive partnership with a much loved animal: the cat.
> D) is a place you must take a look at when you visit the city.

The topic of the entire paragraph deals with cats in the museum and how they came to be there. However, the underlined text says nothing about cats, making it a very awkward introduction to the paragraph. (B) and (D) have the same problems. Only (C) (which was the original text to begin with) provides a clear introduction about cats. Thus, the answer is (C).

Practice Questions

Passage 1

[1] Thomas Edison was responsible for a great number of important inventions, but many people are unaware of how dishonest his "tricks of the trade" could be. [2] There is likely a number of factors that helped Edison, more so than his contemporaries, achieve lasting fame. [3] His natural gift for creativity is certainly one. [4] Sadly, however, another factor was deceit. [5] Edison hoped to ensure himself a lifetime of luxury through his invention of the first direct current generator and, in the process of achieving this goal, compromised his integrity numerous times.

[6] The conflict between his direct current generator and the alternating current generators of his competitors is an embarrassing episode for both business and science. [7] One of the major advantages of alternating current generators is their superior efficiency in transmitting power over long distances, but the patents for alternating current generators were held by Nikola Tesla and George Westinghouse. [8] Technologies often compete for market control, but they usually do not resort to widespread, misinformed campaigns. [9] Public electrocutions of animals were performed by Edison's men in an attempt to discredit the safety of alternating current, which was actually no more dangerous than direct current. [10] Edison, therefore, had to devise a strategy to prove his direct current generators superior.

[11] Then, Edison secretly paid inventor Harold P. Brown to create an execution device using alternating current to further cast doubt on the practicality of his rival invention. [12] However, only alternating current held promise, since the amount of copper wire required for the use of direct current to meet public demand was too costly to be widely implemented. [13] Despite Edison's efforts, alternating current eventually prevailed as the chief means of transmitting electrical energy from power plants into domestic homes. [14] In 1890, Edison officially retired from the electric power business, and the company that he founded merged with its former competitor Thomson-Houston and began fully committing itself to the production of alternating current.

1. In sentence 1, which choice provides the most logical introduction to the passage?
    A) NO CHANGE
    B) and they helped improve the life of millions of people around the world.
    C) but the story of how he invented the light bulb is the most interesting.
    D) but his childhood was anything but normal.

2. To make this paragraph most logical, sentence 2 should be placed
    A) Where it is now.
    B) before sentence 1
    C) after sentence 3
    D) after sentence 4.

3. To make this paragraph most logical, sentence 10 should be placed
    A) Where it is now
    B) after sentence 6
    C) after sentence 7
    D) after sentence 8

4. The writer is considering deleting sentence 8. Should the writer do this?
    A) Yes, because it does not provide reliable information on the technology of Edison's time period.
    B) Yes, because it is an opinionated statement that interrupts the informative explanation on Edison's deceptive strategies.
    C) No, because it provides a detail that proves the author's main point.
    D) No, because it sets up the argument in the next paragraph on Edison's self-centered personality.

5. At this point (after sentence 14), the writer is considering adding the following sentence.

    Needless to say, Edison was bitter that he lost his highly publicized battle against alternating current.

    Should the writer make this addition here?
    A) Yes, because it provides a casual conclusion to the passage.
    B) Yes, because it sheds a new light on the subject matter by taking an emotional perspective.
    C) No, because it undermines the passage's claim about Edison's acts of trickery.
    D) No, because it creates a false impression regarding Edison's remorseful attitude.

Passage 2

[1] At the school where my uncle teaches, his students are really impressed by his skills. [2] At school he always has to make uninteresting subjects exciting for skeptical students. [3] I have seen his classes before; his eyes light up, and he talks with comic enthusiasm about every topic that pops up. [4] His students leave his classroom with true understanding and an increased love of learning. [5] This is the same feeling a person considers when they decide which career path they want to take.

1. The author is considering deleting sentence 5. Should the author make this deletion?
    A) Yes, because it digresses from the topic of the uncle's teaching abilities.
    B) Yes, because it is mostly about students outside of school.
    C) No, because it provides a reason why the students are impressed by the author's uncle.
    D) No, because it is the main point the author is trying to make.

2. The author is considering adding the following sentence after sentence 1.

    He has the skills to really draw in the students and make the subject interesting to everyone.

    Should the writer make this addition here?
    A) Yes, because it explains what skills a teacher needs in class.
    B) Yes, because it provides another example of the uncle's abilities.
    C) No, because it clashes with the ideas of the next sentence.
    D) No, because it makes the next sentence redundant.

Passage 3

[1] Space is controlled by no single country. [2] Outer space is governed by the Outer Space Treaty, drafted and signed in 1967, and since ratified by 100 countries. [3] Additionally, 26 nations have signed the treaty but have not yet ratified it. [4] Almost every nation on earth has allowed that outer space remain a common heritage of humankind for purposes of exploration and use.

[5] Cooperation is easier due to the confined nature of research in space. [6] In space, cooperation amongst scientists and their home nations are made both easier and more complicated than back on Earth. [7] Treaties and contracts signed regarding the International Space Station ensure that no research is military. [8] However, if there is a disagreement regarding a satellite or another outer space mission, there is no legal option for handling it.

1. To make the passage most logical, sentence 4 should be placed
    A) Where it is now.
    B) before sentence 3.
    C) after sentence 1.
    D) before sentence 1.

2. To make the passage most logical, sentence 6 should be placed

    A) Where it is now.

    B) after sentence 8.

    C) before sentence 5.

    D) after sentence 7.

Passage 4

When European explorers first encountered coffee, they remarked on its interesting physical and psychological effects. [2] Until the opening of trade routes between Africa and Italy, coffee was consumed only in the Arab countries. [3] Then, through increased interaction between the Christian and Muslim worlds due to war and trade, coffee spread rapidly throughout Europe. [4] Coffee consumption had a significant influence on many European nations, not to mention on the arts and culture in general. [5]The creation of coffee houses provided places where members of society could gather and exchange ideas. [6]Legendary German composer J.S. Bach wrote one of his most famous pieces, "The Coffee Cantata", about a young woman who had become addicted to the drink.

1. To make the passage most logical, sentence 1 should be placed

    A) Where it is now.

    B) after sentence 2.

    C) after sentence 5.

    D) before sentence 6.

2. To make the passage most logical, sentence 5 should be placed

    A) Where it is now.

    B) before sentence 4.

    C) after sentence 6.

    D) before sentence 1.

Chapter Test

Passage 1

Cordelia

Paragraph 1

Seven playful Border Collie puppies bounded around my legs, a streak of black and white and wagging tails as they leaned their paws against my shins and licked my ankles and bit my toes. Their mother sniffed my hand cautiously before allowing me to pet her. My canine inspectors had all allowed me to pass the doggy test of trust, but only one had let me pass with flying colors. When it was feeding time, both the mother and the puppies flew towards their bowls of smoked salmon – except for one;₁ the sole daughter of the litter was still stubbornly trying to chew off the strap of my left sandal. Instantly I knew that I had found the perfect puppy. [A]

Paragraph 2

[1] In the second week, she had already found her favorite spot: A small circular rug next to my writing table where she would rarely leave my side. [2] Disregarding most suggestions of typical dog names, I decided to name her Cordelia, after the youngest daughter of the eponymous hero in Shakespeare's King Lear. [3] In the first week I brought her home, Cordelia zipped around the house, sniffing madly at everything within the reach of her nose and exploring every nook and cranny. [4] Her burning curiosity matched that of an archaeologist exploring the depths of an archaic temple.

Paragraph 3

And so began Cordelia's regimen of tricks and treats. We started with the most basic commands – sit, shake, roll over. Cordelia was a natural – she got the gist of each trick within the first few hours. Pretty soon, we were moving on from the basics to the advanced. Within three months she mastered a trick that involved playing dead whenever I shot her with my two-fingered gun. Another month, she learned to balance on her hind legs and walk from one end of the lawn to the other. Her level of intelligence wasn't just limited to tricks.₄ [B] She learned to open doors, memorized the names of all thirty-six of her toys, and fetched my slippers at eight in the morning precisely when I woke up.

Paragraph 4

Cordelia's dedication to being with me was only rivalled by her inherent curiosity and boundless energy. At first, I would try to exhaust this massive pool of enthusiasm by taking her for daily runs, but there was a problem: by the end of each run, I wound up feeling more exhausted than my joyful pup, who would clamor for more activity by tackling me when I attempted to rest. My friend recommended that I start teaching Cordelia some tricks.₅ She told me that often, mental stimulation can be just as tiring as its physical counterpart, as well as help to forge stronger bonds between owner and pet. [C]

Paragraph 5

Needless to say, Cordelia quickly became the pride and joy of my life, even more so than my work. Whenever friends or family visited, they would make numerous requests to see her tricks, which she indulged with no hesitation. It was only a matter of time before Mark, a close friend who was an advertiser for a credit card company, approached me and asked if he could star Cordelia in an upcoming ad. I had to think long and hard, but eventually, I had to say no. Though the money would be good, Cordelia was content to perform only on the basis of the trust and love we shared, not as a career. [D]

1. The writer is considering deleting the underlined sentence. Should the sentence be kept or deleted?
    A) Deleted, because it repeats information that has been provided earlier in the paragraph.
    B) Deleted, because it contradicts the information that the dogs trusted the writer.
    C) Kept, because it establishes the difference between Cordelia's and the other dogs' interests in the writer.
    D) Kept, because it foreshadows Cordelia's ability later mentioned in the passage.

2. To make paragraph 2 most logical, sentence 1 should be placed
    A) where it is now.
    B) after sentence 2.
    C) after sentence 3.
    D) after sentence 4.

3. The author wants to add the following sentence to the passage to provide further details.

    And that, truly, was something money couldn't buy.

    The best placement for the sentence is immediately
    A) at point A.
    B) at point B.
    C) at point C.
    D) at point D.

4. Which choice most effectively sets up the information that follows?
    A) NO CHANGE
    B) had its limit though.
    C) has some risk.
    D) was not very astonishing.

5. Before this sentence, the author is considering adding the following sentence.

> Gradually, I found myself too tired to get even a little work done.

Should the writer make this addition here?
A) Yes, because it emphasizes the extent to which keeping Cordelia occupied was a problem for the writer.
B) Yes, because it effectively introduces to us the writer's friend, who plays an important role in the last paragraph.
C) No, because it takes the focus of the passage away from the relationship between the writer and Cordelia.
D) No, because it is not mentioned that the writer has any sort of work.

6. To make the passage most logical, paragraph 3 should be placed:
A) where it is now
B) before paragraph 1.
C) before paragraph 2.
D) after paragraph 4.

Passage 2

Cloud Control

Paragraph 1

A lucid dream is a dream in which you are conscious of the fact that you're dreaming. Lucid dreams are often thought of as the stepping stone to enter the perfect alternate reality, as it is only one small step from being aware of to exerting strong control over the dream. Though random elements do pop up now and then, the dream is mostly open to your command. I was first introduced to lucid dreaming by a friend, who described it as the most surreal experience he had ever had. My curiosity sparked, and I began my research the moment I got home, scouring the Internet for tips for first-time lucid dreamers. Some recommended that I stay absolutely still for thirty minutes. Others advised me to keep a dream diary to recognize common patterns. Also, some others maintained that I perform reality checks when I wasn't sleeping.

Paragraph 2

[1] After a week of lucid-dreamless nights, I finally succeeded. [2] I woke up to find myself in a room with a sunflower in the corner crying, "Marry me! Marry me!" [3] Almost immediately I recognized that something was amiss, and performed a reality check by counting the fingers on my left hand. [4] One, two, three… Four. [5] Hang on, where's the pinky?! [6] Ah, there it is, in the sunflower's mouth! [7] Well-prepared thanks to the tips that experienced lucid dreamers posted online, I immediately summoned a piece of paper with a red circle on it. [8] The circle represented my control over the dream – if my control was fading, the circle would turn from red to blue, a clear indicator to start throwing my weight around.

Paragraph 3

The possibilities were now endless. Keeping the circle tucked behind my left eye, I jumped outside the upside-down room and flew among the clouds. With ease, I began to manipulate their shapes, creating a statue of a girl holding up a pile of diamonds high in the sky. Not long after I was done, a huge Viking ship popped out of nowhere, blasting the statue apart with watermelons and doll heads. I quickly summoned a thundercloud, flicking a finger to strike the hostile Vikings with a thunderbolt. An orchestra of giants looked down at the catastrophe, playing Beethoven's Ninth Symphony as the destruction rained down upon a town.

Paragraph 4

[1] I bounded down the stairs excitedly, turning them into piano keys that played the keyboard solo in The Doors' Light My Fire. [2] Immediately the circle started turning blue. [3] Without a second to spare, I raised a finger and turned her into a winged kangaroo, allowing her to fly out the window. [4] Downstairs I met Mrs. Union, my English Literature teacher, who proceeded to bark, "You're late for school! Hurry up and get going!" [5] The circle slowly returned to red. [6] For good measure I manipulated the laws of gravity and turned the entire room upside-down.

Paragraph 5

"Wake up! Wake up!" As I attempted to save the town by surrounding the debris with a giant cloud, a shrill, familiar cry shrieked into my ear. I turned to see a red parakeet flying by my side, still screaming, "Wake up! You're late for school!" The circle was turning blue again. Before I could turn it into fried chicken, the parakeet lunged forward and grabbed my ear with its beak. An unimaginably real pain sliced into my consciousness, and my eyes flew open. Gone were the Vikings and the giants and the clouds. I was back in the confines of my bed, and my mom was pulling my ear and yelling at me to get up. As I threw my blanket to the side, I realized that I was famished.

7. The writer is considering deleting sentence 8 in paragraph 2. Should the writer do this?
   A) Yes, because it does not serve any rhetorical purpose in the author's story.
   B) Yes, because it provides a redundant explanation of what has been stated before.
   C) No, because it provides an explanation for the writer's act of summoning a red circle.
   D) No, because it foreshadows how the dream is going to end.

8. To make paragraph 4 most logical, sentence 4 should be placed
   A) where it is now.
   B) before sentence 2.
   C) before sentence 3.
   D) before sentence 6.

9. For the sake of the logic and coherence of this essay, Paragraph 3 should be placed
   A) where it is now
   B) before paragraph 1.
   C) before paragraph 2.
   D) after paragraph 4.

10. Which choice most effectively concludes paragraph 5?
    A) NO CHANGE
    B) a bird flew by outside my window.
    C) I found myself wishing that there was such thing as a lucid reality.
    D) my mom exited the room.

12 Graphs & Charts

One-Point Lesson
Some passages from the New SAT Writing section will include a graph or chart. There will be questions that ask you to choose accurate/relevant/effective/etc representation of information provided in a graph. Find the answer *by jumping back and forth* between the answer choice and the graph. *Eliminate* wrong answer choices on the way. Even if you think you've found the correct answer, compare *all* of the choices with the graph to be extra sure.

Graph-specific terms:
INCREASE, DOUBLE, RISE:
- bar graphs: each bar is higher than the one on its left
- line graphs: right side of the line is placed higher than the left

DECREASE, FALL:
- bar graphs: each bar is lower than the one on its left
- line graphs: left side of the line is placed higher than the right

APPRECIABLE/NOTICEABLE change:
- Obvious: obvious change even without reading the numbers on the y-axis
- EXCEED~: check the line or area that the graph is supposed to be exceeding, and see if the bar/line goes above it

Tip: be careful about *generalizations* like "always" or "every year". Even ONE exception to that statement is enough to *eliminate* that answer.

SAT-Style Example

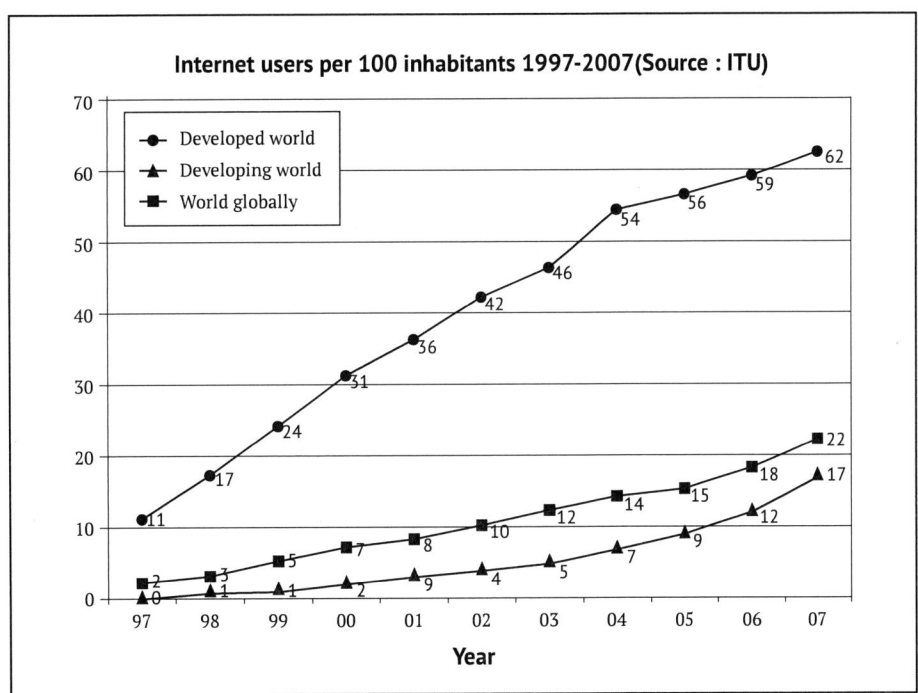

Choose the answer that best replaces the underlined part:

Empathy depends on complex emotions, but the Internet has significantly distanced us from such emotions. In cyberspace, human beings are reduced to one-dimensional profiles, making it much easier for someone to make a hurtful comment. Monica Lewinsky stated in her TED talk about the price of humiliation that the Internet is a place where public shaming is a blood sport, and such shaming is "amplified, uncontained, and permanently accessible." [1] With a steady increase in Internet users around the world, the dehumanizing effects of the Internet seem to have become as potent as ever. Ironically, hope of respite from cyberbullying comes from the fact that too many people have become cyberbullies. Writer Sam Biddle gloried in righteous justice when his post brought Justine Sacco down after she had posted a racist joke on Twitter. [2] Even in the developing world, where the amount of Internet users has quadrupled since 2002, a quick Google search will link Sacco with her tweet for most of her remaining life.

1. Which choice offers the most accurate interpretation of the data in the chart?

    A) NO CHANGE
    B) After the number of Internet users peaked in 2004,
    C) Although the numbers have not increased in the developing world,
    D) With sixty-two people out of a hundred using the Internet,

2. Which choice offers an accurate interpretation of the data in the chart?

    A) NO CHANGE
    B) In the developed world, where sixty-two people out of a hundred lack access to the Internet,
    C) In an era where fifty percent of people still do not have adequate access to the Internet,
    D) While only twelve people out of a hundred use the Internet daily,

Explanation:

The correct answers are (A) and (A).

The graph shows that for the developing world, developed world, and the world combined, the number of Internet users have steadily increased since 1997. Choices (B), (C), (D) are all incorrect interpretations of the chart. Therefore, the answer is (A). For the second question, choice (B) is incorrect because sixty-two percent of people in the developed world do have access to the Internet. Choice (C) is incorrect because more than fifty percent of people do not have adequate access to the Internet. Choice (D) is incorrect because it is impossible to glean information from the chart about daily Internet use. Therefore, the answer is (A).

Practice Questions

Effect of Mutual Gaze Between Pets and Pet-Owners on Oxytocin Levels

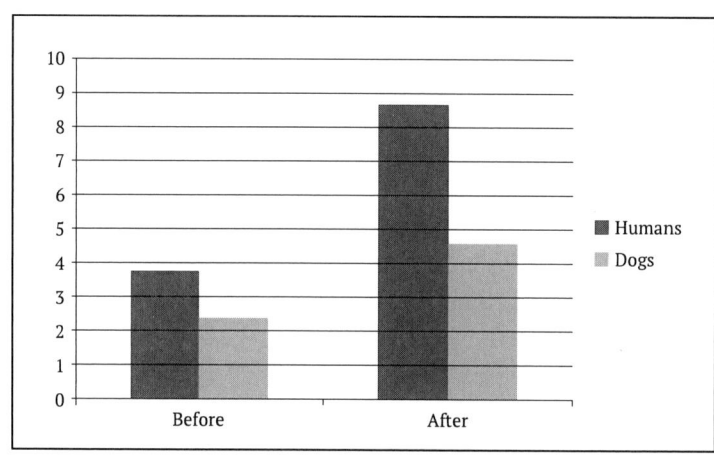

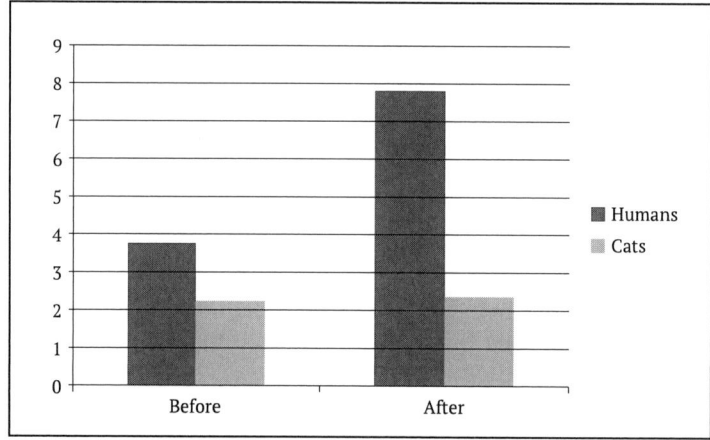

Oxytocin is a hormone known to be associated with emotions of happiness and love.
The two graphs above are the results of an experiment on human-animal interaction. The first graph shows the average oxytocin levels of human pet-owners and their dogs before and after a 30-minute gaze between each pair of pet-owner and pet dog. The second graph shows the average oxytocin levels of human pet-owners and their cats before and after a 30-minute gaze between each pair of pet-owner and pet cat.

1. Choose the option that offers an accurate interpretation of the data in the chart.

    A) Dogs are more capable of expressing emotions of happiness and love.

    B) In general, cats are less affected hormonally by interactions with humans.

    C) Humans show a smaller increase in oxytocin levels after interaction with dogs.

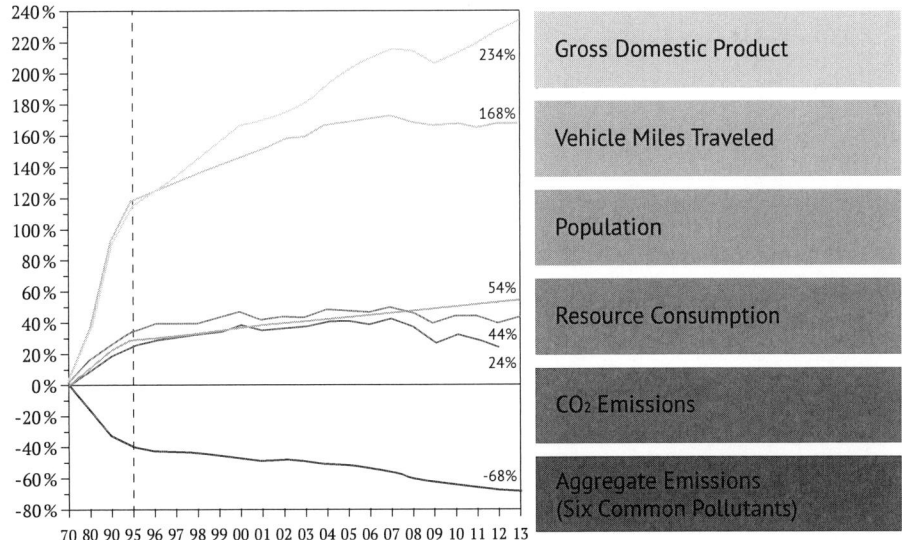

The graph above shows the changes in the growth rates of gross domestic product, vehicle miles traveled, population, resource consumption, CO_2 emissions, and aggregate emissions in the United States from 1970 to 2013.

2. Choose the option that offers an accurate interpretation of the chart.

    A) Vehicle miles traveled is directly proportionate to the gross domestic product.

    B) Aggregate emissions do not include the amount of CO_2 emissions.

    C) The United States has succeeded in finding ways to reduce resource consumption per person in recent years.

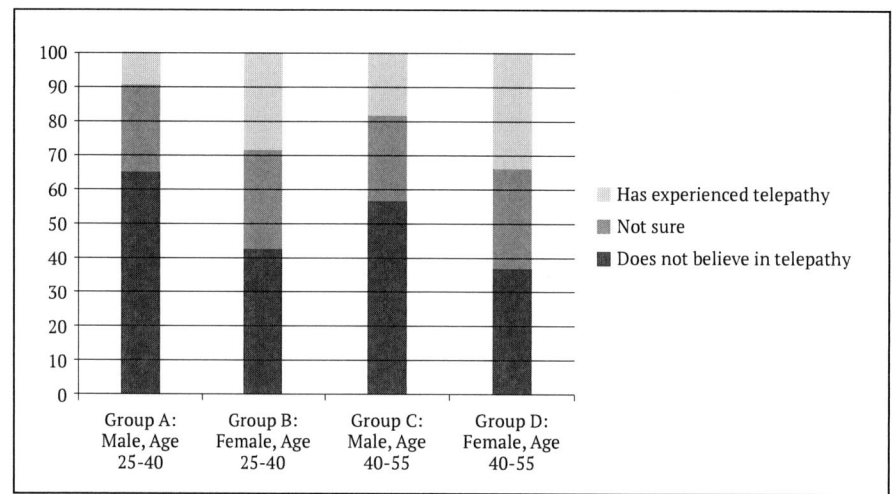

The data above shows the results of a survey conducted on whether telepathy exists. Survey participants were divided into gender and age group and were then asked to choose one of the following three responses: Has experienced telepathy, Not sure, Does not believe in telepathy. Each color shows the percentage of people who chose the corresponding response.

3. Choose the option that offers an accurate interpretation of the data in the chart.

   A) In general, females are more inclined to believe in the existence of telepathy.

   B) Telepathy is more commonly experienced as time progresses, because older generations are more superstitious.

   C) Males do not experience telepathy as often as females because they do not feel as much empathy as females do.

Practice Question Answers & Explanations

1. Number Agreement

1-1. Subject-Verb Agreement

Practice Questions

1. Subject: Kim → singular
   Answer: were → was

2. Subject: Everyone → singular
   Answer: believe → believes

3. Subject: The printing press → singular
   invented around 1440 A.D. → past tense
   Answer: are → was

4. Subject: researchers → plural
   Answer: has been trying → have been trying

5. Subject: Kyle's career → singular
   Answer: no error

6. Subject: Tyler and his sister Ellie → plural
   only plural option → have won
   Answer: A

7. Subject: Anna → singular
   only singular option → shouts
   Answer: C

8. Subject: Anyone → singular
   only singular option → understands
   Answer: A

9. Subject: To Kill A Mockingbird → singular
   only singular option → is
   Answer: B

10. Subject: high school students → plural
    only plural option → hit
    Answer: D

1-2. Noun Agreement

Practice Questions

1. Three → plural adjective
   Answer: no error

2. Fast food, processed meats → plural
   Answer: no error

3. 'Counter-Strike' and 'Call of Duty' → plural
   Answer: an easy computer game → easy computer games

4. All five → plural
   Answer: a doctor → doctors

5. Isaac Newton and Albert Einstein → plural
   Answer: a scientist → scientists

6. Instagram and Snapchat, Two → plural
   only plural option → ways
   Answer: C

7. 'Crowds' implies multiple people → plural
   only plural option → admirers
   Answer: D

8. a patient's ward in a Bosnian hospital → singular
   only singular option → place
   Answer: D

9. Alfonso and Bernadette → plural
   only plural option → gourmets
   Answer: A

10. The professional gamers → plural
    only plural option → experts
    Answer: D

2. Pronouns

2-1. Pronoun Agreement

Practice Questions

1. 'they' → plural
   Answer: alligator → alligators

2. 'they' → plural
   Answer: office position → office positions

3. 'its' → singular
   Answer: Economic depressions → An economic depression

4. 'its' → singular
   Answer: no error

5. 'they' → plural
   Answer: eruption → eruptions

6. 'he' refers to taxi driver
   'them' must refer to underlined part → underlined part must be plural
   only plural option → Emmet and Alfred
   Answer: C

7. 'them' → plural
   only plural option → TV shows
   Answer: A

8. 'it' → singular
   only singular option → delivery
   Answer: C

9. 'his' → singular male
   only singular male option → nephew's
   Answer: B

10. 'he' → singular male
    only singular male option → Every member
    Answer: A

2-2. Pronoun case

Practice Questions

1. The object in possession by 'films' is already stated in noun form – 'plot'. Therefore, the possessive adjective, and not the possessive pronoun, should be used.
   Answer: theirs → their

2. The things being compared are 'your (work)' and 'mine'. Therefore, it is necessary to change the underlined portion to include the object being possessed.
   Answer: your → your work OR your → yours

3. The preposition 'between' requires that the objective case be used.
   Answer: he → him

4. The subjects of the sentence are 'my brother' and 'me'. 'me', therefore, should be changed to the subjective case.
   Answer: me → I

5. The preposition 'to' requires that the objective case be used.
   Answer: she → her

6. It can be inferred that Valentine's day is the speaker's favorite day of the year. Since the object in possession 'favorite day' is already stated in noun form, the possessive adjective, not the possesive pronoun, should be used.
   Answer: C

7. The object in possession by 'novels' is already stated in noun form – 'details, plots'. Therefore, the possessive adjective, not the possessive pronoun, should be used.
   Answer: C

8. The preposition 'between' requires that the objective case be used.
   Answer: C

9. The preposition 'except' requires that the objective case be used.
   Answer: C

10. The preposition 'to' requires that the objective case be used.
    Answer: B

2-3. Pronoun shift

Practice Questions

1. 'our willpower' and 'we can exercise' indicate listener is being referred to in the first person plural
   Answer: you → we

2. pronoun 'one' is being utilized in latter part of sentence → adjust underlined part accordingly
   Answer: we → one

3. Subject: students
   subject is third person plural → use a form of 'they'
   Answer: our → their

4. 'you and me' must be collectively referred to by pronoun 'we'
   pronoun is prepositional object → objective form of pronoun must be used
   Answer: them → us

5. Subject: Seinfeld
   subject is third person singular and refers to a thing, not a person → use a form of 'it'
   Answer: his → its

6. Jonathan, Denise and I → must be collectively referred to by 'we'
   they → cannot refer to first person
   Answer: B

7. Subject has already been referred to by 'you' → continue using 'you' throughout sentence
   Answer: C

8. Subject has already been referred to by 'we' → continue using 'we' throughout sentence
   Answer: B

9. Subject: my new coworkers
   third person plural → a form of 'they' must be used
   Answer: A

10. Object has already been referred to by 'us' → continue using 'us' throughout sentence
    Answer: D

2-4. Ambiguous pronoun

Practice Questions

1. 'she' can refer to either Suzie or Charlotte.
   Change so that it is clear who is at the doctor's office.
   Answer: she → Suzie OR she → Charlotte

2. 'it' can refer to either key or wallet.
   From context, it can be inferred that Bill has left both in the taxi.
   Change pronoun so that it refers to both key and wallet.
   Answer: it → them

3. 'there' can only refer to 'Paris', the only place mentioned in the sentence.
   There is no ambiguity.
   Answer: no error

4. 'he' can refer to either Bill or Charlie. And from context, it is not clear who had work to do.
   Change pronoun so that it is clear who had work to do.
   Answer: he → Susan OR he → Bill OR he → Charlie

5. 'she' can refer to either Darla or Marie.
   Change pronoun so it is clear who is the subject of the second clause.
   Answer: she → Darla OR she → Marie

6. 'He' can refer to either Peter Hwang or Jake Yoo.
   Only option that clarifies which of the two is the subject of second sentence is 'Hwang'.
   Answer: B

7. 'he' can refer to either Daniel or Prahlad.
   Only option that clarifies which of the two is the subject of second sentence is 'Daniel'.
   Answer: C

8. 'she' can refer to either Kendra or her sister.
   Only option that clarifies which of the two is the subject of second clause is 'Kendra'.
   Answer: D

9. 'his' can refer to either Principal Hendricks or Principal Howard.
   Only option that clarifies which of the two is the subject of second sentence is 'The later Principal's'.
   Answer: D

10. 'it' can refer to either watching a documentary or studying for an exam.
    Only option that clarifies which is 'studying for an exam'.
    Answer: B

2-5. Relative Pronoun

Practice Questions

1. The subordinate clause must have 'players' as its subject, so a relative pronoun referring to person must be used.
   Answer: which → who

2. The subordinate clause contains information about 'Germany', so a relative pronoun referring to place must be used.
   Answer: no error

3. The subordinate clause must have 'news helicopter' as its subject, so a relative pronoun referring to a thing must be used.
   Answer: who → which

4. The phrase between the commas modifies 'John Muir', so a relative pronoun referring to person must be used.
   Answer: which → who

5. The relative pronoun must refer to object of preposition 'of', which in this case is 'biodiversity'. A relative pronoun referring to a thing must be used.
   Answer: no error

6. The subordinate clause contains information about 'Las Vegas', so a relative pronoun referring to place must be used.
   Answer: A

7. The subordinate clause contains information about 'Seoul', so a relative pronoun referring to place must be used.
   Answer: D

8. The subordinate clause must have 'girl' as its subject, so a relative pronoun referring to person must be used.
   Answer: C

9. The phrase 'two black holes collided and merged into one' is information about 'a region of space'. A relative pronoun referring to place must be used.
   Answer: A

10. The relative pronoun must refer to the object of preposition 'from', which in this case are 'Native Americans'. A relative pronoun referring to person must be used in the objective case.
    Answer: B

3. Parallelism

Practice Questions

1. Parallel structure: infinitive (take out)
   Answer: no error

2. Parallel structure: infinitive (understand)
   Answer: reconnecting → reconnect

3. Parallel structure: noun (government, play)
   Answer: to have them be pardoned → pardon

4. Parallel structure: -ing (improving, reforming)
   Answer: facilitate → facilitating

5. Parallel structure: infinitive (resolve)
   Answer: they lose interest in → lose interest in

6. Parallel structure: -ing (hitting, threatening)
   mock → mocking
   Answer: B

7. Parallel structure: to + infinitive (to get, to join)
   finding → to find
   Answer: D

8. Parallel structure: to + infinitive (to call, to whimper)
   hug → to hug
   Answer: D

9. Parallel structure: -ing (planting, watering)
   to grow → growing
   Answer: B

10. Parallel structure: infinitive (have, go)
    spending → spend
    Answer: C

4. Comparisons

4-1. Countable vs. Uncountable nouns

Practice Questions

1. 'problems' → countable
   comparative form must be used
   *implicit comparison: there are fewer complex traffic problems (than before, than other places, etc.)
   Answer: no error

2. 'less' modifies 'complex'.
   * This sentence takes on a different meaning from that of problem 1.
   Answer: no error

3. 'information' → uncountable
   no comparison used
   Answer: few information → little information

4. 'money' → uncountable
   no comparison used
   Answer: many → much

5. 'cultures' → countable
   no comparison used
   Answer: much → many

6. 'paintings' → countable
   no comparison used
   Answer: C

7. 'songwriters' → countable
   no comparison used
   Answer: B

8. 'nations' → countable
   comparative form must be used (idiomatic phrase 'no + *comparative* + than~')
   Answer: A

9. 'territories' → countable
   comparative form must be used (in the 1800s than in the 1700s)
   Answer: D

10. 'musicians' → countable
    comparative form must be used (musicians named responsible for the origins of hip hop … than those named responsible for the origins of jazz)
    Answer: B

4-2. Logical Comparisons

Practice Questions

1. 'Michael Moore' cannot be compared with 'documentaries', it must be compared with an equivalent such as 'documentary producers'.
   Answer: documentaries → documentary producers

2. 'Clothing' cannot be compared with 'natural materials', it must be compared with an equivalent such as 'clothing made from natural materials', in parallel with 'clothing made from synthetic materials'.
   Answer: natural materials → clothing made from natural materials

3. Comparison: 'production of a professional theater' vs. 'that of an amateur class'.
   'production' is compared with an equivalent (that)
   Answer: no error

4. 'buses' cannot be compared with 'New York City', it must be compared with an equivalent such as 'those of New York City'.
   Answer: unlike New York City → unlike those of New York City

5. The comparison is between two objects – an 'amphibian' and a 'penny'. 'amphibian' cannot be logically compared to 'the size' of a penny.
   Answer: than the size of a penny → than a penny

6. 'Group' of great warriors cannot be compared with 'a country', it must be compared with an equivalent such as 'armies'.
   Answer: B

7. 'Works' of Van Gogh cannot be compared with 'Picasso', it must be compared with an equivalent such as 'those of Picasso', or 'works of Picasso'.
   Answer: D

8. Comparison: 'later films' vs. 'those produced at the beginning of his career'.
   'films' is compared with an equivalent (those)
   Answer: A

9. Elements being compared should be parallel in structure. 'insuring' is in gerund form, which is not parallel to 'power play'
   Answer: C

10. Elements being compared should be parallel in structure. 'cigarettes' cannot be compared with 'using', it must be compared with an equivalent such as 'nicotine patches'.
    Answer: B

5. Modifiers

5-1. Front Modifiers

Practice Questions

1. Front modifier modifies 'Garfield', not 'the mailman'. 'Garfield' must immediately follow the front modifier.
   Answer: D

2. Front modifier modifies 'the Lilliputians', not 'the giant'. 'the Lilliputians' must immediately follow the front modifier.
   Answer: B

3. Front modifier modifies 'Joshua', not 'the call', or 'Joshua's ears', or 'everyone'. 'Joshua' must immediately follow the front modifier.
   Answer: A

4. Front modifier modifies 'the book and its sequels', not 'generations'. 'the book and its sequels' must immediately follow the front modifier.
   Answer: C

5. Front modifier modifies 'the instructor', so it must immediately follow the front modifier.
   Answer: B

6. Front modifier modifies 'we', not 'the Mississippi River'. 'we' must immediately follow the front modifier.
   Answer: D

7. Front modifier modifies 'the chimpanzee', not 'some researchers', or 'cognitive functions'.
   Answer: A

8. Front modifier modifies 'movies', so it must immediately follow the front modifier.
   Answer: C

9. Front modifier modifies 'Johnny Cash', not 'Johnny Cash's iconoclasm'. 'Johnny Cash' must immediately follow the front modifier.
   Answer: B

10. Front modifier modifies 'I', not 'the new car', or 'a feeling of comfort'. 'I' must immediately follow the front modifier.
    Answer: D

5-2. Back Modifier

Practice Questions

1. Object of sentence is 'kidney'. 'kidney' is the organ 'which removes toxic materials from the body'. Correct sentence must have kidney as object, with back modifier immediately following after comma.
   Answer: C

2. Object of sentence is 'gamers'. 'gamers' are 'eager for the most realistic gaming experience possible', a 'headset' or 'Oculus Rift', cannot be 'eager'. Correct sentence must have 'gamers' as object, with back modifier immediately following after comma.
   Answer: D

3. Object of sentence is 'street arts'. Relative pronoun 'which' can only refer to object and not a person, so modifier 'which combine dark humor with graffiti' must refer to 'satirical street arts'. Correct sentence must have 'street arts' as object, with back modifier immediately following after comma.
   Answer: C

4. Modifier 'which has seemed to focus endlessly on them' must refer to this year's 'debates', not 'this year'. Also, 'focus' is given to 'issues', not 'debates'.
   Answer: B

5. Phrase 'dressed in a Santa Claus outfit' can only refer to Dr. Magnusson himself, not his eggnog or his colleagues. Only option that is unambiguous is C.
   Answer: C

6. Back modifier must use relative pronoun 'where' to refer to 'Berlin'.
   Answer: D

7. 'directs electronics' must clearly modify 'remote control', and not 'Robert Adler'. Only option that is unambiguous is D.
   Answer: D

8. Clarification necessary: who is in the stadium, 'the management' or 'people'? Since verb 'are' indicates plural subject, 'people' must be in the stadium.
   Answer: A

9. Clarification necessary: who is in the restroom, 'the supervisor' or 'employees'? If 'supervisor' is in the restroom, he/she cannot make sure of the belongings of employees. It must be the employees who are in the bathroom.
   Answer: B

10. Object of sentence is 'runes'. Back modifier must refer to 'runes'. Correct sentence must have 'runes' as object, with back modifier immediately following after comma.
    Answer: A

6. Punctuation

6-1. Period, Semi-colon vs. Comma

Practice Questions

1. Sentence structure: two independent clauses. Semicolon or period must be used.
   Answer: semicolon or period

2. Sentence structure: two independent clauses. Conjunction 'and' is present. Comma must be used.
   Answer: comma

3. Sentence structure: two independent clauses. Conjunction 'but' is present. Comma must be used.
   Answer: comma

4. Sentence structure: two independent clauses. Semicolon or period must be used.
   Answer: semicolon or period

5. Sentence structure: two independent clauses with transition 'therefore'. 'Therefore' is not a conjunction. Semicolon or period must be used.
   Answer: semicolon or period.

6. Sentence structure: two independent clauses. Semicolon or period must be used.
   Answer: C

7. Sentence structure: two independent clauses. First clause contains listed elements.
   For listed elements, comma must be used. Between independent clauses, semicolon or period must be used.
   Answer: A

8. Sentence structure: one subordinate adverb clause + independent clause. Comma must be used.
   Answer: D

9. Sentence structure: one adverbial phrase + independent clause. Comma must be used.
   Answer: B

10. Sentence structure: two independent clauses. Semicolon or period must be used.
    Answer: D

6-2. Colons and dashes

Practice Questions

1. Sentence structure: two independent clauses. Second clause provides additional information. Option A is not possible because the usage of comma requires a conjunction be present.
   Answer: B

2. Sentence structure: adverb clause + independent clause + independent clause. Third clause provides additional information. Option B is not possible because the usage of comma requires a conjunction be present.
   Answer: A

3. Sentence structure: two independent clauses. Second clause provides additional information. Option A is not possible because it results in a run-on sentence.
   Answer: B

4. Sentence structure: two independent clauses. Second clause provides additional information.
   Option A is not possible because it results in a run-on sentence.
   Answer: B

5. A nonrestrictive element must be placed between two commas or two dashes. Option A is not possible because nonrestrictive clause is placed between a colon and comma.
Answer: B

6. 'the Joker' is a phrase used to provide additional information. Colon or dash must be used.
Answer: D

7. 'fight or flee' is a phrase used to provide additional information. Colon or dash must be used.
Answer: C

8. An insertion made in the middle of a clause must be made with a pair of dashes or parentheses.
Answer: A

9. An insertion made in the middle of a clause that begins with a dash must end with a dash.
Answer: A

10. An insertion made in the middle of a clause that begins with a dash must end with a dash.
Answer: C

6-3. Various Comma Usages

Practice Questions

1. Sentence structure: front modifier + independent clause. Comma is necessary.
Answer: necessary, front modifier

2. Nonrestrictive element must be placed between two commas.
Answer: necessary, nonrestrictive clause modifying subject

3. Nonrestrictive element must be placed between two commas.
Answer: necessary, nonrestrictive clause modifying subject

4. 'as well as' is not a conjunction. Comma is unnecessary.
Answer: unnecessary, as well as is not a conjunction

5. Sentence structure: two independent clauses. Conjunction 'for' makes comma necessary.
Answer: necessary, before coordinating conjunction

6. Nonrestrictive elements must be placed between two commas. The only option that makes this possible is D.
Answer: D

7. Sentence structure of 2nd sentence: independent clause + incomplete phrase. Comma must be placed before incomplete phrase.
Answer: D

8. Sentence structure: independent clause + incomplete phrase. Comma must be placed before incomplete phrase.
Answer: B

9. Sentence structure: front modifier (adverbial clause) + independent clause (with nonrestrictive element). Adverbial clause necessitates comma, and nonrestrictive element must be placed between two commas.
Answer: A

10. Sentence structure: independent clause + subordinate clause. Subordinate clause must be connected to independent clause with a comma.
Answer: C

6-4. Apostrophes

Practice Questions

1. The 'gift' is from her 'boyfriend', and should therefore be in his possession. Use an apostrophe to indicate possession.
   Answer: boyfriends → boyfriend's

2. The person making the 'return' is the 'father'. Use an apostrophe to indicate possession.
   Answer: father → father's

3. The decision was made by one boy, not several, as can be inferred from the use of pronoun 'he'. Apostrophe placement should be done accordingly.
   Answer: boys' → boy's

4. The 'reaction' was made by 'Temmie', and should therefore be in her possession. Use an apostrophe to indicate possession.
   Answer: Temmies → Temmie's

5. 'Odysseus crew' implies that the crew's name is Odysseus, not that the crew was led by Odysseus. To correctly convey this fact, use an apostrophe to indicate possession.
   Answer: Odysseus → Odysseus's

6. The 'Chinese Water Tank trick' is in possession of Harry Houdini. However, for pronouns such as 'he', the possessive adjective, and not the apostrophe, should be used to indicate possession.
   Answer: D

7. The 'cheek pouch' belongs to 'chipmunk'. Use an apostrophe to indicate possession.
   Answer: C

8. Alan is the one who lost 'nerve'. However, for pronouns such as 'he', the possessive adjective, and not the apostrophe, should be used.
   Answer: D

9. The 'amazing skills' belong to 'Faker and Madlife'. However, for pronouns such as 'they', the possessive adjective, and not the apostrophe, should be used to indicate possession.
   Answer: D

10. The 'gamers' are the ones who dreaded the 'quest', as can be inferred from the pronoun 'they'. Therefore, the apostrophe should be placed after plural noun 'gamers' to indicate possession.
    Answer: C

7. Structure

7-1. Incomplete Sentences

Practice Questions

1. 'being imprisoned' cannot act as verb in this sentence because it is in gerund form.
   Verb must be in past tense because imprisonment of Galilei is historical event.
   Verb must be in passive voice because Galilei is being acted upon by the Catholic church.
   Answer: Galileo Galilei once being imprisoned → Galileo Galilei once was imprisoned

2. 'emigrating' cannot act as verb in this sentence because it is in gerund form.
   Verb must be in past tense because emigration of Jews is historical event.
   Answer: emigrating → emigrated

3. 'showing' cannot act as verb in this sentence because it is in gerund form.
   *NOTE: phrase starting with 'showing' cannot be a modifier to subject 'records' because there is no verb after the comma. 'refuting' also cannot act as verb.
   Verb can be in past or present tense.
   Answer: showing → showed OR show

4. 'adding' cannot act as verb in this sentence because it is in gerund form.
   Verb can be in past or present tense.
   Answer: adding → added OR adds

5. 'Taxi ride' is subject in this sentence. Nonrestrictive element between commas modifies subject, followed by verb 'kept'. Both subject and verb are present in this sentence.
   Answer: no error

6. 'taking place' cannot act as verb in this sentence because it is in gerund form.
   Verb must be in past tense because Industrial Revolution is historical event.
   Answer: C

7. 'Watson, Crick and Wilson' is subject of the sentence, followed by nonrestrictive element between commas modifying subject. Therefore, underlined portion must contain verb. If relative pronoun 'who' is used, clause after comma will become subordinate. 'Who' must be eliminated. Only option satisfying all conditions is B.
   Answer: B

8. 'Paganini' is subject of the sentence, followed by nonrestrictive element between commas modifying subject. Therefore, underlined portion must contain verb. If relative pronoun 'who' is used, clause after comma will become subordinate. 'who' must be eliminated. Only option satisfying all conditions is D.
   Answer: D

9. 'to enter' cannot act as verb in this sentence because it is in the 'to + infinitive' form.
   Verb must be in present tense because sentence refers to event that occurs 'each year'.
   Answer: D

10. 'Red blood cells' is subject of the sentence, followed by nonrestrictive element between commas modifying subject. Therefore, underlined portion must contain verb. If relative pronoun 'which' is used, clause after comma will become subordinate. 'which' must be eliminated. Only option satisfying all conditions is C.
    Answer: C

7-2. Conjunction Errors – General

Practice Questions

1. No. of subjects = 2 (ID badges, they)
   No. of conjunctions = 0
   Results in run-on sentence, must add coordinating conjunction. Cumulative conjunction adding latter statement to former must be used.
   Answer: office, they → office, and they

2. No. of subjects = 2 (J.S. Bach, his work)
   No. of conjunctions = 0
   Results in run-on sentence, must add coordinating conjunction. Conjunction signifying contrast should be used.
   Answer: forms, his work → forms, but his work

3. No. of subjects = 2 (George Lucas, that –clause)
   No. of conjunctions = 1 (but)
   Answer: no error

4. No. of subjects = 2 (Georgia O'Keeffe, she)
   No. of conjunctions = 0
   Results in run-on sentence, must add coordinating conjunction. Cumulative conjunction adding latter statement to former must be used.
   Answer: Southwest, she → Southwest, and she

5. Given sentence combines two sentences with a common subject (National Park Service). In the latter clause subject is omitted for succinctness, but coordinating conjunction is necessary because it is also independent clause. Cumulative conjunction adding latter statement to former must be used.
   Answer: Romanticism, stands → Romanticism, and stands

6. No. of subjects = 3 (ferocity, his army, the army)
   No. of conjunctions = 1 (and)
   Last clause must be connected to rest of the sentence with coordinating conjunction. Conjunction signifying contrast should be used.
   Answer: C

7. No. of subjects = 2 (patients, they)
   No. of conjunctions = 0
   Last clause must be connected to rest of the sentence with coordinating conjunction. Conjunction signifying causality should be used.
   Answer: D

8. No. of subjects = 2 (diet, it)
   No. of conjunctions = 0
   Results in run-on sentence, must add coordinating conjunction. Conjunction signifying causality must be used.
   Answer: B

9. No. of subjects = 2 (curator, she)
   No. of conjunctions = 0
   Results in run-on sentence, must add coordinating conjunction. Cumulative conjunction adding latter statement to former must be used.
   Answer: C

10. No. of subjects = 2 (study, they)
    No. of conjunctions = 0
    Results in run-on sentence, must add coordinating conjunction. Conjunction signifying causality must be used.
    Answer: B

7-3. Adverb Clauses

Practice Questions

1. The adverb clause beginning with subordinating conjunction 'by the time' must be connected to the main clause with a comma because it comes before the main clause.
   Answer: no error

2. The adverb clause beginning with subordinating conjunction 'when' comes after the main clause, and therefore does not need to be introduced by a comma.
   Answer: no error

3. The first clause is introduced with subordinating conjunction 'even though'. 'however' is redundant because 'even though' already signifies a contrast. 'however' should be deleted.
   Answer: however, others describe their dissolution as a result of the plague introduced by Europeans → others describe their dissolution as a result of the plague introduced by Europeans

4. The adverb clause beginning with 'if' is placed before the main clause. It needs to be connected to the main clause with a comma.
   Answer: If the committee had given us permission to implement our plans for animal protection → If the committee had given us permission to implement our plans for animal protection,

5. The adverb clause beginning with 'if' is placed before the main clause. It needs to be connected to the main clause with a comma.
   Answer: no error

6. The two clauses are both introduced by subordinating conjunctions (because, then). One clause must be changed so that it becomes an independent clause. The underlined portion must lose the subordinating conjunction 'then'. Possible options are C and D, but C is wordy due to its use of the passive voice.
   Answer: D

7. The adverbial phrase 'Since 1983' is placed in front of the main clause and therefore needs to end with a comma. The use of 'in' is not possible because the main clause utilizes the present perfect tense.
   Answer: B

8. The adverbial phrase 'since my breakdown last year' is placed after the main clause and therefore does not need to be introduced with a comma.
   Answer: A

9. No. of subjects = 2 (Shelly, she)
   No. of conjunctions = 2 (although, but)
   One conjunction must be deleted for a sound sentence structure. Only possible option is C.
   Answer: C

10. The adverbial phrase 'since its inception' is placed in front of the main clause and therefore needs to end with a comma. The use of 'at' is not possible because the main clause utilizes the present perfect tense.
    Answer: B

7-4. Conjunctions vs. Conjunctive adverbs

Practice Questions

1. 'nevertheless' is a conjunctive adverb and cannot be used in place of a conjunction. It must be replaced by a conjunction signifying contrast. Comma should be eliminated because coordinating conjunctions cannot immediately be followed by a comma.
   Answer: nevertheless, → but

2. 'although' is a conjunctive adverb and cannot be used in place of a conjunction. It must be replaced by a conjunction signifying contrast. Comma should be eliminated because coordinating conjunctions cannot immediately be followed by a comma.
   Answer: although, → but

3. 'nonetheless' is a conjunctive adverb and cannot be used in place of a conjunction. It must be replaced by a conjunction signifying contrast. Comma should be eliminated because coordinating conjunctions cannot immediately be followed by a comma.
   Answer: nonetheless, → but

4. 'accordingly' is a conjunctive adverb and cannot be used in place of a conjunction. It must be replaced by a cumulative conjunction adding latter statement to the former.
   Answer: accordingly → and

5. Two independent clauses are combined with coordinating conjunction 'yet'.
   Answer: no error

6. 'moreover' is a conjunctive adverb and cannot be used in place of a conjunction. It must be replaced by a cumulative conjunction adding latter statement to the former.
   Answer: B

7. 'also' is a conjunctive adverb and cannot be used in place of a conjunction. It must be replaced by a cumulative conjunction adding latter statement to the former.
   Answer: D

8. 'since' is a conjunctive adverb and cannot be used in place of a conjunction. It must be replaced by a conjunction signifying causality.
   Answer: C

9. 'because' is a conjunctive adverb and must be used alongside a coordinating conjunction to connect two independent clauses.
   Answer: D

10. 'still' is a conjunctive adverb and cannot be used in place of a conjunction. It must be replaced by a conjunction signifying contrast.
    Answer: B

8. Tense

Practice Questions

1. 'Now' + 'for three months' signifies the verb must be in present perfect form.
   Answer: trained → has trained

2. 'is' signifies the verb must be in present form.
   Answer: welcomed → welcome

3. 642 AD is a point in past. 'by' + (point in past) signifies the verb must be in past perfect form.
   Answer: has been conquered → had been conquered

4. 'mid-20th century' is a point in past. 'Before' + (point in past) signifies the verb must be in past perfect form.
   Answer: has been → had been

5. 'For the past 10 year (duration)' signifies the verb must be in present perfect form.
   Answer: had been producing → has been producing

6. 'trip to Vietnam' is a point in past. 'Before' + (point in past) signifies the verb must be in past perfect form.
   has never eaten → had never eaten
   Answer: B

7. 'recently' signifies the verb must be in simple past form.
   was releasing → released
   Answer: D

8. 'in the present US' signifies the verb must be in present form.
   has been → is
   Answer: C

9. 'students visit here' signifies the verb must be in present form.
   Answer: A

10. The sentence is talking about the current state of 'Orange Caramel'. Therefore, the verb must be in present form.
    is not owning → does not own
    Answer: C

9. Usage

9-2. Precision and Concision

Practice Questions

1. fulfilled: feeling a sense of achievement
   (ex. feel fulfilled after achieving the dream of becoming an astronaut)

   complacent: feeling satisfied with the current situation and choosing to stay that way (negative connotation)
   (ex. the Romans grew complacent after conquering most of Europe and ended up getting defeated by the barbarians)

   sufficient: having the required amount for a specific purpose
   (ex. there is sufficient amount of water to last the week)

   satiated: feeling of having the needed amount

   Having nutrients inside one's body does not give one a sense of achievement. Having enough nutrients is a positive thing, not negative. There is no given purpose here for consuming the nutrients. However, the sentence clearly says that people can have the needed amount of nutrients from organic food. Therefore, 'satiated' is the correct word to use here.
   Answer: A

2. tight: fitting too close around something
   (ex. the jeans are too tight around my waist)

   stiff: very rigid and inflexible; not moving easily
   (ex. my muscles grew stiff after sitting for hours without moving)

   taut: stretched to a large extent
   (ex. a bow needs to be pulled taut in order to shoot an arrow)

   firm: not changing shape much even when put under pressure

   Apple slices do not fit around something. Neither are they expected to move around or be stretched. An important characteristic of apple people are interested in when choosing what apple to buy is how solid it is. Therefore, 'firm' is the correct adjective to use here.
   Answer: B

3. emphatic: (an emphatic statement) a statement made in a forceful way, because the speaker feels very strongly about it; (an emphatic win) a victory in which a winner has won by a large amount

   paramount: more important than anything else
   (ex. gender equality is an issue paramount to all others)

   eminent: well-known and respected (person)
   (ex. Stephen Hawking is an eminent genius in the field of physics)

   important: significant; valued

   A skill is neither a statement, a victory, or a person. The question implies that taking a class not directly linked to your major can help you learn other helpful skill, not a skill that is more important than other skills. Therefore, 'important' is the correct adjective to use here.
   Answer: D

4. keep going: continue doing something despite difficulty
   (ex. despite the harsh snowstorm, the climbers kept going)

   tolerate: put up with; bear with (something unpleasant)
   (ex. the teacher tolerated the disturbing student only for so long before sending him to the principal's office)

   pursue: carry out or follow an activity, interest, or a plan
   (ex. I pursued my dream of becoming a teacher)

   persist: something undesirable continues to exist

   Termite problem is neither an activity, interest, nor plan. It's the couple who are tolerating the termite problem, not the other way around. 'keep going' is used for people. Therefore, the correct verb to use with 'termite problem' is 'persist' as it is an undesirable situation that continues to exist despite the effort by pest control agency.
   Answer: C

5. sheer: used for emphasizing that a state or situation is complete
   (ex. the taste of her lips is sheer ecstasy)

   limpid: clear, simple, and flowing (used for speech, writing, or music)
   (ex. Shakespeare's plays were written in limpid Elizabethan English)

   crystalline: clear or bright (used for actual objects)
   (ex. the crystalline water flowed from the crack in the iceberg)

   clear: easy to understand, see, or hear
   'couldn't believe that Nina was actually surprised' suggests that the protagonist's intention was very obvious. 'limpid' and 'crystalline' cannot be used since 'intention' is neither a speech, writing, music, or actual object. A noun has to come after 'sheer'. Therefore, 'clear' is the correct adjective to use with 'intention'.
   Answer: D

6. position: a place where someone or something is in relation to other people or things (cannot refer to an area)
   (ex. the position of the hidden nuclear missile silo has been identified)

   orientation: direction a structure or an object is facing
   (ex. the two atoms must collide in a particular orientation to undergo chemical reaction)

   point: a particular place where something happens (the size is an actual dot)
   (ex. the pain originated from a point in my back and will not go away)

   location: a particular place in physical space (used in geography to describe a specific area)

   'position' cannot refer to a specific area. A 'second joint' is going to be opened at a new place, not in a different direction. A restaurant cannot be built on a place the size of a dot, neither is something happening in that place. Therefore, 'location' is the correct noun to use as it is used to describe a specific area.
   Answer: B

7. obstruction: something that blocks a road or a path
   (ex. the car with flat tire is causing an obstruction)

   impediment: something that makes a person's or a thing's movement or progress difficult
   (ex. despite being blind and deaf, Helen Keller did not let such impediment bother her)

   opposition: strong disagreement and disapproval
   (ex. the two teams showed strong opposition to each other's claim)

   challenge: something difficult requiring great effort

   Sticking to the rule of never killing anyone is not acting as an 'obstruction', 'impediment', or 'opposition' to anything. Batman is simply finding it very difficult not to kill the Joker when the Joker has hurt so many of his allies. Therefore, 'challenge' is the correct word to use here.
   Answer: A

8. weighty: serious (used to describe a decision or an issue)
   (ex. the passing of the Antiterrorism Act in Korea is a weighty issue)

   prestigious: respected and admired by many (used to describe a person or an institution)
   (ex. many prestigious people attended the charity ball)

   well-connected: having influential relatives or friends
   (ex. in order to be successful in business, you must be well-connected)

   important: very significant; highly valued

   Benefits is neither an issue, a person, or an institution. Benefits cannot have influential relatives or friends either. Therefore, 'important' is the correct adjective ot use with 'benefits'.
   Answer: B

9. dispatch: kill
   (ex. the assassin dispatched his targets in quick succession)

   overindulge on: have more of something than is good for you because you like it so much
   (ex. do not overindulge on alcohol as you might do something you will later regret)

   dispose of: get rid of; kill
   (ex. the criminal tried to dispose of the evidence)

   devour: eat something quickly out of hunger

   'loss of food' and 'out of hunger' suggests that the mother polar bear 'ate' its cub. While 'dispatch' and 'dispose of' make sense in meaning, they do not fit the context. 'overindulge on' suggests the mother bear enjoyed eating its cub, which is obviously not true. Therefore, 'devour' is the correct verb to use here.
   Answer: A

10. austere: plain and simple
    (ex. in order to save money, my parents lead an austere lifestyle)

    egregious: outstandingly bad; outrageous
    (ex. that is the most egregious abuse of human right)

    unmitigated: absolute; totally (negative connotation)
    (ex. my speech was an unmitigated disaster)

    stark: very obvious

    The difference between 'my school timetable' and 'my brother's' is very obvious as one is filled with academic subjects and one is filled with P.E. and art subjects. Yet, there is no negativity involved with the difference. 'austere' is a word used to describe a person or a lifestyle. Therefore, 'stark' is the correct adjective to use here.
    Answer: D

9-3. Frequently Confused Words

Practice Questions

1. stationery: items used for writing such as paper and pen

   stagnant: not flowing; without activity (used for body of water or a phenomenon)
   (ex. the economy has remained stagnant for months)

   sanctuary: a place of safety provided to those in danger
   (ex. Jean Valjean sought sanctuary in the church)

   stationary: not moving; staying still
   Answer: D

2. principal: person in charge of a school or college
   principate: a state ruled by a prince
   principality: a country ruled by a prince
   principle: a general belief that one has about the way one should behave
   Answer: D

3. loss: a state of not having something; a defeat
   loosen: make less tight or strict
   loose: not firmly held; fixed in place
   lose: (lose something) not have something anymore; forget something
   Answer: B

4. chore: a task that must be done that is boring or unpleasant
   court: place where legal matters are brought before judges and jury
   corps: part of the army with a special duty
   core: central part of an object
   Answer: C

5. pore: (pore over, pore through) look and study something very carefully
   pour: make something flow out of a container
   Answer: A

6. boer: (Boers) descendants of the Dutch people who migrated to South Africa
   bohr: (Bohr) the name of a Danish physicist
   boar: wild pig
   bore: a situation that is not interesting
   Answer: D

7. weather: condition of the atmosphere in one area at a particular time
   when: used to introduce a clause which refers to a time at which something happens
   wither: become very weak
   whether: conjunction used to talk about a choice between two or more alternatives
   Answer: D

8. compliment: a remark that shows someone you like or approve of him or her; a praise
   comment: an opinion or explanation about a subject
   completion: a finished state
   complement: something that goes well with another thing and improves its qualities
   Answer: D

9. precede: happens before
   (ex. the extinction of dinosaurs precedes the appearance of mankind)

   cede: letting someone else have it; giving up
   proceed: continue; go on
   Answer: C

10. die: stop living
    dice: cut into small cubes
    dry: remove moisture from
    dye: change something's color
    Answer: B

10. Style, Tone and Syntax

10-1. Style and Tone

Practice Questions

1. Find the expression downplaying the writer's emotion – A and D are not possible answers because they expressly use words like 'hysterical' and 'agitated'. Choice B is not an understatement, but a contrary statement to what the writer feels.
   Answer: C

2. Find the expression exaggerating the writer's emotion – A and C are not possible answers because a person could reasonably eat a three-course meal or eat for hours if famished enough. B is a contrary statement to what the writer wants to express.
   Answer: D

3. Choice B is not acceptable because it does not express any enthusiasm; Choice C implies that the speaker does not want to accept the award but is obliged to do so; Choice D is inappropriate because it is too colloquial.
   Answer: A

4. The only option including words from the same root is Choice D – 'healthy' and 'unhealthy'.
   Answer: D

5. Although the second sentence is set apart from the previous sentence with a period, it is still appropriate to use the same sentence structure because the two sentences as a whole describe Don's habit of doing certain things when he is drunk. The pattern established in the first sentence is '–ing things' – Choice B is the only option that maintains this structure.
   Answer: B

10-2. Redundancy

Practice Questions

1. There is no redundancy in this sentence.
   Answer: No error

2. 'annually' and 'each year' are redundant.
   Answer: annually planting almost 10 million trees each year → annually planting almost 10 million trees/planting almost 10 million trees each year

3. 'famous' and 'well-known' are redundant.
   Answer: famous for its well-known jazz artists → famous for its jazz artists

4. 'rapturously' and 'enjoyed' are redundant.
   Answer: rapturously enjoyed → enjoyed

5. 'distant' and 'remote' are redundant.
   Answer: distant, remote place → distant place/remote place

6. 'soon', 'imminently', and 'in the future' are redundant.
   happen imminently in the future → happen
   Answer: B

7. 'stronger' and 'greater' are redundant.
   forces greater than her. → forces than hers.
   Answer: B

8. 'dictatorship' and 'tyrant' are redundant.
   ruled by tyrant Josef Stalin → ruled by Josef Stalin
   Answer: D

9. 'discovery' and 'finding' are redundant.
   is the finding that → is that
   Answer: D

10. 'simultaneously' and 'at the same time' are redundant.
    watched TV at the same time → watched TV
    Answer: C

10-3. Wordiness

Practice Questions

1. B is the most concise choice that does not distort the original meaning.
   A, C, D: Too wordy
   Answer: B

2. C is the most concise choice that does not distort the original meaning.
   A, B, D: Too wordy
   Answer: C

3. D is the most concise choice that does not distort the original meaning.
   A, B, C: Too wordy
   Answer: D

4. C is the most concise choice that does not distort the original meaning.
   A, B, D: Too wordy
   Answer: C

5. B is the most concise choice that does not distort the original meaning.
   A, C, D: Too wordy
   Answer: B

6. D is the most concise choice that does not distort the original meaning.
   A, B, C: Too wordy
   Answer: D

7. C is the most concise choice that does not distort the original meaning.
   A, B, D: Too wordy
   Answer: C

8. B is the most concise choice that does not distort the original meaning.
   A, C, D: Too wordy
   Answer: B

9. C is the most concise choice that does not distort the original meaning.
   A, B, D: Too wordy
   Answer: C

10. B is the most concise choice that does not distort the original meaning.
    A, C, D: Too wordy
    Answer: B

10-4. Voice

Practice Questions

1. Active voice is more concise than passive voice.
   Answer: lawmakers are brought together from opposing sides of issues by The Bipartisan Policy Center → The Bipartisan Policy Center brings lawmakers together from opposing sides of issues

2. Active voice is more concise than passive voice.
   Answer: communist uprising was begun → communist uprising began

3. Active voice is more concise than passive voice.
   Answer: are begun as → begin as

4. There is no subject that 'they' is referring to, so the passive voice should be used to describe 'John Sullivan'.
   Answer: they recognized as → was recognized as

5. Active voice is more concise than passive voice.
   Answer: we are always held responsible by the owners → the owners always hold us responsible

6. Active voice is more concise than passive voice.
   Answer: B

7. The passive voice is an apt choice here because it is the 'further funding', not the 'Congress', that is the object of importance here.
   Answer: A

8. Active voice is more concise than passive voice.
   Answer: C

9. Active voice is more concise than passive voice.
   Answer: B

10. It is important to identify exactly who is showing tolerance. Therefore, the active voice is the correct and coherent choice.
    Answer: D

5. A, B: Too informal
   Answer: C

6. A, B: Too informal
   Answer: C

7. A, C: Too informal
   Answer: B

8. B, C: Too informal
   Answer: A

9. A, C: Too informal
   Answer: B

10. A: Too childish
    B: Too formal
    Answer: C

10-5. Register

Practice Questions

1. B, C: Too informal
   Answer: A

2. A: Literary language
   C: Too weak
   Answer: B

3. A, B: Too informal
   Answer: C

4. B, C: Too informal
   Answer: A

11. Insertion/Deletion/Replacement/Content Order

Practice Questions

Passage 1

1. The topic of the passage is how Edison used dishonesty and deception to promote his direct current generator. Information provided by B, C, and D suggest the passage will be about some other topic. Only A mentions 'how dishonest his "tricks of the trade" could be'.
Answer: A

2. Sentence 2 talks about a number of factors that helped Edison achieve lasting fame. Sentence 3 and 4 talk about these factors which are 'gift for creativity' and 'deceit'. Therefore, sentence 2 provides a logical connection to sentence 3 and 4 and should stay where it is.
Answer: A

3. Sentence 10 talks about Edison's plan to prove that direct current generators are superior to alternating current generators. Sentence 7 shows why Edison came up with the plan by talking about how the alternating current generators are superior to direct current generators. Sentence 9 talks about the details of Edison's plan. Therefore, sentence 10 should come after sentence 7 and before sentence 9.
Answer: C

4. The paragraph is focused on Edison's plot to prove the superiority of his direct current generators. Sentence 8 is a general statement about technologies and market that does not belong to the paragraph. Therefore, it should be deleted.
Answer: B

5. The passage lacks a suitable conclusion. The given sentence successfully provides a concluding sentence that is in logical flow with the rest of the passage. Therefore, it should be added.
Answer: A

Passage 2

1. The paragraph is focused on the author's uncle's teaching skills. Sentence 5 talks about a topic that is unrelated with this topic. Therefore, it should be deleted.
Answer: A

2. The sentence being considered is simply repeating what sentence 2 is saying in a different way. Therefore, it should not be added.
Answer: D

Passage 3

1. The sentence talks about how 'almost every nation on earth' has agreed to keep outer space a common heritage of humankind. Sentence 2 mentions how 100 countries have ratified the Outer Space Treaty, which from context can be inferred to be the treaty confirming that no single country controls space. Therefore, it makes sense that sentence 4 be placed right after sentence 2.
Answer: B

2. Sentence 6 introduces the subject of 'cooperation' and how it is 'both easier and more complicated'. Sentence 5 talks about how the 'cooperation is easier' and sentence 8 is talking about how the cooperation is more complicated. Therefore, sentence 6 is best placed before sentence 5.
Answer: C

Passage 4

1. Sentence 2 talks about how 'coffee consumed only in the Arab countries' before the 'opening of trade routes'. Sentence 1 talks about 'European explorers' who 'first encountered coffee'. Therefore, sentence 1 should logically come after sentence 2.
Answer: B

2. Sentence 4 talks about 'coffee consumption' influencing 'European nations'. Sentence 5 talks about how coffee influenced European nations: by 'provid[ing] places where members of society could gather and exchange ideas'. Therefore, sentence 5 should stay where it is now.
Answer: A

12. Graphs & Charts

Practice Questions

1. After a 30-minute gaze with their owners, dogs' oxytocin levels increased by 2 units while cats' oxytocin levels barely increased. Therefore, cats are generally less affected hormonally by interactions with humans.
   Answer: B

2. The graph for resource consumption indicates that the growth rate has in general decreased from year 2007 to 2013. Therefore, it can be concluded that resource consumption per person in the US has decreased in recent years.
   Answer: C

3. For both age groups 24-50 and 40-55, the percentage of females who believe they have experienced telepathy is greater than the percentage of males. Therefore, it can be concluded that females are generally more inclined to believe in the existence of telepathy.
   Answer: A

Chapter Test
Answers & Explanations

1. Number Agreement

1. Subject-Verb Agreement
Subject: most people → plural
plural verbs: agree & were agreeing
agreeing → grammatically incorrect
Answer: A

2. Noun Agreement
Object: You Really Got Me → singular
only singular noun: song
Answer: B

3. Subject-Verb Agreement
Subject: seeds → plural
only plural verb: were
Answer: D

4. Subject-Verb Agreement
Subject: works → plural
only plural verb: are
Answer: C

5. Subject-Verb Agreement
Subject: director and…fans → plural
only plural verb: weren't
Answer: C

6. Subject-Verb Agreement
Subject: drivers → plural
plural verbs: had caused & cause
had caused (past perfect) → wrong tense ('Studies show' → present)
Answer: D

7. Noun Agreement
'a greater number of' must be followed by plural noun.
only plural noun: accidents
Answer: D

8. Subject-Verb Agreement
Subject: driving → singular
only singular verb: hands is
Answer: C

9. Subject-Verb Agreement
Subject: heads → plural
plural verbs: had & have
had (past) → wrong tense ('we don't know' → present)
Answer: D

10. Subject-Verb Agreement
Subject: every fish head → singular
only singular verb: contains
Answer: B

11. Noun Agreement
Subject: fish heads → plural
only plural noun: treasures
Answer: D

12. Subject-Verb Agreement
Subject: many researchers → plural
plural verbs: have been & are
are (present) → wrong tense ('for decades' → present perfect)
Answer: A

13. Subject-Verb Agreement
Subject: most primates → plural
plural verbs: lack & have lacked
have lacked (present perfect) → wrong tense ('are able' → present)
Answer: C

2. Pronouns

1. Pronoun Case
'memory' is a possession of 'you' → use possessive adjective
correct pronoun: your
A: yours (possessive pronoun) → wrong case
Answer: C

2. Relative Pronoun
Precedent: Joachim Bodamer → person
'Joachim Bodamer' is the subject of the dependent clause
'put together' → use subjective clause
correct relative pronoun: who
B: whom (objective) → wrong case
Answer: A

3. Pronoun Case
'implications' is a possession of 'face perception' → use possessive case
correct pronoun: its
A: it (subjective) → wrong case
Answer: D

4. Pronoun Case
'war experiences' is a possession of 'Hemingway' → use possessive case
correct pronoun: his
A: him war experiences (objective), B: he war experiences (subjective) → wrong case
Answer: C

5. Relative Pronoun
Precedent: plane crashes → thing
'plane crashes' is the subject of the dependent clause 'left him in pain' → use subjective case
correct relative pronoun: that
B: in which (possessive) → wrong case
Answer: A

6. Ambiguous Pronoun
'he' can refer to either Plato or Solon.
The only option that clarifies the subject is 'Plato'.
Answer: D

7. Pronoun Agreement
Pronoun referring to: that Greek people... → thing, singular
correct pronoun: it
* 'it is likely' is an idiomatic expression
Answer: C

8. Pronoun Agreement
Pronoun referring to: volcanoes → thing, plural
'effects' is a possession of 'volcanoes' → use possessive case
correct pronoun: their
D: them (objective) → wrong case
Answer: B

9. Pronoun Shift
Subject referred to as 'the participants' in the next sentence.
Use the same subject in the preceding sentence.
Correct subject: participants
Answer: B

10. Pronoun Case
'own judgement' is a possession of 'participants' → use possessive adjective
correct pronoun: their
A: theirs (possessive pronoun) → wrong case
Answer: B

11. Pronoun Case

1st pronoun referring to: many scientists and mathematicians → person, plural
The preposition, 'among', needs an object → use objective case
correct pronoun: them
2nd pronoun referring to: Alan Turing → person, singular
The verb, 'introduced', needs a subject → use subjective case
correct pronoun: He
B: they (subjective), D: they (subjective), him (objective) → wrong case
Answer: A

12. Pronoun Shift

Subject has already been referred to by 'he' → continue using 'he' throughout sentence
Answer: C

13. Pronoun Agreement

Pronoun referring to: a computing machine → thing, singular
correct pronoun: it
Answer: A

3. Parallelism

1. Parallel structure: adjective and adjective (light and entertaining, deep and serious)
non-stop explosions → exhilarating and thrilling
Answer: C

2. Parallel structure: -ing + the adjective with the adjective (combining the amusing with the tragic, marrying the exciting with the poetic)
fuse poignancy with the humorous → fusing the poignant with the humorous
Answer: D

3. Parallel structure: noun and noun (action and meditation, entertainment and art)
comedy and the drama → comedy and drama
Answer: D

4. Parallel structure: adjective + noun (rapid pacing, vivid imagery)
stories on the human condition → humanitarian stories
Answer: B

5. Parallel structure: noun (critics, casual moviegoers)
by fans → fans
Answer: D

6. Parallel structure: possessive + noun (Cream's Disraeli Gears, Aldous Huxley's A Door to Perception)
Spirited Away directed by Hayao Miyazaki → Hayao Miyazaki's Spirited Away
Answer: B

7. Parallel structure: adjective + noun (green apartments, pink condominiums)
we have blue bungalows → blue bungalows
Answer: D

8. Parallel structure: adjective + noun (rainbow colored roads, splashy streets)
wall painted whimsically → whimsically painted walls
Answer: C

9. Parallel, structure: noun (lions, gazelles)
the giraffes → giraffes
Answer: D

10. Parallel structure: -ing + noun (camouflaging themselves, communicating with each other)
purpose of confusing their predators → confusing predators
Answer: C

11. Parallel structure: -ing (poking fun)
Answer: A

12. Parallel structure: literature (The Illiad, The Odyssey)
also Shakespearean works → Shakespearean works
Answer: B

4. Comparisons

1. Logical Comparisons
Elements being compared must be parallel in structure (to motivate people)
brushing their teeth daily → to motivate them to brush their teeth daily
Answer: B

2. Countable vs. Uncountable Nouns
people → countable
no comparison used
Answer: A

3. Countable vs. Uncountable Nouns
education → uncountable
comparative form must be used
* implicit comparison: more public education is needed (than before)
many (non-comparative) → more (comparative)
Answer: C

4. Logical Comparisons
Comparison: coffee vs. other beverage
'coffee' is being compared with an equivalent (other beverage)
Answer: A

5. Countable vs. Uncountable Nouns
places → countable
no comparison used
much (uncountable) → many (countable)
Answer: B

6. Countable vs. Uncountable Nouns
cases → countable
no comparison used
much (uncountable) → many (countable)
Answer: B

7. Logical Comparisons

'sign for choking' in a Paris restaurant cannot be compared to 'an Indian hospital'. It must be compared to an equivalent such as 'that of an Indian hospital' or 'sign for choking in an Indian hospital'.

Answer: D

8. Logical Comparisons

'an answer' cannot be compared to 'other nations'. It must be compared to an equivalent such as 'that of other nations' or 'answer of other nations'.

Answer: C

9. Countable vs. Uncountable Nouns

events → countable

no comparison used

controversial → uncountable

comparison form must be used

Answer: A

10. Logical Comparisons

'event' cannot be compared to 'era'. It must be compared to an equivalent such as 'that of the more recent era' or 'event of the more recent era'.

Answer: C

11. Logical Comparisons

Elements being compared must be parallel in structure

(Diseases)

killed by European warlords → European warlords

Answer: B

12. Countable vs. Uncountable Nouns

people → countable

no comparison used

Many most (grammatically wrong) → Many (countable)

Answer: D

13. Logical Comparisons

'hip hop' and 'electronic music' cannot be compared to 'elements'. They must be compared to an equivalent such as 'rock and roll'.

Answer: B

14. Logical Comparisons

Comparison: rock and roll vs. industrial or new wave

'rock and roll' is being compared with an equivalent (industrial or new wave)

Answer: A

5. Modifiers

1. Front Modifier

Front modifier 'One of nature's most previous gifts' modifies 'honey', not 'we'. 'honey' must immediately follow the modifier.

Answer: B

2. Back Modifier

Back modifier 'creating a dehydrated environment' modifies 'water'. The modifier must immediately follow 'water' after a comma.

Answer: C

3. Front Modifier

Front modifier 'Slathering our wounds and satisfying our sweet tooths' modifies 'honey', not 'jars'. 'honey must immediately follow the modifier.

Answer: D

4. Front Modifier

Front modifier 'Since they are required to drive the quickest path they know' modifies 'taxi drivers', not 'taxi routes'. 'taxi drivers' must immediately follow the modifier.

Answer: B

5. Back Modifier

Back modifier 'like the back of their hands' modifies 'every street route and place of interests', not 'London taxi drivers'. The modifier must immediately follow 'every street route and place of interests'.

Answer: B

6. Front Modifier

Front modifier 'Skis strapped on his back' modifies 'an old man', not 'people'. 'an old man' must immediately follow the modifier.

Answer: D

7. Front Modifier/Back Modifier

'sniffs away at trash cans' modifies 'Golden Retriever', not the 'woman'. The modifier must immediately follow 'Golden Retriever'. 'impeccably dressed' modifies 'woman', not the 'Golden Retriever'.

Answer: C

8. Back Modifier

Back modifier 'remembering the bittersweet moments of her past' modifies 'elderly woman', not 'chest'. The correct conjunction, 'while', must be used to show this relationship.

Answer: C

9. Front Modifier

Front modifier 'With utmost tenderness' modifies 'woman', not 'a picture'. 'woman' or 'she' must immediately follow the modifier.

Answer: C

10. Front Modifier

Front modifier 'Presented in a bright pink tutu' modifies 'the girl', not 'innocence'. 'the girl' must immediately follow the modifier.

Answer: B

11. Front Modifier

Front modifier 'Three stories high and filled with all sorts of fascinating things' modifies 'the History of the Future museum', not 'the dreams and imaginations'. 'the History of the Future museum' must immediately follow the modifier.

Answer: C

12. Back Modifier

Back modifier 'when pulling a lever' modifies 'the model kitchen', not 'oven'. The modifier must be rephrased to show this relationship.

Answer: D

6. Punctuation

1. Period/Semi-colon vs. Comma
Sentence structure: two independent clauses with the transition 'however'
'however' is not a conjunction.
Semicolon or period must be used.
Answer: B

2. Various Comma Usages
Sentence structure: incomplete phrase + independent clause
Comma must be used after the incomplete phrase.
Answer: C

3. Period/Semi-colon vs. Comma/Apostrophes
Sentence structure: two independent clauses
Semicolon or period must be used.
'symptoms' belongs to 'radiation poisoning' → its
Answer: A

4. Period/Semi-colon vs. Comma
Sentence structure: two independent clauses with the conjunction 'but'
Comma must be used.
Answer: A

5. Colons and Dashes
An insertion made in the middle of the clause that begins with a dash must end with a dash.
Answer: D

6. Period/Semi-colon vs. Comma
Sentence structure: two independent clauses
Semicolon or period must be used.
Answer: A

7. Colons and Dashes
The second sentence is a list of factors scholars 'have attempted to draw a line between'.
Colon must be used.
Answer: A

8. Period/Semi-colon vs. Comma
Sentence structure: two independent clauses with the conjunction 'but'
Comma must be used.
Answer: C

9. Colons and Dashes/Apostrophes
The second sentence is a list of Rome's 'long and interesting history'.
Colon must be used.
The sentence should start with 'it is' as 'it' is referring to 'The city of Rome' → it's
Answer: C

10. Apostrophes
'hall is' is grammatically incorrect in the sentence and nothing is possessed by 'hall'.
'halls' belong to 'Rome', which is one city.
Use singular possession of 'city' → city's
cities halls → city's halls
Answer: D

11. Apostrophes
'street is' is grammatically incorrect in the sentence and nothing is possessed by 'street'.
'streets' belong to 'Rome', which is one city.
Use singular possession of 'city' → city's
Answer: A

12. Various Comma Usages
Sentence structure: Subject + incomplete phrase + verb + object
Commas must be used before and after the insertion modifying the subject.
Answer: D

13. Various Comma Usages

Sentence structure: incomplete phrase + independent clause

Comma must be used after the incomplete phrase.

Answer: A

14. Period/Semi-colon vs. Comma

Sentence structure: two independent clauses with the transition 'however'

'however' is not a conjunction.

Semicolon or period must be used.

Answer: B

7. Structure

1. Conjunction Errors - General

\# of subjects: 2 (reading, it)

\# of conjunctions: 2 (While, and)

\# of subjects - # of conjunction = 0

and it is → it is

Answer: D

2. Conjunction Errors - General

\# of subjects: 2 (advantages, peace)

\# of conjunctions: 2 (Although, but)

\# of subjects - # of conjunction = 0

Although the → The

Answer: C

3. Conjunctions vs. Conjunctive Adverbs

'consequently' is an adverb and cannot be used as a conjunction. A conjunction is needed to complete the sentence.

consequently → and

Answer: C

4. Incomplete Sentences

No verb

full → is (verb) full

C: are full (plural) → wrong form ('news' is always singular)

Answer: D

5. Adverb Clauses

Adverb clause: 'inadequate planning…revolutions'

Main clause is 'many ineffectual…unrest', not 'Also, even if… happen'.

Since the adverb clause is placed in front of the main clause, the two clauses are correctly connected by a comma.

Answer: A

6. Incomplete Sentences
No subject, no verb
wondering → you (subject) could (verb) wonder
Answer: C

7. Conjunction Errors - General
of subjects: 2 (air conditioner, it)
# of conjunctions: 2 (Even though, but)
# of subjects - # of conjunctions = 0
but it → it
Answer: C

8. Incomplete Sentences
No verb
showing → shows (verb)
D) show (plural) → wrong form
Answer: B

9. Conjunction vs. Conjunctive Adverbs
'moreover' is an adverb and cannot be used as a conjunction.
A conjunction is needed to complete the sentence.
moreover → and
Answer: D

10. Conjunction Error – General
of subjects: 2 (it, gym)
# of conjunctions: 2 (Because, so)
# of subjects - # of conjunctions = 0
so the → the
Answer: C

11. Conjunction vs. Conjunctive Adverbs
'Eventually' can be a modifier and start a sentence on its own. The usage is adequate.
Answer: A

12. Incomplete Sentences
No verb
being → is (verb)
Answer: D

13. Adverb Clauses
Adverb clause: 'it is now…existed'
Main clause: 'the legend…invasion'
Since the adverb clause is placed in front of the main clause, the two clauses are correctly connected by a comma.
Answer: A

14. Conjunction vs. Conjunctive Adverbs
'therefore' is an adverb and cannot be used as a conjunction.
A conjunction is need to complete the sentence.
therefore → and
B) but → wrong relationship between clauses
Answer: C

8. Tense

1. 'Ming dynasty' is a point in past. 'in' + (point in past) signifies the verb must be in simple past form.
beared (incorrect simple past form) → bore
Answer: C

2. 'After they counted (simple past)' signifies the verb must be in simple past form.
have discovered → discovered
Answer: D

3. 'the time the scientists realized' is a point in past. 'by' + (point in past) signifies the verb must be in past perfect form.
D) deaded (incorrect past perfect form)
Answer: A

4. 'Once' signifies 'the corn + verb' occurred before 'Father was ready (past)' and that the verb must be in past perfect form.
had rose → had risen
Answer: B

5. 'We had (simple past)' signifies the verb must be in simple past form.
will all be → were all
Answer: C

6. 'In the past eleven years (duration)' signifies the verb must be in present perfect form.
Answer: A

7. 'it starts (simple present)' signifies the verb must be in simple present form.
accelerated → accelerates
Answer: B

8. 'the time a doctor diagnosed cancer' is a point in the past. 'by' + (point in past) signifies the verb must be in past perfect form.
has already began → had already begun
Answer: D

9. '16th century' is a point in past. 'in' + (point in past) signifies the verb must be in simple past form.
has invented → invented
Answer: D

10. 'when' signifies 'you + verb' occurs after ' you learn (simple present)' and that the verb must be in future form.
Answer: A

11. 'then' is a point in past. 'Since' + (point in past) signifies the verb must be in present perfect form.
has took → has taken
Answer: D

12. 'I have (simple present)' signifies the verb must be in simple present form.
Answer: A

13. 'I could remember' is a point in past. 'Ever since' + (point in past) signifies the verb must be in present perfect form.
Answer: A

9. Usage

1. Precision and concision
From context, the fact that the sphinx is 'one of the most well-known' wonders of the world is well-established, not open to debate. Therefore, that fact is not 'debatable', 'controversial', or 'disputable', it can be argued for – and thus 'arguable'.
Answer: B

2. Diction
The Sphinx of Giza is being compared with all other sphinxes, not one other sphinx in particular. Therefore, 'between' cannot be used. Instead, use 'among'.
Answer: D

3. Precision and concision
The passage is discussing where the sphinx itself is located, not its direction or orientation relative to some other object. Also, 'position' cannot be used because it cannot refer to an area.
Answer: A

4. Diction
Here the builders of the sphinxes are being referred to, and therefore it makes sense to use the possessive adjective. 'they're' is the contracted form of 'they are', and 'there' refers to a point in space.
Answer: C

5. Precision and concision
The passage is talking about how easy it is to understand why the Egyptians would have named the sphinx after the Sun God's daughter Sekhmet. The only choice that carries the connotation of 'easy to understand' is C, clear.
Answer: C

6. Precision and concision
The Egyptians held a stalwart belief, one that is not easily changed – a 'firm' belief. 'tight' or 'taut' means stretched out as to be strained; 'stiff' is used with a physical attribute.
Answer: D

7. Precision and concision
The Egyptians believed that the sphinxes would keep the tomb safe from harm. 'sequestered' and 'reclusive' mean shut out from external events; 'restricted' means to have limited access. 'sheltered' comes closest to the meaning of 'safe'.
Answer: A

8. Diction
'raise' is a transitive verb and requires an object – in this case, the Sun God must 'raise himself' from the dead. Since there is no reflexive pronoun, a form of 'rise' must be used. The past participle alone cannot be used as a verb; thus the only possible option is C.
Answer: C

9. Frequently confused words
The Sun God would rise and 'rule' his kingdom. The only option close to the meaning of 'rule' is 'reign'.
Answer: B

10. Frequently confused words
The Germans would have risen up to the ranks of the major powers. The only option that carries the meaning to 'ascend', or 'rise up' is 'ascent'.
Answer: B

11. Diction

The sentence is talking about the people who lived at the time of the Second World War. 'than' is used for comparison. 'then' is the option that carries the meaning of 'at that time'. 'when' on its own cannot refer to a specific point in time. 'there' cannot be used because it refers to place.

Answer: A

12. Frequently confused words

It can be inferred that each pair was made up of one leader and one wingman. Therefore, the wingman completes the team by acting as the remaining half of the team, or 'complementing' the leader. 'completes' cannot be used because the 'leader' is not completed by the 'wingman', the 'team' is.

Answer: C

13. Frequently confused words

The two pairs of aircraft would make it seem like there is only one pair, when in reality there are two. Therefore, they are making something that is not really what it seems to be – an 'illusion'. A 'delusion' is a 'belief in something that is not true', and is not used for visual or auditory sensations. It is used for mental confusion.

Answer: B

14. Frequently confused words

It is by way of the aerial tactic that Germany achieved air superiority. The option that comes closest to 'by way of' is D, through.

Answer: D

15. Frequently confused words

The RAF would have expanded because the dangers Germany posed were looming closer; 'imminent' is the most appropriate option to express this fact. 'eminent' does not fit because it simply means the dangers Germany posed were already predominant.

Answer: B

16. Frequently confused words

The squadrons would have been equipped with radar to make sure accurate communication would be possible. The only option that carries the meaning of 'make sure' is 'ensure'.

Answer: C

17. Precision and concision

The Axis powers were the losing side in the war; 'defeated' should be used to explain this fact. Choices B and C all suggest that one side performed better than the other, which is not necessarily synonymous with winning or losing. Choice D, 'relinquished', means to give up or surrender. However, it cannot be used in this case because the verb is in the passive voice.

Answer: A

18. Diction

The sentence begins with a question, asking who is to blame for air pollution in California. Therefore, the interrogative pronoun 'who' should be used. Choice C is not possible because then the sentence would lack a verb. Choice B includes both the pronoun and the verb in contracted form.

Answer: B

19. Precision and concision

People would have been making determined efforts to counter the difficulties posed by air pollution. The only option that conveys this meaning is A, 'struggle'. Choice B, 'scuttle', means to move about in a confused fashion. Choice C, 'melee' simply refers to a confused crowd of people. D, 'bout' is a sudden burst of activity that is not geared toward a specific purpose.

Answer: A

20. Frequently confused words

'dust clouds and smog' would be covering up the clean air of California. The only option that conveys this meaning is D, 'enveloped'.

Answer: D

21. Diction

Here 'to' must carry the meaning of 'in order to'. 'too' means 'excessively', and cannot be used. Choice C, 'through' requires that a noun come after it, and is grammatically incorrect.

Answer: B

22. Precision and concision

The bills would be setting limits on how much of the atmosphere pollutants can be allowed - the amount of pollutants relative to the amount of clean air. The only option that implies a ratio is B, 'concentration'. Choices A, C, and D all simply refer to a building up of material.

Answer: B

23. Frequently confused words

The guidelines would be limiting 'too much' consumption of fuels. The only option that conveys that meaning is 'excessive'. 'recessive' means passive or dormant. 'successive' means consecutive.

Answer: C

24. Frequently confused words

The consumption of fuels would influence air pollution. The only option that carries the meaning of 'to influence' is 'affect'.

Answer: A

25. Precision and concision

The context suggests that the residents of California think the efforts to reduce air pollution have not 'yielded substantive results'. The only option that conveys this meaning is 'unfruitful'. 'unfinished' simply means the work has not been completed; 'inconclusive' means that the results have not been decisive or definite; 'deficient' means to lack some element or characteristic.

Answer: C

26. Precision and concision

The context suggests nothing is being done to specifically address the health problems. Choices A and B mean 'untested or in the early stages'. Choice C, 'serviceable' means 'generally helpful'. Only Choice D carries the meaning of 'relevant and useful to the situation at hand'.

Answer: D

27. Precision and concision

It can be inferred that addressing the health issue is something that is 'necessary' and 'must be done'. The only option that precisely conveys this meaning is B, 'imperative'. Choice A, 'momentous', also means significant, but it does not imply that it is necessary.

Answer: B

10. Style, Tone and Syntax

1. Wordiness
A: Too wordy and provides unnecessary details
C, D: Too wordy
Answer: B

2. Redundancy
'collecting' and 'gathering' are redundant.
collecting, gathering, and examining → collecting and examining/gathering and examining
Answer: B

3. Register
The use of 'I' is acceptable here because the writer already said the painting is 'one of my favorite'.
B: Too formal
C: Too informal
Answer: A

4. Wordiness
A, C, D: Too wordy
Answer: B

5. Style and Tone
The pattern of the passage is: adjective related to calmness + but + adjective related to energy.
Answer: B

6. Wordiness
B, C, D: Too wordy
Answer: A

7. Wordiness
'are illogical' is the most concise way among the choices to express the writer's intention.
Answer: C

8. Style and Tone
'makes it difficult' and 'guide' are both phrases that are formal but casual.
A, C, D: Phrases such as 'bumpy ride', 'grimace and groan', and 'real hard' are too informal
Answer: B

9. Wordiness
A, C: Too wordy
D: Grammatically incorrect
Answer: B

10. Register
A, B: Too informal
Answer: C

11. Voice
The active voice is the best and most concise choice here.
Answer: B

12. Wordiness
A, B, D: Too wordy
Answer: C

13. Redundancy
'identical twins' and 'exact same genetic material' are redundant.
Answer: D

14. Voice
The active voice is the best and most concise choice here.
Answer: D

15. Wordiness
A, B, D: Too wordy
Answer: C

11. Insertion/Deletion/Replacement/Content Order

1. Deletion

Without this sentence, the reason why Cordelia was different from the other dogs and why 'only one had let me pass with flying colors' cannot be identified. Therefore, the sentence should be kept.

Answer: C

2. Content Order

Sentence 2 feels out of place as it begins talking about 'the second week' when the writer has not even talked about the first week. Sentence 3 talks about 'the first week [the writer] brought her home' and sentence 4 adds additional detail about Cordelia's action in sentence 3. Therefore, sentence 2 should be placed after sentence 4.

Answer: D

3. Insertion

The sentence is talking about money and a quality that even money cannot buy. The last sentence of paragraph 5 is the only sentence in the whole passage that talks about money. Therefore, the sentence should be added at point D.

Answer: D

4. Replacement

The following information is about how Cordelia was capable of executing more than just simple tricks. 'wasn't limited to tricks' effectively provides the transition for this information.

Answer: A

5. Insertion

This sentence emphasizes how tired the writer got from keeping Cordelia occupied and explains why her 'friend recommended that [the writer] start teaching Cordelia some tricks'. Therefore, the sentence should be added.

Answer: A

6. Content Order

Paragraph 3 begins with 'And so', suggesting that the previous paragraph should provide a reason for the details in paragraph 3. Paragraph 3 talks about the writer teaching Cordelia tricks. Paragraph 4 talks about why the writer started teaching Cordelia tricks: 'My friend recommended that I start teaching Cordelia some tricks'. Therefore, the paragraph should come after paragraph 4.

Answer: D

7. Deletion

Sentence 7 of paragraph 2 talks about how the writer 'summoned a piece of paper with a red circle on it'. Without sentence 8, the readers will never know why the writer did this and what the circle represents. Therefore, the sentence should not be deleted.

Answer: C

8. Content Order

Sentence 2 feels out of place as there is no explanation as to why the circle turned blue. '[T]urning [stairs] into piano keys' is an act that should show that the writer is exerting control over his dream and turn the circle red. However, sentence 4 is a real-life detail that should show the writer is losing control of the dream, which should turn the circle blue. Therefore, sentence 4 should be placed before sentence 2.

Answer: B

9. Content Order

Paragraph 3 begins with talking about the writer 'jumped outside the upside-down room'. Paragraph 4 ends with how the author 'turned the entire room upside-down'. Therefore, paragraph 3 should be placed after paragraph 4.

Answer: D

10. Replacement

In order to most effectively conclude the paragraph, information regarding the author's experience with lucid dreaming should be present. Only Choice C presents such information.

Answer: C

4 Practice Tests

Practice Test 1

Passage 1

Classy Quinoa

In the last five years, quinoa - a type of grain which tastes like a mixture of oats and beans - has increased wildly in popularity around the world. **1** With individual grains that are quite small, quinoa is clearly desirable, because it provides many benefits such as high protein and fiber content. Despite originally being grown only in South America, it has become a hot commodity from China to Europe and beyond.

From 2000 to 2015, production of Quinoa in Peru, Bolivia and Ecuador has increased by over 60 percent. This dramatic increase in demand, which has surprised some observers, **2** has caused world health organizations to take a step back and consider the **3** social well-being results from this change in status for the simple crop. Thankfully, the issues surrounding the growing of quinoa are not related to environmental impacts, but rather the end of quinoa as a crop **4** to be consumed by farmers.

1

Which of the following best suits the examples provided in the sentence?
A) NO CHANGE
B) As far as unusual crops go,
C) While it is relatively new,
D) In a time of increased health consciousness,

2

A) NO CHANGE
B) who have
C) who has
D) have

3

A) NO CHANGE
B) community results on health
C) public health consequences
D) impacting results on society

4

A) NO CHANGE
B) to consume by farmers
C) for farmers' consumption
D) for farmers to be consuming

Twenty years ago, quinoa was an important source of cheap and healthy nutrition for local farmers. It can be grown in a wide variety of agricultural conditions, and is very healthy. **5** At that time quinoa was not yet a worldwide phenomenon, and prices for the crop were quite low. The low price allowed the farmers to eat the quinoa themselves without worrying about the loss of profit from not selling it abroad. **6** Therefore, as popularity and demand for quinoa grew, the increasing price of the crop made it much more tempting to sell quinoa rather than eat it.

The farmers received much more money than before, which was undoubtedly beneficial. However, the situation has created health issues since farmers now replace the healthy calories of quinoa with unhealthy calories from less expensive processed foods, like pasta and rice. This problem extends even into cities in South America where middle-class families can no longer afford to buy quinoa from the farmers and are also switching to less healthy options. In some places, the price of quinoa has undergone **7** inflating to become twice as expensive as the same weight of chicken, and four times as expensive as rice.

5

At this point, the writer is considering adding the following information.

, having comparatively high levels of nutritional fiber, vitamins and protein.

Should the author add this information here?
A) Yes, because it explains exactly how quinoa is healthy.
B) Yes, because it proves why quinoa has risen in popularity.
C) No, because it distracts the reader with information that is unconnected to the main idea.
D) No, because it moves the topic of the passage away from the increasing price of quinoa.

6

A) NO CHANGE
B) However,
C) Once,
D) Regardless,

7

A) NO CHANGE
B) inflation
C) influxing
D) influxes

Anthropologist Pablo Laguna, who has studied this issue at length, said during an interview on National Public Radio that despite concerns, the increased income and quality of life provided by the rise in quinoa's popularity offsets the negative effects of increasing its price. **8** South American farmers may have some initial difficulty maintaining a healthy diets. Many of these will be wealthier and allow them to make healthier choices for their diets. Besides, all over the world there is a need for people to eat healthier food, and the rise of quinoa is one symptom of this trend. **9** While it damages the lives of the farmers who grow it, quinoa will be beneficial for everyone else.

8

Which choice most effectively combines the underlined sentences?

A) Eventually, the benefits of many farmers being wealthier will allow them to make healthier choices for their diets; however, some farmers may have initial difficulty maintaining them.

B) South American farmers may have some initial difficulty maintaining healthy diets; however, many farmers will be wealthier and healthier choices for their diets will eventually be made by them.

C) At first, South American farmers may have some difficulty in maintaining a healthy diet, while eventually healthier choices will be allowed by greater wealth.

D) While there may be some initial difficulty for South American farmers in maintaining a healthy diet, eventually the benefits of greater wealth will allow them to make healthier choices.

9

Which of the following ends the paragraph with a summary of the topics described in the passage so far?

A) NO CHANGE

B) Despite some transitional difficulties, more quinoa consumption means a healthier diet for everyone, and a better life for farmers as well.

C) The quick rise in popularity of quinoa is no surprise given how long South American farmers have grown it, but it will take years for it to reach everyone around the world.

D) Without quinoa, health conscious consumers will have to look to other grains such as oats and barley for their dietary needs.

100 calories' worth of quinoa has more complete protein than the same amount of brown rice, potatoes, barley or millet, and is also high in essential amino acids. While health food experts tout the benefits of the grain, [10] however it does contain a small amount of toxin known as saponin, which can cause eye irritation. They say those who properly prepare the grain, washing, [11] those rinsing, and cooking it thoroughly, can avoid these dangers.

10

A) NO CHANGE
B) so
C) because
D) DELETE the underlined word

11

A) NO CHANGE
B) rinse,
C) rinsing,
D) to rinse,

Passage 2

Operation: Operatic Reputation

When many people think of opera, images of large women in Viking helmets singing comically loud may come to mind. Not to mention they may think they have to wear uncomfortable formal clothes like tuxedos and ball gowns in order to watch it, or have to be able to speak German, Italian, or French to understand what is going on. With these misconceptions so common, it is no wonder that opera **12** carries a reputation for being old-fashioned at best and downright painful at worst.

This widespread public reputation is based largely on a style that was made popular in the 19th century by composers like Richard Wagner. It was made to be enjoyed by audiences that had deep appreciation for musical complexity, knowledge of the history of music, and, more often than not, a great deal of money in the bank. **13** While this style of opera has left an unfortunate legacy for opera today, it could not be further from the art form's humble origins.

12

A) NO CHANGE
B) promotes
C) upholds
D) enjoys

13

At this point, the writer is considering adding the following sentence.

Some of Wagner's most successful operas involved references to Norse mythology, which was well known among all classes of German society.

Should the writer make this addition here?

A) Yes, because it provides a specific example of the paragraph's main focus.
B) Yes, because it confirms the idea that 19th century opera was intended only for elite audiences.
C) No, because it provides information that distracts from the paragraph's main idea of opera elitism.
D) No, because discussion of the classes of German society is not relevant to the author's main idea.

Setting story and theater to music is one of the oldest forms of public entertainment. Music historians have discovered that [14] their are many works written by ancient Greek playwrights like Aristophanes and Euripides that contain passages intended to be sung. This tradition continued until opera in its modern form developed in the merchant cities of Renaissance Italy, like Venice and Genoa. At that time, opera was [15] popularly and as a result not aristocratically enjoyed. Much like modern day sports teams, the best soloists in the city would develop passionate fans who would attend the performances of competitors just to boo them. [16]

14

A) NO CHANGE
B) there were
C) their were
D) there are

15

A) NO CHANGE
B) popularly enjoyed
C) enjoyed by people thought not to be elites
D) enjoyed by common people, attending after they finish work

Over time, in order to draw bigger and bigger crowds, operatic productions **17** had to grow bigger and bigger themselves, and wealthy investors spent money to hire the best talent and provide the biggest spectacle. By the 18th century, a composer was considered unserious until he had attempted to write an opera. From Hayden to Beethoven, nearly all famous composers from this era wrote at least one, **18** also.

16

At this point, the author wants to provide further proof of the passion of early opera fans. Which choice best accomplishes this goal?

A) Wagner might have chosen a different subject for his operas if he had been present for such performances.
B) This is similar to enthusiastic fans today who often make angry posts to social media in support of their favorite artists.
C) It is hard to imagine this kind of passion now, given the reputation that opera has among the public.
D) In fact, there are police records of riots that broke out between groups that disagreed as to which tenor soloist had the most beautiful voice.

17

A) NO CHANGE
B) have had to
C) are having to
D) have to

18

A) NO CHANGE
B) though.
C) as a result.
D) in addition.

By the 19th century, opera was perceived socially as the "highest" form of art, and the amount of money required to stage a performance of the best works ensured that only the "highest" and best-educated classes would be able to enjoy them. This all changed with the technological advances of the twentieth **19** century: radio, film, and television. Popular tunes played on the phonograph were more easily available than **20** the high society who attended expensive performances at the opera house. Because of these changes, the popularity and prestige of opera began to decline.

Today, opera attendance and revenue are at the lowest point ever recorded. **21** For example, there is a growing movement to combat this trend. For the health of the art form, **22** taking opera back to its roots and make it relevant for people again. For example, the opera *Cold Mountain*, composed by Jennifer Higdon and performed by Santa Fe Opera, makes a conscious effort to use simple melodies, storyline, and language to be accessible to people who may not have a deep understanding of musical history but still want to enjoy musical theater.

19
A) NO CHANGE
B) century,
C) century
D) century;

20
A) NO CHANGE
B) the attending of
C) attending
D) DELETE the underlined words

21
A) NO CHANGE
B) Unfortunately,
C) However,
D) Similarly,

22
A) NO CHANGE
B) having taken
C) some composers take
D) to take

Passage 3

Protecting Our Best Friends

Dogs have been domesticated for thousands of years, and they have been bred for special jobs like herding and hunting for almost as long. The dachshund and terrier were chosen for **23** it's small size so they could more easily chase small game like rabbits and badgers into their holes. Collies and sheepdogs were chosen for their intelligence so they could follow commands well. Nearly every known dog breed has unique attributes that are tied to some function that humans wanted them to perform.

(1) **24** Therefore, today most people who own dogs do so because they enjoy the companionship, comfort and entertainment that dogs provide. (2) While this has not been a problem historically, in the last few decades this specialized breeding has become problematic for a number of reasons. (3) Unfortunately, people no longer expect **25** that they will be used for sport or work. (4) Dogs do not spend all day running alongside livestock or fighting wild animals in holes. (5) Most modern owners are unable to **26** see—that their dogs are unhealthy and unfit for the jobs for which they were originally bred. (6) This leads to individuals amongst breeds like the dachshund being **27** optimized for their long body length, or bulldogs for their unusual face shape, without any concern for whether the animal is healthy. **28**

23

A) NO CHANGE
B) its
C) their
D) there

24

A) NO CHANGE
B) Similarly,
C) However,
D) Additionally,

25

A) NO CHANGE
B) that dogs will be used
C) that it will be used
D) how their use will be applied

26

A) NO CHANGE
B) see; that
C) see that
D) see, that

27

A) NO CHANGE
B) selected
C) elevated
D) elected

28

The writer wants to add the following sentence to the paragraph.

Consequently, dog owners choose the animals they purchase for their aesthetic appeal, rather than for their value as tools on the farm or on the hunt.

The best placement for the sentence is immediately

A) before sentence 1.
B) before sentence 3.
C) before sentence 6.
D) after sentence 6.

Even 50 years ago, this was not a problem, as the breeding stock of most dogs stayed relatively close to their original working ancestors. However, if one compares a photograph of a dachshund taken in 1908 to one of the breed today, it is easy to see that **29** much of it has changed. The animal in the old photograph appears 30 percent larger, has legs that are longer and stronger, and looks generally more proportionally healthy than a dachshund sold today. These changes make clear that an unhealthy shift has developed **30** and persisted in the breed, even if neither the public nor the breeders intended harm.

29

A) NO CHANGE
B) a dramatic shift from the photograph to the animal.
C) the animal's transformation.
D) the animal's features have changed dramatically.

30

A) NO CHANGE
B) and persisted; in
C) and persisted in,
D) and, persisted in,

Since the 1990s, pets have become big business. The amount of money spent on pets and pet services has more than tripled **31**. In order to make as much money as possible, some dog breeding farms select dogs based only on their appearance and these specific traits. They also engage in unhealthy and unsafe breeding practices to reduce their costs. This leads to bulldogs with respiratory problems and many different breeds that develop problems with their hips and legs due to unnatural length and shape. Not to mention animal populations develop genetic weaknesses to specific diseases and behavioral disorders. **32** In fact, purebred dogs have shorter lifespans compared to mixed breed dogs.

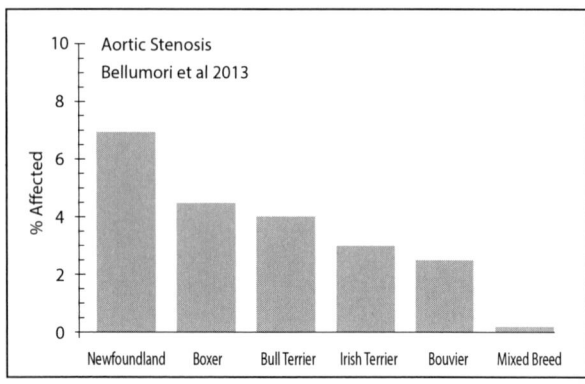

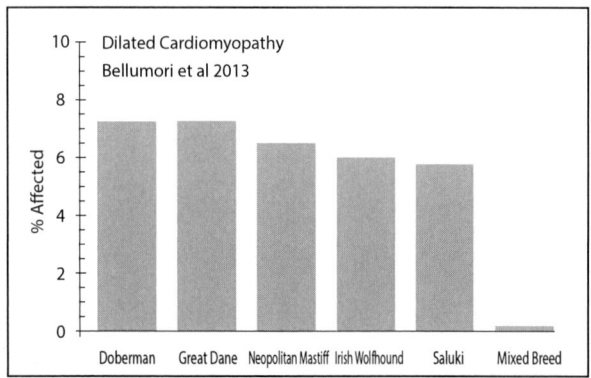

Percentage of dogs affected by certain diseases, by breed
Source: http://www.instituteofcaninebiology.org/purebred-vs-mixed-uc-davis.html

31

At this point, the writer is considering adding the following information.

,from $17 billion in 1994 to over $60 billion in 2015

Should the writer add this information here?

A) Yes, because it confirms that the pet industry has had three times more business over a twenty year period.
B) Yes, because it provides concrete numbers that make clear the large scale at which the pet industry operates.
C) No, because it disproves the prior assertion that the pet industry is in fact increasing in size.
D) No, because the introduction of figures and dates digresses from the paragraph's focus on business practices.

32

Here the author wants to include accurate, relevant data from the graph. Which choice best accomplishes this goal?

A) NO CHANGE
B) According to a study, purebred dogs are more prone to various types of disorders compared to mixed breed dogs.
C) Actually, purebreds are only in danger of developing atopy or allergies.
D) Mixed breed dogs and purebreds show a similar incidence rate for cardiomyopathies.

Dog breeders and animal rights groups [33] beginning to make strides in this area work to change public perception of dog breeding and force the industry to respond accordingly. More and more people choose to adopt from shelters rather than purchase from puppy farms, but there is still a long way to go to turn the trend of unhealthy breeding around. Hopefully, increased awareness of these issues will lead to better lives for dogs in the future.

33
A) NO CHANGE
B) that begin to make strides in this area and work to
C) that begin to make strides in this area, where they work
D) beginning to make strides in this area, they work

Passage 4

Science Fiction to Fact with Artificial Intelligence?

Robot research facilities and software developers are making great strides toward artificial intelligences (AIs) that would be able to think and act for themselves. This achievement, a milestone in technological development and the history of **34** humankind; could change your world in fundamental ways. Current indicators in the industry and economy point to the need for intelligent and hardworking AI experts to solve some of the current obstacles to creating the first machine that thinks as well as, if not better than, a human. With the field developing rapidly every day, with the right credentials and training, it is possible that you could actually be the one to make AI a reality.

(1) There are professionals in mainly two different fields working on the tricky problem of artificial intelligence, and thus two different approaches you could take if you wanted to pursue a career in the field. (2) One profession is tackling the question from the software and processing perspective. (3) Programmers and cognitive specialists work **35** diligently to create programs that can think and act like humans. (4) The other side of the field deals with hardware and the physical capabilities of robots. (5) Once intelligent programming is developed, the robots will need to be able to perform physical tasks as well.

34

A) NO CHANGE
B) humankind,
C) humankind
D) humankind—

35

A) NO CHANGE
B) emphatically
C) stringently
D) dispassionately

(6) Creating a program that can play card games is very different from creating one that can provide proper emotional responses, react appropriately to unexpected events, or recognize shapes in a picture **36** also. **37**

If you are eagerly **38** waiting a conversation with a computer, you are not alone. Most often when people think of artificial intelligence, they think of robot movie characters like C-3PO from *Star Wars*, or Data from *Star Trek*, **39** whom moves, looks, thinks, and acts like people. Whatever form happens to be the one **40** how we first produce AI, it will be more **41** plain than what we have imagined in film, at least at first. Most likely the first AI will be a computer program that can respond to human and environmental input as fast as or faster than a human can.

36
A) NO CHANGE
B) additionally.
C) besides.
D) DELETE the underlined word and end the sentence with a period.

37
To make this paragraph most logical, sentence 6 should be placed
A) where it is now.
B) after sentence 1.
C) after sentence 3.
D) after sentence 4.

38
A) NO CHANGE
B) waiting to
C) awaiting
D) awaiting for

39
A) NO CHANGE
B) moving, looking, thinking, and acting
C) who move, look, think, and act
D) they move, look, think, and act

40
A) NO CHANGE
B) therefore
C) from
D) through which

41
A) NO CHANGE
B) plain then
C) plane than
D) plain, then

If a program truly does achieve what we think of as 'artificial intelligence', it will be able to satisfy certain [42] criteria, consequently: fooling humans, improving itself, and reliability. If you spoke with an 'official' artificial intelligence online, you would not be able to tell the difference between it and a human being. So far, this achievement is still in the future.

This difference between a human response and a computer response is currently one of the most important problems facing the development of AI. While many programs exist that can do simple tasks and recognize basic patterns, versatile robots and programs that can creatively interpret input still elude researchers. If you want to pursue a career in this field, you will need to be intrigued by these problems and [43] have a strong understanding of philosophy.

The field of AI research is growing, and a number of well-respected universities have already developed dedicated artificial intelligence majors. Even if you don't pursue a dedicated AI major, computer programming, cognitive theory, or mechanical engineering would all be good potential fields to consider if you are interested in the subject. [44] If you are not interested in a career in artificial intelligence, it will still be important to understand the technology in order to successfully navigate the jobs of the future.

42

A) NO CHANGE
B) criteria:
C) criteria, however:
D) criteria, besides:

43

Which of the following best ends the sentence with a suggestion that suits the topic of the sentence?

A) NO CHANGE
B) be uninterested in other fields entirely.
C) be excited about looking for their solutions.
D) have a good eye for detail when it comes to working with small mechanical parts.

44

At this point, the author is considering adding the following sentence.

Other fields such as medicine, finance, and education will continue to be practical career paths, even if the use of artificial intelligence becomes widespread.

Should the writer make this addition here?

A) Yes, because it provides examples of fields which could lead to greater understanding of artificial intelligence.
B) Yes, because it supports the main idea of the paragraph with proof of the growing importance of artificial intelligence.
C) No, because it introduces a discussion of fields outside of artificial intelligence that is not further addressed.
D) No, because it refutes the central argument of the passage by proving the value of pursuing a degree in other fields.

Practice Test 2

Passage 1

Vacation Time

It is no secret that employees in the US are stressed out. Compared to other nations around the world, Americans **[1]** spend much more time on smartphones and other media devices. With nearly 50 percent of employees at companies in the United States not taking or even being allowed vacation days during the year, according to The Huffington Post, companies in the US lose $23 billion a year due to decreased productivity, worker stress, and accidents. **[2]** Employees who have not taken a vacation or have worked overtime for extended periods tend to have more accidents and decreased quality of life compared to those who regularly take or are allowed vacation.

One of the causes of stress and dissatisfaction is the amount of hours employees are required to work. **[3]** In the end, job requirements have reached a point where workers who do take vacations are thought by their colleagues to be slacking off. The days the average employee spends on vacation have decreased substantially in the last 30 years, leading many to consider vacation time an impossible luxury. So long as businesses require excessive work from employees, supervisors should provide appropriate rest to keep everyone working smoothly and contentedly.

[1]

Which of the following serves as the best introduction to the passage?

A) NO CHANGE
B) engage in much less time with friends and family in the evening, so they are more depressed.
C) spend more money on gasoline and travel expenses, which means they have less to spend on vacations.
D) take far fewer vacation and sick days, and this is hurting their health and productivity.

[2]

At this point, the writer is considering adding the following sentence.

> While rates of work fatalities are decreasing, there were still 3.4 deaths for every 100 thousand workers last year.

Should the writer make this addition here?

A) Yes, because it supplies statistical proof that supports information that follows it.
B) Yes, because provides the rationale for the actions taken later in the passage.
C) No, because it interrupts the discussion of the negative effects of lack of vacation time.
D) No, because it fails to mention the number of lives that are saved every year by improved safety practices.

[3]

A) NO CHANGE
B) Regardless,
C) On the other hand,
D) For example,

It may seem like increased vacation time would hurt a **[4]** company's overall profit's, but research shows that this is not the case. Being able to reliably look forward to a break from day-to-day responsibilities serves to boost motivation, while upcoming vacation can act as a deadline to help work be completed faster. **[5]** Vacation time is also beneficial even beyond raising worker morale. It might also contribute to improved employee health and decreased sick days.

[4]

A) NO CHANGE
B) companies' overall profits',
C) company's overall profits,
D) companies overall profits,

[5]

Which choice most effectively combines the underlined sentences?

A) Even beyond raising worker morale, vacation time is beneficial in other ways, possibly contributing to improved employee health and decreased sick days.
B) The benefits of vacation time, even beyond raising worker morale, possibly contribute to improved employee health and decreased sick days.
C) Possibly contributing to improved employee health and decreased sick days, vacation time is beneficial and raises worker morale.
D) Vacation time, which raises worker morale and is beneficial in other ways, possibly contributes to improved employee health and decreased sick days.

Even companies who regularly hire part-time workers, like fast food restaurants, retail outlets, and call centers can benefit from increased vacation time for employees. Offering part-time vacation is a means **6** to increasing retention rates and reducing employee turnover. Lowe's Home Improvement, **7** they are considered one of the top part-time employers in the country, is one such company taking this step. The company allows vacation time after 180 days with the company, provides healthcare benefits, and generously matches retirement contributions. Since they instituted the vacation policy, they **8** have seen a 6 percent reduction in the need for new recruits.

6
A) NO CHANGE
B) by
C) of
D) DELETE the underlined word

7
A) NO CHANGE
B) which is
C) it being
D) they are

8
Which of the following best supports the claims made in the paragraph?
A) NO CHANGE
B) experienced an 8 percent boost in sales.
C) saved a great deal of time and effort.
D) decreased their expenses on employee morale programs.

There are a number of other companies who are exploring the benefits of increased vacation time. PriceWaterhouseCoopers tracks employee vacation time and sends stern annual reminders to employees and supervisors when it is time to take a trip **9** once a year. Netflix, an online media streaming provider, has done away with vacation time entirely for their workforce, which, in turn, **10** are reporting record job satisfaction. Rather than having only a set number of days per year, Netflix has found improvement not only of employee satisfaction but also of customer satisfaction with their simple policy. "As long as employees get their work done, they can take off as much time as they want," said one company representative. If a company wants employees that cheerier, **11** happy, and more engaged with their work, then increased vacation time just might be the answer.

9

A) NO CHANGE
B) each year.
C) every year.
D) DELETE the selection and end with a period.

10

A) NO CHANGE
B) is
C) can be
D) have been

11

A) NO CHANGE
B) happier, and more
C) happier, and they are
D) happier, becoming more

Passage 2

Appropriate Technology, the Next Step for Engineers

For most of the 20th century, the field of engineering had been associated with things big and high-tech. Engineering built skyscrapers and airports as well as satellites and smartphones. This will continue to be true in the future, but in recent years a new avenue of engineering has been gaining momentum. **12** As a result of fears over international trade imbalance and concern about the environmental impacts of economic growth, some engineers have switched their focus to a field known as appropriate technology. Developing simple and inexpensive ways to solve resource problems in developing **13** nations, and these inventors have already made many amazing developments.

12

In the context of the paragraph, which of the following best serves as an introduction to the sentence?

A) NO CHANGE
B) Due to increasing interest in the issue of economic inequality and
C) Fearing that their field was losing relevance and
D) DELETE the underlined portion

13

A) NO CHANGE
B) nations;
C) nations:
D) nations,

For example, one success of the appropriate tech movement is a new building method developed by **14** NGOs. This is a cost-effective and durable way to build homes in places where there is a need for housing but a lack of affordable materials. **15** Food preservation is another important, almost pivotal, issue, as in places with little electricity and warm climates it can be difficult to safely store foods, leading to much waste, hunger, and disease. To this end, researchers at the University of Calgary developed a device that cools air underground using the difference in temperature above and below the surface, allowing refrigeration at levels of a modern industrial refrigerator. **16**

14

The writer is considering revising the underlined portion of the sentence to read:

NGOs, involving plastic bottles, sand, and clay.

Should the writer add this information here?

A) Yes, because it makes clear how the building process uses readily available resources.
B) Yes, because it allows the paragraph to flow naturally from one topic to another.
C) No, because it should come later in the paragraph.
D) No, because it weakens the main argument of the passage.

15

A) NO CHANGE
B) Important, almost pivotal, is the issue of food preservation,
C) Food preservation is another important issue,
D) There is an important, almost pivotal, issue with food preservation

16

Which of the following most effectively concludes the paragraph?

A) The best part is that this refrigerator can be constructed with relatively inexpensive materials in almost any location.
B) Refrigerators were one of the most important inventions of the 20th century, allowing for greater food safety and more leisure time for women.
C) They are not as big as modern electrical refrigerators, however, and do not look as sleek and decorative.
D) Any engineer that can find a way to produce these refrigerators on a large scale will certainly be hugely successful.

Water sanitation is possibly the biggest issue faced by underdeveloped regions, and one of the success stories in the field of appropriate technology. Ceramic water filtration systems, easy to **17** manufacture: use only clay pots combined with the right consistencies of sand and rocks in the right order. This method of filtration, which can be constructed in many sizes and configurations, **18** are prized for their ability to mimic the natural filtration of water that occurs in hills and mountains. It can be installed in almost any home at very low cost. The devices not only remove harmful bacteria and toxins, **19** but also save hours of labor that would have been spent gathering and burning wood to boil and purify the water.

17

A) NO CHANGE
B) manufacture; use
C) manufacture. Use
D) manufacture, use

18

A) NO CHANGE
B) has been prized for their
C) is prized for its
D) is prized for their

19

A) NO CHANGE
B) also saving
C) but they also save
D) but also saving

Engineers who pursue this path must be ready to sacrifice short term personal gain for long term social betterment. **20** The biggest problem regarding the development and spread of appropriate technology is not the ability of researchers to create simple machines and devices or find useful solutions, but rather their ability to push **21** himself or herself to find inventions that are economical, practical and convenient enough to encourage widespread use by populations that need it. Even if a device like the underground refrigerator works well, if it is unreliable or difficult to use, then it will not gain widespread acceptance. This concern is one aspect of development that any engineer of appropriate technology will have to think about while designing.

At the moment the field of appropriate technology may not seem the best career path to follow if one hopes to make a lot of money. After all, the places and people for whom these technologies are being developed have little or no money to begin with. However, if one thinks about the numbers of people who might be helped out of poverty with such **22** inspiring inventions, quality of life around the world will improve and further progress be made.

20

The writer is considering deleting the previous sentence. Should the writer make this change?

    A) Yes, because it presents information that is not related to the topic of the rest of the paragraph.
    B) Yes, because it contradicts the main argument of the passage.
    C) No, because it serves as a relevant introduction to the paragraph.
    D) No, because it supports assertions that are made later in the paragraph.

21

    A) NO CHANGE
    B) oneself
    C) themselves
    D) him or herself

22

Which choice best maintains the tone established in the passage?

    A) NO CHANGE
    B) joyful
    C) delightful
    D) good

Passage 3

Biofuels: Miracle Cure?

Fossil fuels—which include coal, oil, and natural gas—provide 80 percent of world energy consumption as of 2015 and produce **23** cruel pollutants that threaten the ability of humans to live comfortably on the Earth. Our reliance on these resources has increased exponentially since the Industrial Revolution, and as developing countries grow more and more, so too does our use of fossil fuels. Nations around the world agree that this situation needs to change, and have struggled for decades to find fuels that could allow industrial society to enjoy its current prosperity without harming the environment. Two such fuels that have been explored as potential solutions in the last two decades have been biodiesel and ethanol, **24** they are chemicals which produce significantly fewer emissions than traditional resources. However, research suggests that these miracle fuels may not be quite as miraculous as previously thought.

In the 1990s, the US government spent millions of dollars to assist in the production of ethanol and biodiesel. **25** These fuels are produced by processing biological material called biomass, which is gathered from corn, sugarcane, or certain types of grass. Once processed, the resulting fuel can be added to gasoline, reducing automobile emissions.

23
A) NO CHANGE
B) hurtful
C) venomous
D) toxic

24
A) NO CHANGE
B) those being
C) these are
D) DELETE the underlined words

25
Which choice most effectively combines the underlined sentences?

A) These fuels are produced by processing biomass, which is biological material that is gathered from corn, sugarcane, or certain types of grasses, processed, and then added to gasoline to reduce automobile emissions.

B) Fuels produced from processed biomass reduce automobile emissions when added to gasoline, once the biological material is gathered from corn, sugarcane and certain types of grasses.

C) Processed biomass—which is gathered from corn, sugarcane or certain types of grasses and added as an emissions reducer to gasoline—is what produces these fuels.

D) Added to gasoline after being processed from biological materials, these fuels are produced from biomass gathered from corn, sugarcane, or certain types of grasses.

Due to its growing popularity, [26] ethanol is projected to account for an increasing amount of total fuel use. Refining and burning biofuels produce much less pollution than traditional sources [27] do, but there is a problem. [28] The amount of corn cultivated has risen by 90 percent; because increased demand for corn increases the price for the crop, this in turn creates more demand for land to grow it, which means more trees get cut down to create farmland. Consider the [29] rainforest, for example, one of the biggest natural sources of carbon dioxide reduction, it is being deforested at an alarming rate by farmers eager to profit from the increased price of corn. As a result, the benefits of reduced emissions are offset by the environmental harm. Many scientists are now arguing that we should stop focusing on biofuels as alternative fuel sources.

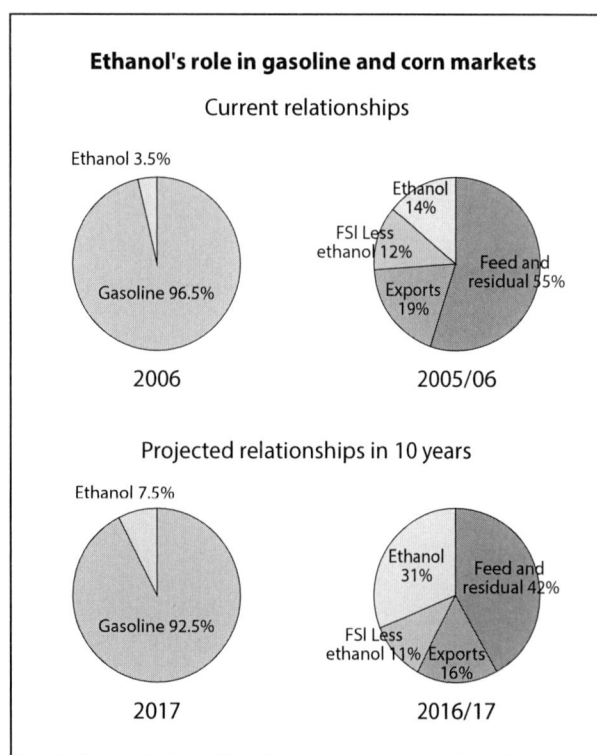

Note: FSI=food, seed, and industrial
Source: USDA Agricultural Projections to 2016, February 2007

26

Which choice most effectively completes the sentence with relevant and accurate information based on the graph?

A) NO CHANGE
B) ethanol will cease to be a major energy source by 2017.
C) gasoline has remained the dominant source of energy thus far.
D) corn will be exploited as a new fuel, starting from 2017.

27

A) NO CHANGE
B) have,
C) did,
D) had,

28

Which choice most effectively completes the sentence with relevant and accurate information based on the graph?

A) NO CHANGE
B) The price of corn is expected to decrease in 2017 because of the increase in demand;
C) Larger proportions of corn harvests are expected to be used for the creation of ethanol;
D) The use of corn for feed will diminish greatly by 2017;

29

A) NO CHANGE
B) rainforest, for example
C) rainforest. For example,
D) rainforest, for example:

(1) The original rationale behind pursuing these fuels as alternatives to coal was that they might serve as a "bridge" between our fossil fuel past and our renewable energy future. (2) Fortunately, advances in solar and wind power are starting to make it seem more feasible than previously thought. (3) As we can see, however, from the findings about the unforeseen environmental impacts of biofuels, it is clear that we must find a way to make the transition without burnable fuels at all if we want to avoid warming the Earth to dangerous levels. (4) Some of the most interesting advances have come from work done by these 'true renewables' scientists, **30** which focus their efforts on technologies that require less extraction and resource depletion. (5) Experts argue that funds that are currently being spent on the production of biofuels would be better spent on these options. **31**

In any case, a great deal of work still needs to be done in order to protect ourselves and the environment from further harm. While biofuels have not proven to be the ultimate solution to our problems, the exploration of **32** its possibilities show that humans can attempt to overcome their dependence on fossil fuels through innovative and exciting ideas. This is true even if their results ultimately turn out to be less exciting than expected. **33** There are now newer technologies that will make our efforts at attempting to use fossil fuels look foolish and misguided.

30

A) NO CHANGE
B) who
C) that
D) they

31

To make this paragraph most logical, sentence 3 should be placed

A) where it is now.
B) after sentence 1.
C) after sentence 4.
D) after sentence 5.

32

A) NO CHANGE
B) their
C) it's
D) there

33

The writer wants to end the passage with a summary of his or her discussion of biofuels and a call for future environmental efforts. Which choice best accomplishes this goal?

A) NO CHANGE
B) Only by continuing to pursue biofuels and other "bridge" solutions can we ever hope to overcome the challenges that we face as a global community.
C) Even though one possible solution has unfortunately proven unfruitful, as long as we carefully monitor our efforts and keep trying, we will eventually find our way to a cleaner and more prosperous world.
D) Clearly, the efforts of those in the field of renewable energy have proven that it is possible to profit and grow as a society with the help of biofuels.

Passage 4

A New Haven for Pet Lovers

More and more people have moved to cities in the last decade and as a result, costs of living in major population centers like New York and San Francisco have risen dramatically. While it is possible to live and work there, accommodations for those who arrive are **34** binding compared to the less densely populated regions from which they came. This leads to a desire among city-dwellers for a simulation of some of the aspects of the lifestyle they left behind in order to make their fortunes in the city. Two examples of this are the city park and the **35** zoo, amenities meant to provide calming green spaces and connection to nature have been popular throughout history, and no one living in the city would want to do without them. The pet cafe is a modern form of this impulse that is catching on around the world.

34
A) NO CHANGE
B) limited
C) surrounded
D) strict

35
A) NO CHANGE
B) zoo; these amenities
C) zoo. These amenities
D) zoo. Amenities

For decades, more and more families have appreciated the joys of pet ownership, finding it to contribute greatly to quality of life as well as **36** reducing stress. Unfortunately, when they arrive in New York or other densely populated cities, they find that they cannot afford the space necessary to provide a comfortable life for their furry friends. **37** Previously, these new urbanites would have just gone without the animals, but entrepreneurs are finding that there is a market for places where people can come and have a cup of coffee and spend some time with a collection of cats or dogs.

36

A) NO CHANGE
B) have reduced
C) reduce
D) reduced

37

At this point, the writer is considering adding the following sentence.

> Since the growth of Silicon Valley, rents in San Francisco have skyrocketed, presenting a daunting barrier to new residents.

Should the writer make this addition here?

A) Yes, because it links the housing issues of New York and San Francisco.
B) Yes, because it explains why San Franciscans might be interested in pet cafes.
C) No, because it does not give information about why the growth of Silicon Valley would cause rents to increase.
D) No, because it provides background information that only serves to reiterate a previously explained fact.

(1) This trend—popular outside of the US for quite some **38** time; had its first examples **39** paving the way for a wide variety of animal-based cafes. (2) The very first business of this **40** type, the Taiwanese Cat Flower Garden, opened in in 1998 and spread rapidly through Japan and South Korea. (3) The great success of these establishments eventually inspired international imitators. (4) The first American cat cafe opened in New York in 2014, and dog cafes began opening in Los Angeles soon after. (5) The trend is spreading beyond the US and Canada as well, with a few European cities claiming their own cafes. (6) Further locations in North America are expected to open soon, also on the East and West Coasts. (7) At each of these locations, patrons are able to socialize with the animals, as many as 20 different breeds at some locations, **41** and enjoy a fine selection of teas or coffee available at reasonable prices. **42**

38

A) NO CHANGE
B) time
C) time:
D) time—

39

Which of the following best introduces the examples given in the paragraph?

A) NO CHANGE
B) including breeds representative of cultures all over the world.
C) opening in highly urbanized nations in East Asia.
D) exciting foreign investors following successful North American openings.

40

A) NO CHANGE
B) type, the Taiwanese, Cat Flower Garden
C) type, the Taiwanese, Cat Flower Garden
D) type the Taiwanese Cat Flower Garden,

41

In the context of the paragraph, which of the following CANNOT be placed in the underlined part?

A) NO CHANGE
B) with an equal mix of small and large breeds of dogs and well-behaved cats.
C) a fact that may alarm government regulators.
D) which will certainly cause excitement among pet enthusiasts.

42

To make this paragraph most logical, sentence 6 should be placed

A) where it is now.
B) after sentence 2.
C) after sentence 3.
D) after sentence 4.

While most people are at least intrigued by the idea of spending time with a lot of animals in a safe and controlled environment, and being able to drink coffee or tea while doing so, there are some concerns when it comes to mixing animals with food and drink. Anyone who would like to open a restaurant that also is home to so many lovable pets needs to be sure that they are not in violation of any health codes. An establishment that serves food in the US, including one that involves unique circumstances, **43** facing tight restrictions when it comes to the presence of animals. Any potential pet cafe needs to provide separate areas for animal interaction and food service. This increases the cost for opening the business, which might account for the length of time it has taken for the trend to arrive in the states. However, now that it has, pet lovers in the city finally have the chance to **44** participate in the vibrant economies of these cities and their new businesses.

43

A) NO CHANGE
B) faces
C) have faced
D) face

44

A) NO CHANGE
B) enjoy the company of animals while protesting the unfairness of city health codes.
C) determine whether or not they would actually like to have a pet in the city.
D) experience the joys of having a pet, even if only for an afternoon at a time.

Practice Test 3

Passage 1

Let's Get this Show Started

My friends and I have been in a band together for about a year and a half now. We mostly play covers by some of our favorite artists, but none of us have any interest in being professional musicians. You can see our posters hanging everywhere in downtown, most near the restaurant district but even at bus stops, on benches, or **1** they are plastered on bulletin boards at the university. Our shows regularly sell out, and the owner of a local venue has asked us to perform on a weekly basis. We love the idea, and would love to keep playing, **2** in addition there is a significant problem. Next summer, our drummer and our bassist will be transferring to another university, so the band will basically be **3** defunct no matter what happens.

1
A) NO CHANGE
B) plastered on
C) on
D) DELETE the underlined words.

2
A) NO CHANGE
B) although
C) but
D) and

3
A) NO CHANGE
B) abolished
C) obsolete
D) vanquished

Twenty or even ten years ago, our little group of musicians would have come and gone and our fans would have drifted away, barely remembering us. The costs of recording and printing an album of cover songs by a nearly unknown band would have been impossible to afford without the backing of even a minor record label. Fortunately, in the modern era we have a few more options for [4] that. [5] One of those options is a new method of online investment that is rapidly gaining popularity. It is crowdfunding. Even with only the small fan base we have created, we should be able to raise just enough money to pay for studio time and enough copies of our record for ourselves and a few dozen of our fans.

4

A) NO CHANGE
B) this
C) them
D) such a project

5

In context, which choice best combines the underlined sentences?

A) One of those options is crowdfunding, a new method of online investment that is rapidly gaining popularity.
B) A new method, crowdfunding, of online investment is one of those options that is rapidly gaining popularity.
C) A new method of online investment rapidly gains popularity and it is called crowdfunding.
D) Crowdfunding, one of those options, rapidly gains popularity and is a new method of online investment.

[6] The owner of the venue we often perform at was unable to ensure that a project like ours can get off the ground. Websites specializing in this practice, such as Kickstarter and Indiegogo, provide an avenue for the funding of a project or business outside the traditional pathways like bank loans or big investors. There are many ways to run a crowdfunded project, but the most common way is to set up a project, like our album, and post on the website the project and how much money will be required to complete it. Most projects allow any level of contribution, and [7] increase the quality of rewards given depending on how much people contribute. For our album, if someone pledges less than 15 dollars, we send them a thank you email and a picture of the band in concert. For 15 dollars, we send them a copy of the album, and for 30 dollars we send them a t-shirt. The highest reward is set at 100 dollars and [8] entitled the donor to a live performance of our band at a location of their choosing. It is a simple but effective system for many different types of projects.

6

Which choice provides the most appropriate introduction to the paragraph?

A) NO CHANGE
B) Crowdfunding is the process of collecting small investments from interested customers
C) Sometimes bands like ours find it difficult to raise funds
D) Recording cover songs might not seem like motivation enough

7

Which choice provides the best link to the information that follows?

A) NO CHANGE
B) include more tracks on the album
C) list the number of available investors
D) increases the cost of the final product

8

A) NO CHANGE
B) entitling
C) has entitled
D) entitles

It has proven effective for us. We messaged our fans about the project and we have already raised half of the money we need to get it done. As I write this, there are still two weeks to go before the deadline, but I think we will be able to raise all the money we need. **9** Some people have criticized crowdsourcing for not having protections in place for consumers who pay but don't receive what they paid for, which has happened in many cases. This usually happens when a person promises much more than they can actually deliver, but in our case we don't think it will be a problem. Our project, **10** appropriately we named it "Thanks to the **11** Crowd"— would never have happened without crowdsourcing, so we definitely appreciate it.

9

At this point, the writer is considering adding the following sentence.

Crowdfunding can provide an alternative for organizations that don't have access to traditional means of funding a project.

Should the writer make this addition here?

A) Yes, because it appropriately summarizes the main ideas of the passage.
B) Yes, because it more clearly explains the purpose and background of crowdfunding.
C) No, because it restates information from previous paragraphs for no clear purpose.
D) No, because there is no information in the passage that supports this statement.

10

A) NO CHANGE
B) we appropriately named it
C) it was named appropriately
D) which we appropriately named

11

A) NO CHANGE
B) Crowd",
C) Crowd";
D) Crowd

Passage 2

The Martian

Space travel and exploration have been dreams of humankind even before flight was possible. Jules Verne and H.G. Wells, legendary writers of early science fiction, both wrote stories that filled the public imagination with new ideas about [12] space such as: what space travel might be like and what we might find on distant planets once we got there. The early successes of the space race and NASA stoked public imagination, and science fiction at the time of and following the moon landing generally assumed that our destiny lay in the stars. [13] Unfortunately, legendary science fiction writers Isaac Asimov and Arthur C. Clarke as well as astronomer Carl Sagan put forward in their work the extreme likelihood of humanity's future in space. [14] As a result, since the 1980s, public fascination with space travel has dwindled, and government funding for NASA in general and manned space programs in particular [15] have dropped to a small fraction of the amount set aside in the 1960s.

[12]
A) NO CHANGE
B) space, such as,
C) space such as,
D) space, such as

[13]
A) NO CHANGE
B) For example,
C) Yet,
D) On the other hand,

[14]
A) NO CHANGE
B) Finally,
C) However,
D) In addition,

[15]
A) NO CHANGE
B) has dropped
C) dropping
D) dropped

[16] There are some who would argue that this deceleration of space exploration is either a good thing, given the problems that need to be tackled down here on the ground, or that it is a natural result of the difficulty or impossibility of going to space. Elon Musk, founder of PayPal and Tesla motors, belongs to neither of these groups. With his private company SpaceX, Musk has a long term plan to put a human colony on Mars before the end of the century. **[17]** Given the current state of space exploration, it is easy to dismiss his goal as science fiction, but the case he makes for Martian tourism is surprisingly convincing.

16

A) NO CHANGE
B) Their are
C) Their is
D) There is

17

At this point, the writer is considering adding the following sentence.

> The atmosphere of Mars is composed primarily of carbon dioxide and most contemporary research suggests that water once flowed on the planet's surface, even if only briefly.

Should the writer add this sentence here?

A) Yes, because it supports the views of modern scientists regarding environmental conditions on Mars.
B) Yes, because it strengthens the passage's argument that colonizing Mars will be difficult.
C) No, because it presents information that is unrelated to the focus of the paragraph.
D) No, because it repeats information presented earlier in the passage.

First, he argues that the reason we have not yet colonized Mars is that it is too expensive. He says space travel has been monopolized by government mistakes, expensive defense contracts and restricted participation without accountability. For the sake of tradition, **18** having continued problem solving methods that only slowly and painfully make progress. Through his company SpaceX, Musk hopes to bypass this inefficient system. Already the company is responsible for a number of contracts to launch communication and observation satellites. The company has developed revolutionary thruster and rocket designs that have decreased the cost of an individual launch by 80 percent of the cost of a rocket that is **19** launched traditionally, and hopes to decrease it even further. This is causing many to reconsider the possibility of flights to Mars.

18

A) NO CHANGE
B) to continue
C) continuing
D) these methods continue

19

A) NO CHANGE
B) launched in such a way that it is traditional,
C) launched in a traditional way, with inefficient government investment and oversight,
D) traditionally and as a result not efficiently launched,

Prohibitive cost is the most important barrier to Martian travel, and Musk **20** clarifies that if he can decrease the cost of a "ticket" to mars to $100,000 per person, there will be enough interest that the creation of a colony will be possible. Currently, the cost per person is estimated at nearly $1 billion per person, but given the success of SpaceX at reducing rocket costs, Musk is optimistic that they can accomplish a similar reduction in the price per individual. Potential colonists will be more likely to go to Mars if homes there are more affordable and exciting than **21** the choice of their suburban equivalents, which are less adventurous and subject to property taxes.

Perhaps the most important cause for optimism is Musk's motivation for undertaking the project in the first place. Rather than looking for a financial advantage or potential market to exploit, Musk claims he wants to go to Mars to protect the future of the human race. "I think we need an insurance plan for our species," he said. "Throughout history there have been natural events that led to massive extinctions, and if humans live on two different planets, then we will have a much better chance to survive."
22

20
A) NO CHANGE
B) spouts off
C) confesses
D) asserts

21
A) NO CHANGE
B) those who choose
C) choosing
D) DELETE the underlined portion.

22
At this point, the writer wants to add a statement providing qualified support for the quote from Elon Musk. Which choice best accomplishes this goal?

A) Visions like these give me hope that someday humanity will spread throughout the stars.
B) This perspective presents a new and compelling argument for space travel, though time will tell if it will be enough to motivate humanity to the stars.
C) Governmental space programs around the world face growing competition from businessmen like Musk.
D) To this end, petitions to be on the first official trip have begun circulating around the internet and seem to only be growing longer.

Passage 3

Save the Sea

Most people would say that global warming is the most important environmental issue that we face as a species. Unfortunately, the unrestricted release of the byproducts of industrial activity impacts not only our skies (due to a variety of emissions) but also [23] affecting our seas. The most harmful effects of global warming are expected to take place decades from now, [24] but surprisingly some speculate that the ecosystems of oceans and seas around world might collapse well before the worst of those temperatures occur. There are three factors currently affecting the ocean that are most dangerous to [25] the future of both humanity and the sea; ocean acidification, waste dumping, and overfishing. Acidification can be linked to global warming, but the other two are side-effects of human resource mismanagement, and problems that could be solved if nations worked more closely together. If not, [26] their oceans might become aquatic wastelands their children will be unable to use.

23

A) NO CHANGE
B) is affecting
C) affects
D) DELETE the underlined portion.

24

Which of the following best establishes the contrast within the statement and accurately reflects the information in the passage?

A) NO CHANGE
B) but there is a real danger that
C) while there is a heated debate whether or not
D) though some continue to claim

25

A) NO CHANGE
B) the future of both humanity and the sea
C) the future of both humanity and the sea:
D) the future of both—humanity and the sea,

26

A) NO CHANGE
B) they're oceans might become aquatic wastelands they're
C) there oceans might become aquatic wastelands their
D) their oceans might become aquatic wastelands there

Scientists call ocean acidification the "evil twin" of global warming, because as more CO_2 is released into the atmosphere, the oceans absorb more of it as well. This is a natural process that usually finds a balance, but the dramatic increase in atmospheric CO_2 has led to an equally dramatic increase in oceanic CO_2. When the seawater absorbs CO_2, it reacts chemically and creates more hydrogen ions, increasing the acidity of the water. Scientists think the average pH of the oceans has decreased by 30 percent since the beginning of the industrial revolution. This is a trend which has serious consequences for ocean life, especially the tiny animals that make up the foundation of the oceanic food chain like phytoplankton and other shelled animals. In fact, **27** the number of crabs in Alaska is expected to remain unchanged with the current state of ocean acidification. If the food chain breaks down, it could **28** disrupt human food sources and biodiversity beyond anything we have yet experienced.

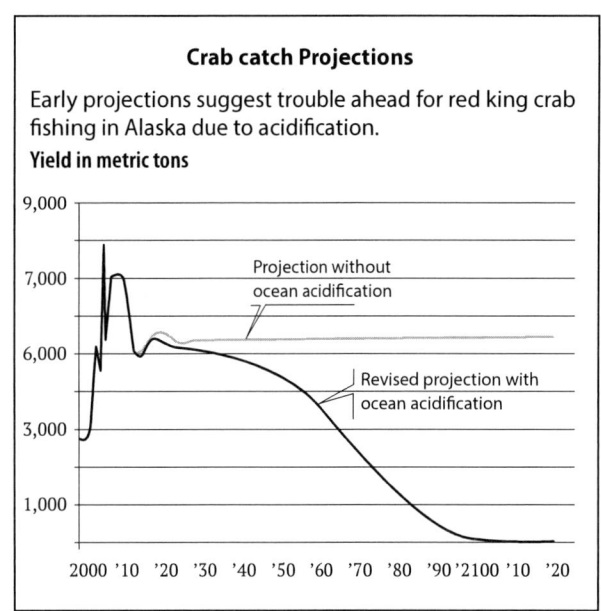

27

Which choice offers an accurate interpretation of the data in the chart?

    A) NO CHANGE
    B) the number of crabs caught in Alaska is expected to diminish dramatically by 2100.
    C) fishers in Alaska are expecting a greater yield of crabs by 2050
    D) crabs in Alaska are developing a resistance to acidification

28

The writer wants to convey the impact of acidification on the food chain so that readers understand its dramatic significance. Which choice best accomplishes this goal?

    A) NO CHANGE
    B) deplete
    C) decrease
    D) devastate

(1) Along with this tragic impact of global warming, human garbage production is leading to the deaths of hundreds of thousands of fish and sea animals every year, and the problem is only getting worse. (2) Many people know that plastic does not break down easily in nature. (3) However, many more are unaware that much discarded plastic eventually ends up in the ocean as a result of dumping and runoff from the land. (4) Possibly the most damaging impact of plastic pollution is the fact that it does not break down even when it is nearly microscopic. (5) A greater focus on recycling and reusing materials could help mitigate these effects according to **29** researchers, and these researchers have been looking for ways to curb this type of pollution for decades. **30**

29

A) NO CHANGE
B) researchers, but researchers
C) researchers, who
D) researchers. Researchers

30

The writer wants to add the following sentence to the paragraph.

These invisible pieces of plastic can absorb toxins which poison the animals that unknowingly consume them, or possibly even people who consume the animals.

The best placement for the sentence is immediately

A) after sentence 1.
B) after sentence 2.
C) after sentence 3.
D) after sentence 4.

Finally, there is the simple fact of overfishing. 3.5 billion people in the world rely on the ocean for their livelihood, but populations of traditional food fish have dropped upwards of 90 percent and in some cases even become extinct in the 20th century. Methods used for commercial fishing [31] involve huge nets that cannot discriminate between the types of fish they hope to catch. This results in the "bycatch" of non-commercial wildlife, up to 20 million tons a year that is simply dumped back into the sea. It is difficult to monitor and police fishing operations, but if these trends continue [32] ocean acidification will become a much worse problem.

With all these factors affecting the health of the ocean, it is clear that more action needs to be taken to ensure that the oceans, home to 99 percent of all life on earth, are still alive and thriving for generations to come. If not, we will need to find a different way to feed the vast majority of humanity, a task that could be in [33] a vein that a world without oceans might not be possible.

31

A) NO CHANGE
B) are involving
C) have involved
D) involves

32

Which choice most effectively ends this sentence and paragraph?

A) NO CHANGE
B) many more types of fish will be discovered and categorized.
C) funding from international organizations will be difficult to obtain.
D) there may soon be no more fish for anyone catch.

33

A) NO CHANGE
B) vain since a world
C) vein since a world
D) vane that a world

Passage 4

Nothing Lasts Forever, Even Languages

Language changes over time, sometimes dramatically. To see how true this is in writing, just compare the style of Shakespeare's plays to the average text message sent between friends today. These changes **34** was equally true in accents and dialects, perhaps even more so. Anyone coming face to face with a time traveler from their hometown from 100 years ago would have a hard time being **35** both effective speakers and listeners. Research seems to suggest that spoken language is susceptible to sudden and dramatic shifts over a short period of time. **36**

34

A) NO CHANGE
B) were
C) had been
D) are

35

A) NO CHANGE
B) an effective speaker and listener.
C) effective speakers and listeners.
D) effective both as speakers and listeners.

36

At this point, the writer is considering adding the following sentence.

Dramatic linguistic change may not happen over a long period of time after all, with some studies indicating just the opposite, in fact.

Should the writer make this addition here?

A) Yes, because it lends support to the ideas presented in the following paragraph.
B) Yes, because it gives a concrete example of the ideas presented in preceding sentences.
C) No, because it serves only to restate the information in the previous sentence.
D) No, because it introduces information that is unrelated to the topic under discussion.

(1) We don't often deal with travelers from the past, however. (2) So why it would be important to find out about past languages and dialects at all? (3) Those who study such things, [37] studying historical linguistics, would argue that by studying changes in language over time we will be better able to understand how language itself works. (4) This is where communities like the town of Tangiers in Virginia can be of great assistance. (5) If we know why words mean what they mean then we can [38] understandably comprehend one another. (6) There is almost no recorded audio dating from more than 100 years ago, so the difficulty in studying past dialects comes from actually finding examples of it. [39]

Located on a remote island in the middle of Chesapeake Bay, Tangiers was settled by English colonists as far back as 1670. Due to its location, the island is difficult to reach even by boat, and there is enough food and water that historically, the local inhabitants rarely had to venture out to the mainland for trade. [40] Despite this, there has been relatively little [41] immigration to or emigration from the island over the years, and a local dialect not far removed from the speech patterns of the 17th century colonists persists. The English of these "Hoi Toiders" (taken from their pronunciation of 'high tiders') is so thickly accented that it can be nearly unintelligible to visitors from off the island.

37

A) NO CHANGE
B) known as historical linguists
C) they are called historical linguists since they,
D) called historical linguists,

38

A) NO CHANGE
B) better know to figure each other out.
C) better understand each other.
D) conceive our interactions.

39

To make this paragraph most logical, sentence 4 should be

A) where it is now.
B) located before sentence 3.
C) located after sentence 6.
D) DELETED from the paragraph.

40

A) NO CHANGE
B) However,
C) Similarly,
D) Fortunately,

41

Which of the following best supports the ideas discussed in the paragraph?

A) NO CHANGE
B) interest in trade or tourism with
C) motivation to consider economic trends of
D) environmental impact on plants and animals on

By studying the speech patterns of Hoi Toiders, linguists have been able to learn more about the accents of the early English speaking [42] colonists: British, Scottish, and later Irish fishermen— and connect them to the American Standard English that is spoken today. To speak with a resident of the town is somewhat similar to actually having a conversation with one of the time travelers mentioned earlier, at least in a linguistic sense. Hidden within the differing vowels or added and dropped consonant sounds are links to our shared history and a greater understanding of the effects that time has on us all.

Economic changes and media saturation are slowly removing the dialects from Tangiers and other similarly isolated [43] communities, sadly. Losing the connection to the past provided by Hoi Toiders and their language feels particularly [44] excruciating, even if the change of languages is a natural part of the flow of history.

[42]
A) NO CHANGE
B) colonists—British, Scottish, and later Irish fishermen—
C) colonists; British, Scottish, and later Irish fishermen;
D) colonists; British, Scottish, and later Irish fishermen,

[43]
A) NO CHANGE
B) communities, sadly losing
C) communities sadly losing
D) communities—sadly, losing

[44]
A) NO CHANGE
B) poignant
C) touching
D) caustic

Practice Test 4

Passage 1

A to Zydeco

(1) The United States is home to a diverse population and diverse cultures that have given birth to myriad genres of music. (2) Jazz, rock and roll, hip hop, country, and bluegrass music all originate in the United States and enjoy popularity across a wide cross-section of the modern population. (3) But there are genres resulting from other less known fusions that do not capture the public imagination quite as thoroughly as those listed above. (4) Like the nation itself, they represent a fusion of the cultures and viewpoints of cultures from around the world coexisting in their adopted home. (5) One such music is Zydeco, which originated from French Creole and Cajun cultures intermingling **1** between the various swamps of the Mississippi Delta. **2**

Historical events were **3** huge influences going to the eventual development of Zydeco. From 1756 to 1763, during what was called the 7 Years War in Europe and the French-Indian War in the United States, British forces took control of the St. Lawrence River in Canada. The French communities there, known as Acadians, **4** were forced by the British to relocate to Louisiana.

1

A) NO CHANGE
B) among
C) into
D) with

2

To make this paragraph most logical, sentence 4 should be placed

A) where it is now.
B) before sentence 2.
C) after sentence 2.
D) after sentence 5.

3

A) NO CHANGE
B) the big things that led to
C) the important things that cause
D) the primary factors in

4

A) NO CHANGE
B) have been forced
C) are forced
D) forced

5 Once they were resettled, they influenced and were influenced by the Louisiana Creole who were already living in the area, a population of freed slaves and European settlers. Influences from this cultural melting pot eventually resulted in Cajun (short for Acadian) culture and Zydeco music.

Part of the appeal of Zydeco music involves its unique instruments, time signatures, and language. For example, percussion is handled by a musician who plays the rubboard, a washboard worn over the head, strummed by hand or tool, and **6** rhythmically scratching out. The songs are most often played in a syncopated, high speed waltz-like style that is unlike any other form of popular music. Lyrics of the music are filled with Cajun and Creole turns of phrase and imagery, like the famous "laissez les bon temps roulez", which in English means "let the good times roll". Few types of music in the United States give their listeners such **7** welcome relief from the struggles of daily life.

5

At this point, the writer is considering adding the following sentence.

Nearly 12,000 people were forcibly removed from their lands and shipped across the continent.

Should the writer make this addition here?

A) Yes, because it explains why Acadians were so eager to create new forms of music and develop their new culture.
B) Yes, because it shows the magnitude of Acadian deportation, which provides context for their influence once they arrive in Louisiana.
C) No, because the number of deported Acadians is unrelated to the main subject of the paragraph.
D) No, because it disproves the author's point about the importance of historic events.

6

A) NO CHANGE
B) rhythmically scratched out
C) rhythmic scratching out
D) rhythmically to scratch out

7

Which option best summarizes the main point of the paragraph?

A) NO CHANGE
B) a complex and challenging music to perform.
C) a diverse and unusual collection of attributes.
D) historically rich and culturally significant artifacts.

Zydeco maintains a niche following, though [8] annually popularity of the genre is increasing every year. Accordingly, there are pockets of Zydeco performers around the world. Performers respond not only to the music's infectious rhythms [9] in addition its carefree spirit, even if they have never called Louisiana home. As long as people enjoy unique sounds that are easy to dance to and a spirit of [10] freedom; Zydeco musicians will have no trouble finding audiences at live jazz clubs and other music venues around the world. [11] Clearly, anyone who enjoys music will enjoy listening to Zydeco, a fact that makes it superior to most other American genres.

8

A) NO CHANGE
B) it has a yearly increase of popularity annually.
C) it experiences an annual increase of popularity every year.
D) its popularity increases every year.

9

A) NO CHANGE
B) but they also enjoy
C) but also to
D) as do they also to

10

A) NO CHANGE
B) freedom, and Zydeco musicians
C) freedom, Zydeco musicians
D) freedom, Zydeco musicians,

11

The writer wants to conclude the passage with a sentence that summarizes the main points of the article. Which choice best accomplishes this goal?

A) NO CHANGE
B) Despite its current lack of renown, Zydeco will no doubt again reach the levels of popularity it enjoyed during the Seven Years War.
C) With its unusual instruments and sound, Zydeco will continue to present a challenge to any performer who decides to give it a try.
D) The music's rich history and inimitable style make it unlike anything else, and enjoyable to all.

Passage 2

Greenhouse Gases

Anthropogenic climate change, more commonly [12] it is referred to as global warming, is associated in the public imagination mainly with carbon dioxide, or CO_2. As the gas comprises over 80 percent of US greenhouse gas emissions, it is certainly of great concern. However, there are other gases which play a role in the process of heating the planet, and in some ways [13] its impact [14] may be of greater concern in the short-term plan for reducing emissions and controlling temperature increases. CO_2 does indeed lead to the trapping of heat within the atmosphere, but its potency as one of these gases pales in comparison to others, namely methane, nitrous oxide, and fluoridated gases.

[12]
A) NO CHANGE
B) it is global
C) it is known as global
D) known as global

[13]
A) NO CHANGE
B) they're
C) their
D) there

[14]
A) NO CHANGE
B) are maybe pretty important
C) might be big players
D) possibly worth a look

[15] Worrying and widespread, for climate scientists methane represents a problematic gas. It is currently responsible for 10% of warming that is being experienced. Though there is much less of the gas present in the atmosphere compared to CO_2, methane, or CH_4, is 25 times more effective at trapping heat, and is released from similar sources as CO_2, such as the burning of fossil fuels and industrial processes. [16] Methane is released when tundra, permafrost, and arctic ice melt due to rising [17] temperatures, a fact that may greatly accelerate warming effects if action is not taken soon.

Nitrous Oxide, or N_2O, is 300 times more powerful than carbon dioxide. The production of N_2O and other non-greenhouse gases [18] exemplify the unintended negative effects of unchecked growth and industrialization. More than 40% of the nitrous oxide in the atmosphere today is a result of human activity, particularly its use in fertilizers.

15

A) NO CHANGE
B) One of the most widespread and worrying gases for climate scientists is methane.
C) Among widespread and worrying gases, one of the most is methane for climate scientists .
D) Climate scientists, widespread and worrying, find methane one of the most.

16

At this point, the writer is considering adding the following sentence.

Also, as global warming intensifies, so too will the amount of methane in the atmosphere.

Should the writer make this addition here?

A) Yes, because it provides important context for the information that follows it.
B) Yes, because it undermines the argument of those who do not agree with the main idea of the passage.
C) No, because it makes more logical sense if placed in later paragraphs.
D) No, because it serves to weaken the main argument of the paragraph.

17

A) NO CHANGE
B) temperatures
C) temperatures;
D) temperatures, this is

18

A) NO CHANGE
B) exemplify the unintended negative affects
C) exemplifies the unintended negative effects
D) exemplifies the unintended negative affects

Finally, and perhaps most frightening of all the global warming gases are the F-gases, HFCs and SF₆. Created as substitutes for CFCs, which interact with and destroy the ozone layer that protects all life on earth from ultraviolet [19] radiation; HFCs are not entirely harmful. However, while they do not destroy ozone, HFCs do have the unfortunate distinction of being 12,000 times more effective at trapping heat than CO_2. SF₆ does not have the same positive characteristics as HFCs, and traps 22,000 times more heat than CO_2. [20] They are used in the manufacture of semiconductors. Experts see the increase in the popularity of devices like smartphones and other portable electronics as having given rise to the increase of this toxic and heat-trapping chemical.

19

A) NO CHANGE
B) radiation, this shows HFCs are not entirely harmful.
C) radiation; thus HFCs are not being considered entirely harmful.
D) radiation, HFCs are not entirely harmful.

20

A) NO CHANGE
B) It is
C) Its
D) Their

[21] Currently F-gases only account for 3% of the total emissions, but that number is expected to increase.

These unfamiliar chemicals and the startling numbers around them may seem intimidating. [22] However, the final effects of global warming are still unknown, and the prospects for humanity might be good or bad no matter what we do about gases besides CO_2.

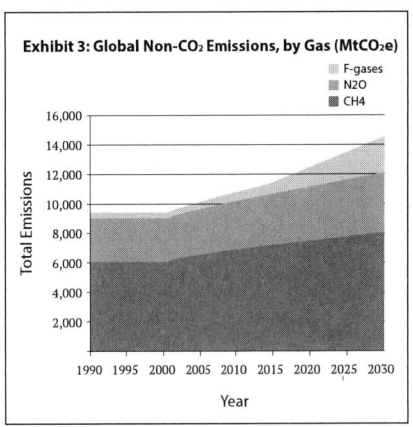

Note: Each colored section represents the percentage of total emissions for each gas.

21

Here the writer wants to include accurate, relevant data from the graph. Which choice best accomplishes this goal?

A) NO CHANGE
B) Total greenhouse gas emissions have plateaued in the last few years, and this trend is expected to continue.
C) The percentage of F-gases is expected to surpass that of N2O by the year 2030.
D) The increase in the use of such devices is expected to lower total greenhouse gas emissions.

22

The writer wants to conclude the article with a summary of the larger issue he or she is discussing while offering hope for the future. Which choice best accomplishes this goal?

A) NO CHANGE
B) The challenges that lay ahead for climate scientists, government officials, and everyday citizens are great, but they are aware of them and already taking steps to meet them.
C) Regardless, there are even greater obstacles to educating and motivating policymakers to reduce or ban global use of these gasses and the behaviors that create them.
D) Accordingly, rising temperatures will also create new shipping lanes in the Arctic, allowing significant increase in global trade.

Passage 3

As SLow aS Possible

One key feature of any piece of music is the tempo. This is usually marked at the top of the page following traditional Italian musical **23** notation: like *largo* and *allegro*, meaning slow and fast respectively. Over time, these traditional markings have given way to more straightforward and descriptive tempo markings, such as *fast, but not too fast* or *furiously*. While sometimes humorous, these markings are vitally important as they indicate the style in which the composer intended for the song to be played. Without them, the conductor or musician would not know if a song was intended **24** to last only a second or even a whole day. Postmodern composer John Cage took this fact to an extreme in his 1987 composition *Organ²/ASLSP (As SLow aS Possible)*. As one might expect, the tempo for this piece is *as slow as possible*.

23
A) NO CHANGE
B) notation
C) notation—
D) notation;

24
Which of the following uses exaggeration/hyperbole to consolidate the writer's point regarding the importance of time signatures?
A) NO CHANGE
B) to be played for a long or short time.
C) to proceed at a particular speed.
D) to be performed at a fast or slow tempo.

[25] This is a remarkable time signature for a modern composer. In fact, conventional performances of the eight-page composition do generally range from 20 to up to 70 minutes, which is not at all strange. However, the open notation of the piece allows the performer to determine exactly how long they want to hold each note before moving onto the next, and Cage himself has purposefully refused to reveal how long he expects the piece to last. This results in no two performances of the piece being the same length or even close to the same length. In 2009, organist Diane Luchese gave [26] appropriately, a performance that lasted for over 14 hours. Someone could perform the piece in less than five minutes and still be giving a proper performance, [27] but critics will not be impressed.

25

Which of the following best introduces the paragraph?
- A) NO CHANGE
- B) Now, this might not seem like that unusual of a tempo at first.
- C) John Cage was not the first composer to challenge audience endurance.
- D) Critical response to Cage's composition was mixed because of the tempo.

26

- A) NO CHANGE
- B) though,
- C) therefore,
- D) for example,

27

The writer wants to end the paragraph effectively, while also stressing the most important aspect of the music being discussed in the paragraph. Which choice best accomplishes this goal?
- A) NO CHANGE
- B) although John Cage would no doubt be disappointed.
- C) if you were performing as slow as you possibly could.
- D) even though the song is extraordinarily difficult to play.

This [28] subjectivity, which has multiple interpretations, was part of Cage's original intention for the piece, and has led some professional musicians to be mystified by its possibilities. Nowhere is this more apparent than the performance of *ASLSP* that has been ongoing at the Halberstadt Cathedral in Halberstadt, Germany since 2001 and is not scheduled to end until the year 2640. So far only 12 chord changes have taken place, with the next scheduled for September 2020. [29] Even though the piece is being played to a specific tempo, no matter how slow, the exact times for each note can be calculated.

[28]
A) NO CHANGE
B) subjectivity
C) subjectivity — the aspect of a work which is open to interpretation —
D) subjectivity, which anyone can interpret as they wish,

[29]
A) NO CHANGE
B) Since
C) Thus
D) DELETE the underlined words and start the sentence with a capital letter.

While we may not be around for the final notes of the performance, the idea is elegant in **30** it's connection to both music history and cathedrals themselves. When medieval church leaders and workers began constructing a cathedral, they did not expect to see it built **31** within their lifetime, and instead left completion of the project in future **32** generation's hands. A Halberstadt fan on hand for a note change in 2008 told the New York Times he loved the performance and had high hopes for its impact. **33** "It's a way for us to feel connected to the future, and for the future to be connected to the past," he said.

30

A) NO CHANGE
B) their
C) its
D) these

31

A) NO CHANGE
B) on
C) inside
D) with

32

A) NO CHANGE
B) generations
C) generations's
D) generations'

33

Which of the following best provides support for the idea that the Halberstadt performance will be successful despite its length, as described in the preceding paragraph?

A) NO CHANGE
B) He has filled two bags with purchases from a nearby gift shop, and continues to take photographs of the area.
C) He stands with his ears covered against the strength of the sound, wincing in pain.
D) Behind him outside, his two children make fast friends with tourists from other countries, chatting with obvious ease.

Passage 4

Automated Automobiles

Some of the most eagerly anticipated technological developments in contemporary technology and culture center around [34] social media, artificial intelligence alternative, energy, and robots. Drones have already become an [35] excepted part to everyday life, though they still carry a certain air of excitement and futuristic wonder. Apps on our phones can automatically determine our location and route goods and services to us as needed, a development that has had tremendous consequences for the businesses of [36] traditional services such as taxis and hotels. However, there is one eagerly anticipated futuristic tech that may be more disruptive still: the automated car [37] —a vehicle controlled by a computer without the need for any human input whatsoever. This technology has the potential to be one of the most important developments that society has seen in a very long time. So important, in fact, that many questions and concerns are already being raised about the technology before it [38] has even been released for public use.

[34]

A) NO CHANGE
B) social media, artificial intelligence, alternative
C) social media artificial intelligence, alternative,
D) social, media, artificial, intelligence, alternative,

[35]

A) NO CHANGE
B) excepted part of
C) accepted part to
D) accepted part of

[36]

A) NO CHANGE
B) old-fashioned entrepreneurship
C) superannuated trades
D) mom-and-pop labor forces

[37]

The writer is considering deleting the underlined portion and ending the sentence with a period. Should the writer make this change?

A) Yes, because it adds information that distracts the reader from the technology that the paragraph focuses on.
B) Yes, because the information in the section is already given earlier in the paragraph.
C) No, because the section clearly defines a concept that is important for the passage.
D) No, because the section provides the first example of the kind of technology the author is discussing.

[38]

A) NO CHANGE
B) was even released
C) had even been released
D) could even have been released

(1) Are driverless cars dangerous? (2) There are few things people fear more than not having control over their environment. (3) This is especially true when passengers are travelling at speeds fast enough to cause **39** him or her harm, **40** but research must be conducted to decide if it is safer to allow human control or not. (4) Currently, companies like Tesla and Google claim that the only accidents that have occurred in such vehicles happened when humans rather than computers were in control. **41**

Will it lead to better environmental circumstances, or worse? Automated car technology could dramatically reduce the number of automobiles on the road if it becomes possible for a driverless vehicle to simply appear whenever one is requested. **42** In opposition to the increased availability and success of these vehicles, demand for vehicles of all kinds might therefore increase, leading to even more manufacturing and possibly even more pollution. It is truly impossible to tell at so early a point in development. **43** In addition, any claims made about the environmental consequences of the technology should be taken with a grain of salt until more data becomes available.

39
A) NO CHANGE
B) him
C) it
D) them

40
A) NO CHANGE
B) so
C) for
D) or

41
The writer wants to add the following sentence to the paragraph.

It will take more than the word of the companies trying to sell the technology to convince the public, however.

The best placement for the sentence is immediately
A) after sentence 1.
B) after sentence 2.
C) after sentence 3.
D) after sentence 4.

42
A) NO CHANGE
B) Unrelated to
C) Without
D) As a result of

43
A) NO CHANGE
B) Therefore,
C) However,
D) Regardless,

Either way, we may not have much choice in the matter if driverless vehicle technology becomes feasible. If they are not more effective or efficient than traditional automobiles, the technology is unlikely to catch on, and thus all these **44** questions would be irrelevant. By the same token, if the technology is cheaper and more efficient than automobiles, we may find ourselves in a driverless future regardless of the potential safety and environmental concerns.

44

A) NO CHANGE
B) questions about the impacts of the technology
C) technological impact questions
D) consequential questions regarding technological impact

Practice Test
Answers & Explanations

Practice Test 1

PASSAGE 1

1. 11 Replacement
The underlined portion is followed by examples of health 'benefits', such as 'high protein and fiber content'. The underlined portion should indicate that quinoa's popularity is due to some reason related to health or health consciousness.
Answer: D

2. 1-1 Subject-Verb Agreement
The subject of the sentence is singular noun 'increase in demand', followed by nonrestrictive element between two commas, which should then be followed by the verb. The verb should be in singular form. Relative pronoun 'who' creates a subordinate clause, making the clause a sentence fragment. Only option satisfying these conditions is A.
Answer: A

3. 9-2 Precision and Concision
The underlined portion should be as concise and clear as possible, and use idiomatic language. The passage talks about what results will occur when quinoa is no longer consumed by farmers. This is idiomatically referred to as a 'public health' issue. Therefore, choice C is most idiomatic. Choice A is erroneously nuanced because of the word 'well-being'. Choice B is awkward due to the word 'community'. Choice D is redundant because of the words 'impacting', and 'results'.
Answer: C

4. 10-3 Wordiness
The underlined portion should be as concise and clear as possible. Choice A utilizes the passive voice, making the phrase unnecessarily wordy. Choice B is grammatically incorrect. Choice D is unnecessarily wordy. Choice C is the most concise answer.
Answer: C

5. 11 Insertion
The phrase should be added because it follows from a discussion of why quinoa is good nutrition for farmers. Additional information on why quinoa is exceptionally healthy would help the reader understand why it would be a health issue if farmers stopped consuming quinoa.
Answer: A

6. 11 Replacement
The transition should convey contrast, because the sentence provides contrasting information from what was discussed in the previous sentence. The previous sentence states that quinoa could be consumed by farmers because it was not popular. The underlined sentence states that farmers are tempted to sell quinoa rather than eat it.
Answer: B

7. 9-3 Frequently Confused Words
Prices do not 'influx', they 'inflate'. 'influx' refers to a flowing in of something. Also, when a noun form exists (such as 'inflation'), it is preferable to use the noun form over the gerund form ('inflating').
Answer: B

8. 10-3 Wordiness
A contrast must be established between the 'initial difficulty' farmers will face and the 'healthier choices' they will be able to eventually make. The most concise way to combine these sentences is to create a subordinate clause including a conjunction indicating contrast. Choices A and B are unnecessarily wordy. Choice C distorts the intended meaning.
Answer: D

9. 11 Replacement

The passage mainly discusses the impact of the rise in quinoa's popularity. The health consequences created for farmers indicates a 'transitional difficulty', and the eventual wealth resulting from the popularity of quinoa indicates 'a better life for farmers'.

Answer: B

10. 10-2 Redundancy

The sentence already contains a subordinating conjunction 'while', and therefore another word conveying contrast is redundant. 'however' should be deleted.

Answer: D

11. 3 Parallelism

Parallel structure: -ing (washing, cooking)
those rinsing → rinsing

Answer: C

PASSAGE 2

12. 9-2 Precision and Concision

The context indicates that opera 'has' a reputation for being old fashioned. A synonym of 'has' is necessary. Choice A and D are the only viable choices. Choice D 'enjoys' is possible to use with 'reputation', but an 'old-fashioned', 'painful' reputation is not a reputation to be 'enjoyed'.

Answer: A

13. 11 Insertion

The paragraph asserts that Wagner's compositions were enjoyed by audiences with 'a great deal of money in the bank'. The insertion states that operatic references were 'well known among all classes of German society', and thus takes the focus away from the elitist nature of opera as a genre.

Answer: C

14. 8 Tense

The past tense 'there were' cannot be used because it implies that 'works' by ancient Greek playwrights do not exist any longer – which is not the case. The present tense 'are' should be used. 'their' should not be used because it is the possessive case of 'they'.

Answer: D

15. 10-2 Redundancy

'popularly' is synonymous with 'not aristocratically', so one should be deleted to avoid redundancy. Choices C and D are unnecessarily wordy.

Answer: B

16. 11 Replacement

The answer must refer to early opera fans – choices A, B, and C are eliminated immediately because there is no mention of early opera fans. Choice B may be confusing, but it takes the focus away from 'early fans' to 'fans today', and therefore is not a viable answer.

Answer: D

17. 8 Tense

The sentence is referring to a period in the past. Also, the tense used in context is the past tense ('spent money', 'was considered'). Therefore, the past tense must be used.

Answer: A

18. 11 Replacement

The underlined portion must indicate causality, because the reason composers wrote at least one opera was due to the fact that 'a composer was considered unserious until they had attempted to write an opera'. The only option conveying causality is C.

Answer: C

19. 6-2 Colons and Dashes
'century' is followed by a list of elements (radio, film, and television), and therefore should be accompanied by a colon.
Answer: A

20. 4-2 Logical Comparisons
The comparison being made should be between 'tunes being played on the phonograph' and another way music can be consumed, such as 'expensive performances'. Choice A compares 'tunes' with 'high society'. Choice B and C compares the act of 'attending' and 'tunes'. Choice D is the only logical comparison.
Answer: D

21. 11 Replacement
The underlined portion must convey contrast, because the paragraph is making a transition from the minimal popularity opera enjoys ('lowest point ever recorded') to the movement emerging to combat this unpopularity.
Answer: C

22. 7-1 Incomplete Sentences
The sentence lacks both a subject and a verb. The only option that adds both a subject and a verb is C.
Answer: C

PASSAGE 3

23. 2-1 Pronoun Agreement
The underlined portion should be a pronoun in the possessive case referring to both 'dachshund' and 'terrier'.
Answer: C

24. 11 Replacement
The underlined portion should convey contrast, because the passage is transitioning from the discussion of unique breed traits that were continued for 'functions', to the fact that people do not own dogs for their 'functions' anymore.
Answer: C

25. 2-4 Ambiguous Pronoun
The pronoun 'they' is ambiguous because it can refer to both 'people' and 'dogs'. To eliminate ambiguity, 'dogs' should be used instead of 'they'.
Answer: B

26. 6 Punctuation
The that-clause serves as the object of the verb 'see' and therefore should not be separated from 'see' with a punctuation mark.
Answer: C

27. 9-2 Precision and Concision
The sentence is attempting to explain how individuals among breeds are preferred over, and therefore chosen over others due to specific traits they possess. The word that best conveys this meaning is 'selected'. Choice D, 'elected' is not possible because it implies that individuals are being chosen by vote.
Answer: B

28. 11 Content Order
The reason dog owners choose dogs for their 'aesthetic appeal' is the fact that modern owners do not need to consider whether dogs can do their jobs well. Also, the insertion must be followed by a discussion of why such 'selection' is unhealthy. Therefore, the sentence should be placed after sentence 5.
Answer: C

29. 4-2 Logical Comparison

'it' is ambiguous because it can refer to 'photograph', or 'dachshund'. Also, the transformation that is occurring is between the animal in the old photograph to the animal in the photograph today. Choices A and B are thus eliminated. Choice C is not possible because 'that' must be followed by a clause including both subject and verb.

Answer: D

30. 6-3 Various Comma Usages

'persisted' and 'in' cannot be separated by a punctuation mark because it is an idiomatic phrase. Also, a comma should not follow 'in' because the verb and the object cannot be separated by punctuation.

Answer: A

31. 11 Insertion

The inclusion of the phrase would effectively inform the reader of how large the pet industry is, because it provides large numbers such as '$60 billion'. The reader must be helped to understand the scale of the pet industry because it places the problem of selective breeding into an economic context.

Answer: B

32. 12 Graphs & Charts

The graphs indicate that the percentage of purebred dogs that are prone to certain diseases (dilated cardiomyopathy, aortic stenosis) is higher than that of mixed breed dogs. The only correct option is B.

Answer: B

33. 10-3 Wordiness

Choices B, C, and D are unnecessarily wordy. Choice A is the most concise and clear way to modify 'animal rights groups'.

Answer: A

PASSAGE 4

34. 6-3 Various Comma Usages

The phrase 'a milestone in … humankind' is a nonrestrictive element used to modify the subject. Therefore, it should be placed between two commas.

Answer: B

35. 9-2 Precision and Concision

Programmers and cognitive specialists would be working hard to create programs. The option that comes closest to this meaning is A. Choice B, 'emphatically', means to emphasize. 'stringently' could be confusing, but it implies that the programmers are working under strict supervision. Choice D, 'dispassionately', means 'noncommittal', and thus the opposite of what we are looking for.

Answer: A

36. 10-2 Redundancy

'or' already acts to add the last statement to the list, and therefore 'also' is unnecessary.

Answer: D

37. 11 Content Order

Sentence 6 attempts to explain how difficult it is to create a program that acts human (provide proper emotional responses, react appropriately to unexpected events, …). Therefore, it should be placed after sentence 3.

Answer: C

38. 9-1 Diction

'wait' must be used with the preposition 'for'. 'await', however, does not require a preposition to connect it with its object. Therefore, the correct option should either be 'waiting for', or 'awaiting'.

Answer: C

39. 2-5 Relative Pronoun

The latter clause must be connected to the main clause via a subordinating conjunction or relative pronoun. Choices B and D are ruled out. 'move', 'look', 'think', and 'act' are all actions done by robot characters. Therefore, they are the subject of the clause and 'whom' cannot be used.

Answer: C

40. 2-5 Relative Pronoun

A relative pronoun must be used to begin the modifier 'we first produce AI'. We produce AI 'through' a 'form'. 'how' refers to a method and therefore cannot refer to 'form'.

Answer: D

41. 9-3 Frequently Confused Words

The sentence attempts to explain that the actual AI we create will be considerably less sophisticated than the examples we see in films. Therefore, the adjective 'plain' should be used to convey the meaning of 'simple'. 'plane' is a homonym of 'plain', but it means 'a two-dimensional surface', not 'simple'. Similarly, 'than' needs to be used for comparison, not 'then'.

Answer: A

42. 11 Replacement

The sentence seeks to provide certain conditions that a program must satisfy in order to be classified as 'artificial intelligence'. It introduces a topic (criteria) different from what was put forth in the previous sentence, so 'consequently' is unnecessary. There is no need to establish a contrast.

Answer: B

43. 11 Replacement

The suggestion must include a statement on how the reader should be interested in addressing the 'problems' discussed in the paragraph. The only viable option is C. Choices A and D include irrelevant details; Choice B takes the logic to an extreme.

Answer: C

44. 11 Insertion

The paragraph is mainly discussing the majors that bear some relation with the field of AI. It does not seek to give career advice on fields that are not related to AI, such as 'medicine, finance, and education'. The insertion, therefore, is an irrelevant detail that will not be discussed further.

Answer: C

Practice Test 2

PASSAGE 1

1. 11 Replacement

The passage as a whole is concerned with the vacation time of American employees, and the costs of not having enough vacation days are mentioned immediately after this sentence. Therefore, the best option is D.

Answer: D

2. 11 Insertion

The insertion provides a detail on work fatalities; it is a topic that will not be discussed further in the passage and thus takes the focus of the paragraph away from the cons of not having enough vacation days.

Answer: C

3. 11 Replacement

This sentence provides a concrete example of the claim put forth in the previous sentence – that employees are required to work too much. Therefore, option D is most appropriate.

Answer: D

4. 6-4 Apostrophes

Here, the indefinite article 'a' requires a singular noun come after it, so 'companies' is not appropriate. The 'profits' belong to the 'company', so a possessive determiner must be used. An apostrophe is necessary after 'company'. 'profits' is a plural noun, so the apostrophe must be eliminated.

Answer: C

5. 10-3 Wordiness

The first sentence discusses one benefit of vacation – raising worker morale. The latter sentence discusses further benefits of vacation time. To appropriately combine these two sentences, a phrase must be used to clarify that 'improved employee health and decreased sick days' are 'further', 'additional' benefits. Choices C and D are thus eliminated. Choice B is less clear than choice A because subject and verb are separated by a nonrestrictive element.

Answer: A

6. 9-3 Frequently Confused Words

'means of' is the idiomatical phrase.

Answer: C

7. 2-5 Relative Pronoun

The underlined portion is part of a nonrestrictive element that modifies the subject, Lowe's Home Improvement. Therefore, it must refer to the subject with a relative pronoun. The only option utilizing a relative pronoun is B.

Answer: B

8. 11 Replacement

The paragraph is discussing the effects of increased vacation time on employee turnover. Therefore, the underlined portion must mention how increased vacation time has decreased the number of employees leaving Lowe's Home Improvement.

Answer: A

9. 10-2 Redundancy

The sentence mentions that PriceWaterhouseCoopers sends 'annual' reminders. The phrases 'once a year', 'each year', and 'every year' are thus redundant and should not be included in the sentence.

Answer: D

10. 1-1 Subject-Verb Agreement

The subject of the sentence is 'workforce', a singular noun. The verb has to be in the singular form, eliminating choices A and D. Choice C is not possible because 'can be' suggests that 'record job satisfaction' has not taken place yet.

Answer: B

11. 3 Parallelism

Parallel structure: comparatives (cheerier)
happy → happier, engaged → more engaged
Choices B and D both satisfy the parallel structure, but B is the more concise option.

Answer: B

PASSAGE 2

12. 11 Replacement

Appropriate technology is a field that seeks solutions for resource problems in developing nations. Therefore, the underlined portion should include some information on the economic disparity between nations despite technological advances.

Answer: B

13. 6-3 Various Comma Usages

The phrase beginning with 'developing' is a front modifier for the subject 'these inventors'. Therefore, it should be connected to the main clause with a comma.

Answer: D

14. 11 Insertion

The insertion about 'plastic bottles, sand, and clay' is necessary to explain why this new building method is 'cost-effective', and appropriate for places where there is a 'lack of affordable materials'.

Answer: A

15. 10-2 Redundancy

'important' and 'pivotal' mean the same thing. Therefore, using both words creates redundancy. Choice C is the only option that utilizes one and not both.

Answer: C

16. 11 Replacement

The device developed by researchers at the University of Calgary must serve as an example of appropriate technology that can be built in developing countries with readily available resources. The only sentence that provides such information is A.

Answer: A

17. 6-3 Various Comma Usages

'easy to manufacture' is a nonrestrictive element modifying the subject 'Ceramic water filtration systems', and must be placed between two commas.

Answer: D

18. 1-1 Subject Verb Agreement

The subject of the sentence is 'filtration', a singular noun. The verb must be in singular form, and thus choice A is eliminated. The possessive pronoun must also be in singular form, and thus choices B and D are eliminated.

Answer: C

19. 3 Parallelism

The use of 'not only ... but also ...' construction necessitates a parallel structure. 'not only' is followed by the verb 'remove', so 'but also' should also be followed by a verb and not a noun. Choices B and D use the gerund form instead of the infinitive. Choice C inserts noun 'they' between 'but' and 'also'.

Answer: A

20. 11 Deletion
The paragraph in general talks about how the engineer must be prepared to design reliable and convenient solutions instead of simply finding easy and simple solutions. Sacrificing 'short term personal gain for long term social betterment' is not related to this topic, and the sentence should be eliminated.
Answer: A

21. 2-1 Pronoun Agreement
The antecedent of the underlined portion is 'researchers', so the pronoun must be in plural form. The only plural option is C.
Answer: C

22. 10-5 Register
The tone of the passage as a whole is informative, but not overly optimistic or lighthearted. 'joyful', 'delightful', and 'good' all convey a tone of lightheartedness and positivity that is not in accordance with the overall tone.
Answer: A

PASSAGE 3

23. 9-2 Precision and Concision
'pollutants' cannot be cruel or hurtful; both words imply a malicious intent, which inanimate objects cannot hold. 'venomous' is used to describe poisonous substances secreted by animals or insects. Thus, 'toxic' is the most appropriate word to use in context.
Answer: D

24. 2-5 Relative Pronoun
The underlined part begins a back modifier providing information about 'biodiesel and ethanol'; it cannot introduce a new subject (they, those, these). It should begin with a relative pronoun referring to 'biodiesel or ethanol', or be rid of the pronoun altogether to immediately connect the modifier to the object.
Answer: D

25. 10-3 Wordiness
The combined sentence should do two things:
1: make it clear that biomass = biological material gathered from corn, sugarcane, or other types of grasses.
2: combine the two sentences with a common subject = these fuels, the resulting fuel.
The only option that does both is A.
Answer: A

26. 11 Replacement
The underlined portion must include some indication of the 'growing popularity' of biodiesel or ethanol. The only option that provides such information is A.
Answer: A

27. 3 Parallelism
A parallel structure must be maintained when making comparisons. 'Refining and burning biofuels PRODUCE' vs. 'traditional sources DO'. Choices C and D are in the past tense and thus ruled out. Traditional source do not 'have' pollution, they 'produce' pollution.
Answer: A

28. 12 Graphs & Charts
It can be inferred from context that the rise in the demand for corn is resulting from the increasing amounts of biodiesel being created from corn. Thus, the underlined portion should include information from the graph that conveys this fact. Choices A and D are inaccurate; Choice B does mention an 'increase in demand', but there is no information in the chart about decreased prices.
Answer: C

29. 6-2 Colons and Dashes

The first part of the sentence, 'consider the rainforest', is asking the reader to consider the rainforest as an example of how trees are being cut down for farmland. The clause beginning with 'one of the biggest ...' serves to provide more information on how rainforests are being destroyed for farmland. Therefore, a colon must be placed after 'for example' to create such a structure.

Answer: D

30. 2-5 Relative Pronoun

A relative pronoun should be used to create a subordinate clause, and the relative pronoun must refer to the 'scientists' mentioned immediately before it. Relative pronoun 'that' cannot be used after a comma, and 'which' cannot refer to a person(s).

Answer: B

31. 11 Content Order

Sentence 3 talks about how biofuels cannot be used to make the transition to renewable energy. The conjunctive adverb 'however' indicates that the previous sentence must contain contrasting information. Sentence 1 mentions how biofuels had been expected to serve as an appropriate 'bridge' between fossil fuels and renewable energy. Sentence 3 must be placed right after sentence 1.

Answer: B

32. 2-1 Pronoun Agreement

The antecedent of the possessive adjective is 'biofuels', so the pronoun must be in plural form.

Answer: B

33. 11 Replacement

The passage mentions how 'biofuels have not proven to be the ultimate solution'. This is the conclusion on the discussion of biofuels, and must be mentioned in the answer choice. Choices A and B are eliminated. Choice D cannot be the answer because it fails to provide 'a call for future environmental efforts'.

Answer: C

PASSAGE 4

34. 9-2 Precision and Concision

The underlined word must convey the fact that the available accommodations in regions like New York have less to offer, therefore being 'limited' in the number of benefits provided. 'binding' is used for a physical limitation, like being bound with a rope. 'surrounded' is mainly used to refer to a spatial dimension, and 'strict' implies that rules are being enforced.

Answer: B

35. 6-1 Period, Semi-colon vs. Comma

The sentence contains two independent clauses. The usage of a comma results in a run-on sentence, so a semicolon or period must be used. Choices B and C are ruled out because the word 'amenities' is not just referring to city parks and zoos. It refers to the whole range of amenities that provide 'calming green spaces', so pronoun 'these' should not be used.

Answer: D

36. 3 Parallelism

To maintain a parallel structure, the verb infinitive form must be used – 'contribute' as well as 'reduce'.

Answer: C

37. 11 Insertion
The insertion talks about rent in a densely populated city. However, the previous sentence already mentions that rent is a problem for people who want pets in densely populated areas. Therefore, it only serves to reiterate an already stated fact.
Answer: D

38. 6-2 Colons and Dashes
'popular outside of the US for quite some time' is a nonrestrictive element modifying subject 'trend'. Nonrestrictive elements must be placed between two commas or two dashes. Since it began with a dash in front of 'popular', it must end with a dash.
Answer: D

39. 11 Replacement
The next two sentences mention how pet cafes began in Taiwan and South Korea. Therefore, the underlined portion must mention these regions.
Answer: C

40. 6-3 Various Comma Usages
'the Taiwanese Cat Flower Garden' is a nonrestrictive element and must be placed between two commas.
Answer: A

41. 11 Replacement
The underlined portion should provide some kind of information about pet cafes. Choice C cannot be placed in the underlined portion because we have no evidence that pet cafes would alarm government regulators.
Answer: C

42. 11 Content Order
Sentence 4 mentions the first few locations pet cafes were opened in the US – New York and Los Angeles. Sentence 6 explains that 'further locations' will be opening in North America, so it should be placed after sentence 4. Sentence 5 goes onto state that the trend will be moving further from North America to Europe, the location of sentence 6 after 4 fits nicely into the logical flow of the paragraph.
Answer: D

43. 1-1 Subject-Verb Agreement
The subject of the sentence, 'establishment' is singular, so a singular verb form must be used. Choice A, 'facing', is ruled out because then the sentence would lack a verb.
Answer: B

44. 11 Replacement
The underlined part should indicate some benefit of pet cafes for pet lovers in the city. Choice A is a benefit that is not specific to pet lovers. Choice B states that pet cafes are a way to protest against city health codes, which is not in accordance with the claims of the passage. Choice C may seem plausible, but we have no evidence that pet cafes serve to help pet lovers decide whether they want a pet or not.
Answer: D

Practice Test 3

PASSAGE 1

1. 3 Parallelism
Parallel structure: preposition + location (at bus stops, on benches)
they are plastered on bulletin boards → on bulletin boards
Answer: C

2. 7-4 Conjunctions vs. Conjunctive Adverbs
'in addition' is an adverb and cannot be used as a conjunction. Therefore, we need a conjunction instead. The sentence structure is: independent clause + independent clause + independent clause. This eliminates choice B as 'although' is usually placed in front of a dependent clause. Of the leftover choices, choice C 'but' best represents the relationship between the two independent clauses.
Answer: C

3. 9-2 Precision and Concision
defunct: no longer existing
abolish: put an end to a system or a practice
obsolete: no longer needed because something better has been created
vanquish: defeat something in a battle or a competition
The author's band is not a system or a practice. It is not disappearing because some better band has appeared. It was not defeated in a battle or a competition. Choice A 'defunct' best describes the situation the author's band is facing.
Answer: A

4. 2-4 Ambiguous Pronoun
It is not clear what the pronoun is referring to. It can be referring to 'recording and printing' or 'minor record label' or even something else. The only choice that removes this ambiguity is choice D 'such a project'.
Answer: D

5. 10-3 Wordiness
Choice B is wordy and 'crowdfunding' is placed awkwardly. Choice D is unnecessarily wordy. Choice C is wordy and does not provide a smooth transition from 'few more options' in the previous sentence. Choice A is the most concise sentence that also provides a smooth transition from the previous sentence.
Answer: A

6. 11 Replacement
Providing details about crowdfunding is the main subject of the paragraph. Choices A, C, and D can all be eliminated because none of them introduce this topic.
Answer: B

7. 11 Replacement
The rest of the paragraph talks about different levels of rewards the author's band is offering to its supporters depending on the amount of their contributions. Choices B, C, and D can be eliminated because none of them introduce this topic.
Answer: A

8. 8 Tense
The sentence begins with 'The highest reward is set...' which uses the verb in present tense. Since there are no other signifiers, the verb should stay in present tense which is choice D 'entitles'.
Answer: D

9. 11 Insertion

In paragraph 2, the author has already talked about how crowdfunding is 'a new method of online investment'. The new sentence is repeating this information without a clear reason and should not be added.

Answer: C

10. 7-2 Conjunction Errors – General

The number of subjects is 3 (project, we, we). The number of conjunctions is 1 (so). Since this results in a general conjunction error (number of subjects – number of conjunctions = 2), another conjunction is needed to correct the sentence. Only choice D begins with 'which', a relative pronoun that can also act as a conjunction.

Answer: D

11. 6-3 Various Comma Usages

The sentence structure is: subject + modifier + verb + object. Commas should be placed before and after the modifier.

Answer: B

PASSAGE 2

12. 6-2 Colons or Dashes

'such as' already acts like a colon as it is used to introduce or list a series of items. Therefore, a colon is not needed. The underlined phrase should be written as either 'space such as' or 'space, such as'.

Answer: D

13. 11 Replacement

The previous sentence is talking about how 'science fiction at the time…generally assumed that our destiny lay in the stars'. The following sentence is providing examples of writers who wrote such science fiction stories believing that humans will explore outer space. Only choice B 'For example' effectively transitions from the previous sentence to this one.

Answer: B

14. 11 Replacement

The sentence is talking about how the people and the government's attitudes about space travel changed from positive to indifferent. Only choice C 'However' effectively transitions from the previous sentence to this one.

Answer: C

15. 8 Tense

'1980s' is a point in past. 'Since' + (point in past) signifies the verb must be in present perfect form, which is choice B 'has dropped'.

Answer: B

16. 9-1 Diction/1-1 Subject-Verb Agreement

Since the subject 'some' is plural, the plural verb 'are' is correct. 'Their' is a possessive case of 'they' and cannot be used in this sentence.

Answer: A

17. 11 Insertion

The focus of the paragraph is on 'Elon Musk' and his plan to build a human colony on Mars. The new sentence is providing a general description of Mars but does not mention whether the planet is habitable or not. Therefore, it is presenting information unrelated to the focus of the paragraph and should not be added.

Answer: C

18. 7-1 Incomplete Sentences

The sentence has no subject. Only choice D 'these methods (subject) continue (verb)' results in a complete sentence.

Answer: D

19. 10-3 Wordiness

Choices B, C, and D are all too wordy and provide unnecessary information.

Answer: A

20. 9-2 Precision and Concision

clarify: makes something easy to understand, usually by explaining it

spout off: talk about something in a boring or annoying way

confess: admit to doing something wrong

assert: state a fact or belief

Musk is not making something easy to understand as there is nothing to explain. Neither is he talking in a boring or annoying way or admitting to doing something wrong. He is simply stating his belief that the 'creation of a colony will be possible'. Choice D 'asserts' best describes what Musk is doing.

Answer: D

21. 4-2 Logical Comparisons

'homes' in Mars cannot be compared to 'the choice'. It must be compared to an equivalent such as 'homes on Earth' or 'suburban equivalents'. Therefore, the underlined phrase should be deleted.

Answer: D

22. 11 Insertion

'qualified support' means the support is not absolute because there are reasons for doubt. Choice A is a personal statement that cannot support Musk's quote. Choice C shifts the focus away from the conclusion, which is Musk's motivation for space travel. Choice D shows too much positive support without any qualification. Only choice B provides qualified support.

Answer: B

PASSAGE 3

23. 3 Parallelism

The use of 'not only ... but also ...' construction necessitates a parallel structure. Since 'our skies' comes after 'not only', 'our seas' should come after 'but also'.

Answer: D

24. 10-1 Style and Tone

The contrast within the statement is between the possible danger in the far future and the probable danger in the near future. The passage is talking about human activities that are not just limited to global warming and how they are quickly destroying Earth. Choice C effectively establishes this contrast with the use of transition word 'but' and the phrase 'real danger'. Choice A and choice D are incorrect because 'some' are not mentioned anywhere in the passage. Choice C is also incorrect as there is no mention of a 'debate'.

Answer: B

25. 6-2 Colons or Dashes

The sentence is immediately followed by a list of 'three factors'. Therefore, a colon should be used to introduce this list.

Answer: C

26. 9-1 Diction

'oceans' and 'children' are both in possession of 'nations'. Therefore, the use of 'their', possessive case of 'they', is correct.

Answer: A

27. 12 Graphs & Charts

The graph shows that by the end of the 21st century, the yield from crab fishing in Alaska is expected to reach near zero with ocean acidification. All the other choices offer an incorrect interpretation of the graph.

Answer: B

28. 10-1 Style and Tone

'deplete' and 'decrease' both mean 'reduce' without any additional negative connotation. 'disrupt', which means to 'cause difficulty' is slightly better but still not enough to convey the dramatic significance the author is looking for. Only choice D 'devastate', which means 'to damage badly or to totally destroy' fits the requirement the author is looking for.

Answer: D

29. 10-3 Wordiness

Choice A, B, and D are all too wordy by repeating 'researchers'. Only choice C concisely combines the two sentences by using 'who' and turning the latter sentence into a modifier.

Answer: C

30. 11 Insertion

Since the sentence is talking about effects of plastic, it has to come after a sentence that mentions plastic. This eliminates Choice A. The sentence is also talking about how the plastic is 'invisible', and this is only mentioned in sentence 4 by saying how the plastic can become 'nearly microscopic'. Therefore, the sentence should come after sentence 4.

Answer: D

31. 1-1 Subject-Verb Agreement/8 Tense

The subject 'Methods' is plural, so a plural verb should be used. Choice B is incorrect because the use of '-ing' is unnecessary. Choice C is incorrect because it can be seen from context that the tense should be in present form, not present perfect.

Answer: A

32. 11 Replacement

The paragraph is talking about the dropping number of fish in the ocean and how some may 'even become extinct'. The only choice that mentions this fact is choice D.

Answer: D

33. 9-3 Frequently Confused Words

vein (n.): thin tubes in your body through which your blood flows toward your heart

vain (adj.): failing to achieve what was intended

vane (n.): flat blade which pushes or is pushed by wind or water

The author is trying to say that trying to feed a majority of the population when there might not even be a world for them to live on is purposeless. The only word that conveys this meaning is 'vain'.

Answer: B

PASSAGE 4

34. 1-1 Subject-Verb Agreement/8 Tense

The subject 'changes' is plural, so a plural verb should be used. Also, as the rest of the passage is written in present tense, it can be seen that the verb must be in present tense.

Answer: D

35. 1-2 Noun Agreement/3 Parallelism

Since the subject 'Anyone' is singular, the objects 'speaker' and 'listener' also have to be singular. Also, the usage of construction 'both A and B' necessitates a parallel structure. This eliminates choices A, C, and D.

Answer: B

36. 11 Insertion

The sentence only serves to paraphrase what was said in the previous sentence. Therefore, it should not be added.

Answer: C

37. 6-3 Various Comma Usages

The sentence structure is: subject + modifier + verb + object. Commas should come before and after the modifier. This eliminates choice B. Choice A is incorrect because it does not clearly describe who 'Those' are. Choice C is incorrect because it results in a conjunction error.

Answer: D

38. 10-2 Redundancy

'understandably' and 'comprehend' are redundant in choice A. 'know' and 'figure out' are redundant in choice B. Choice D omits a keyword 'better' and is also too formal.

Answer: C

39. 11 Content Order

It is awkward for sentence 4 to be placed where it is now when no explanation about the 'town of Tangiers' appears until the third paragraph. Therefore, sentence 4 should be placed after sentence 6.

Answer: C

40. 11 Replacement

The sentences before and after the transition are both talking about how the local inhabitants seldom leave their island. The only transition that points out this common link is choice C 'similarly'.

Answer: C

41. 11 Replacement

The paragraph is talking about how the lack of change in the local population has caused the speech pattern to remain unchanged for several decades. The fact that there has been little 'immigration to or emigration from the island' reinforces the idea that the local population has not changed much since the 17th century.

Answer: A

42. 6-3 Colons and Dashes

A nonrestrictive element that begins with a dash must end with a dash. On the same note, a phrase that begins with a colon cannot end with a dash. Choices C and D are wrong since a complete sentence has to come after a semi-colon.

Answer: B

43. 5-2 Back Modifier

'sadly' acts as a modifier describing the act of 'removing the dialects'. Therefore, it should come at the end of the sentence following a comma. Choices B and C are incorrect because they result in run-on sentences. The use of a dash is also incorrect for choice D because the sentence after is not placed within a clause or used as an interruption.

Answer: A

44. 10-3 Precision and Concision

excruciating: extremely painful, either physically or emotionally

touching: causing sympathy

caustic: extremely cruel, critical, or bitter

poignant: making you feel sadness or regret

From context and the use of 'sadly', it can be assumed that the author is describing the process of 'losing the connection to the past' as 'sad'. Choice D 'caustic' can be easily eliminated. Choice A 'excruciating' is too strong. We can eliminate choice C 'touching' as there is no specific target for the feeling of sympathy to be directed at. Choice B 'poignant' is the fitting choice.

Answer: B

Practice Test 4

PASSAGE 1

1. 9-1 Diction
Choice C and D are incorrect because it is the French Creole intermingling *with* Cajun cultures *inside* the various swamps, not French Creole *and* Cajun cultures intermingling *with* the various swamps. Choice A is incorrect because 'various swamps' implies that there are more than two, and 'between' can only be used when there are two objects.
Answer: B

2. 11 Content Order
Look at sentence 3. The phrase 'other less known fusions' implies that 'fusion' was previously mentioned in the paragraph. Such 'fusion of the cultures and viewpoints of cultures' is only mentioned in sentence 4, logically placing sentence 4 in front of sentence 3. This also makes sense because sentence 4 talks about 'the nation itself', and the nation of 'the United States' is mentioned in sentence 2.
Answer: C

3. 10-5 Register
The whole passage is written quite formally. Choices A, B, and C are all too informal to join the rest of the passage. Choice D is the most concise and formal.
Answer: D

4. 8 Tense
The whole second paragraph is written in simple past tense. Also, since the '7 Year War' took place 'from 1756 to 1763', a point in past. 'during' + (point in past) signifies the verb must be in simple past tense. Therefore, 'were forced' is the correct tense.
Answer: A

5. 11 Insertion
The main idea of the second paragraph is how the Acadians influenced and were influenced by Louisiana Creole. Adding the new sentence will provide a context to understand the magnitude of the Acadians' influence on the Louisiana Creole. For example, had the author said 'only a few dozen Acadians were forced to move to Louisiana', then the readers would understand their influence to be small, compared to the '12,000 people' as provided in the new sentence. Therefore, the sentence should be added.
Answer: B

6. 3 Parallelism
Parallel structure: verb (past tense & passive voice) rhythmically scratching out → rhythmically scratched out
Answer: B

7. 11 Replacement
The main idea of the third paragraph is the uniqueness of Zydeco music. This can be seen from phrases such as 'unique instruments' and 'unlike any other form of popular music'. Choice C successfully captures this by saying 'unusual collection of attributes'. Other choices are either not mentioned or not the focus of the paragraph.
Answer: C

8. 10-2 Redundancy
'annually' and 'every year' are redundant. Only choice D removes this redundancy.
Answer: D

9. 9-1 Diction
The usage of 'not only … but also …' construction necessitates a parallel structure.
Answer: C

10. 6-1 Period, Semi-colon vs. Comma/6-3 Various Comma Usages

A semicolon can only be used to connect two complete sentences. The current structure involves an incomplete sentence followed by a complete sentence, so a comma should come right after the incomplete phrase, not a semicolon. Choice B can be eliminated because it creates a run-on sentence and choice D can be eliminated because a comma is unnecessarily placed after 'musicians'.

Answer: C

11. 11 Replacement

The whole passage talks about Zydeco music's history and unique style. Choice D successfully captures this through the phrase 'rich history and inimitable style'. Other choices are either not true or not mentioned in the passage.

Answer: D

PASSAGE 2

12. 6-3 Various Comma Usages

The sentence structure is: subject + modifier + verb + object. Since the modifier has to be an incomplete sentence, choices A, B, and C can be eliminated.

Answer: D

13. 2-1 Pronoun Agreement

The pronoun is referring to 'other gases' which is plural. Therefore, 'their' should be used instead of 'its'.

Answer: C

14. 10-5 Register

The whole passage is written quite formally. Choices B, C, and D are too informal to join the rest of the passage due to the use of 'pretty', 'big players', and 'worth a look'. Choice A is the most formal.

Answer: A

15. 5-1 Front Modifiers

'widespread and worrying' is a front modifier modifying 'methane', not 'climate scientists'. Therefore, choices A and D can be eliminated. Between choices B and C, choice B is the more concise.

Answer: B

16. 11 Insertion

The last sentence of the second paragraph talks about how rising temperature can cause more methane to be released. Adding the new sentence will provide a context to understand this fact in, as it mentions how global warming can result in an increased amount of methane.

Answer: A

17. 6-1 Period, Semi-colon vs. Comma/6-3 Various Comma Usages

A semicolon can only be used to connect two complete sentences. The current structure involves a complete sentence followed by an incomplete phrase providing additional information, so a comma should come right after the complete sentence, not a semicolon. Choice B is incorrect because it results in a run-on sentence and choice D is incorrect because a comma alone cannot connect two complete sentences.

Answer: A

18. 1-1 Subject-Verb Agreement/9-1 Frequently Confused Words

The subject, disregarding all the modifiers, is 'the production', which is singular. Therefore, the verb must be in singular form, which is 'exemplifies'. Choice D is incorrect because 'affects' is a verb.

Answer: C

19. 6-1 Period, Semi-colon vs. Comma/6-3 Various Comma Usages

A semicolon can only be used to connect two complete sentences. The current structure involves a modifier followed by another modifier followed by a complete sentence, so a comma should come after each modifier, not a semicolon. Choice B is incorrect because 'created as substitutes for CFCs' is modifying 'HFCs', not 'this'.
Answer: D

20. 2-1 Pronoun Agreement

The pronoun is referring to 'SF_6' which is singular. Therefore, 'it is' should be used instead of 'they are'.
Answer: B

21. 12 Graphs and Charts

The graph shows that the amount of F-gases relative to total emissions, as represented by the uppermost section of the graph, is expected to increase significantly by 2030.
Answer: A

22. 10-1 Style and Tone

Choices A and C do not necessarily offer any kind of hope for the future. Choice D fails to summarize the larger issue discussed in the passage. The only choice that summarizes the issue discussed in the passage and offers a hope for the future is choice B.
Answer: B

PASSAGE 3

23. 6-2 Colons and Dashes

Even though a colon is used to introduce a list or series of items, it is unnecessary here as the word 'like' already performs that function. Choice C is also incorrect as the sentence is not placed within a clause. Choice D is incorrect because a semicolon has to connect two complete sentences.
Answer: B

24. 10-1 Style and Tone

The question asks for the use of a 'hyperbole'. Choices B, C, and D are all far from being exaggerative. Only choice A is an example of a hyperbole, as it is unlikely that a song would last only a 'second' or a 'whole day'.
Answer: A

25. 11 Replacement

The use of transition 'In fact' signifies that the second sentence supports the previous sentence. Since the second sentence states that the performance 'is not at all strange', the previous sentence should state something in a similar vein. This eliminates choice A as 'remarkable' is the opposite of 'not at all strange'. Choices C and D are not mentioned. Only choice B is correct as 'this might not seem like that unusual' is similar to 'not at all strange'.
Answer: B

26. 11 Replacement

The previous sentence talks about how 'no two performances of the piece [are] the same length'. The writer then gives examples of how the performances can be different by saying how one organist's performance can be over 14 hours while another can be as short as five minutes. Therefore, choice D 'for example' provides the most appropriate transition.
Answer: D

27. 10-1 Style and Tone

The most important aspect of the music is that it has to be played '*as slow as possible*'. Only choice C mentions this.
Answer: C

28. 10-2 Redundancy

'subjectivity' and 'has multiple interpretations' are redundant. The only choice that eliminates this redundancy is choice B.
Answer: B

29. 11 Replacement

Read the sentence carefully to understand its logic. The sentence states that *even though* the piece is being played very slowly, the exact time for each note can be calculated *because* it is still being played to a specific tempo. The transition word has to have a similar meaning to 'because', which is choice B 'since'.

Answer: B

30. 6-4 Apostrophes

The 'connection' belongs to 'idea', so the possessive case of 'idea' should be used, which is 'its'.

Answer: C

31. 9-1 Diction

'within … lifetime' is an idiomatic expression.

Answer: A

32. 6-4 Apostrophes

Since there is no 'a' in front of 'future' and 'hands' is plural, the noun should be plural, which is 'generations'. Since 'hands' belong to 'generations', an apostrophe should be used to indicate possession. Choice C is incorrect because when a noun is plural, an apostrophe follows it without an additional 's'.

Answer: D

33. 10-1 Style and Tone

Choices B, C, and D all provide details that are unrelated to the topic of the paragraph, which is the connection of past and future through continuation of an unfinished work. Only choice A provides a quote that captures this idea.

Answer: A

PASSAGE 4

34. 6-3 Various Comma Usages

'social media', 'artificial intelligence', and 'alternative energy' are all separate words. Commas should come between the words, not within the words themselves.

Answer: B

35. 9-1 Diction/9-3 Frequently Confused Words

except (prep.): apart from
accept (v.): say yes or agree to; recognize something as necessary
The author is saying that people have already recognized 'drones' as being part of their everyday life. Therefore, 'accept' is the correct choice here. Also, 'part of' is an idiomatic expression.

Answer: D

36. 10-5 Register

The tone of the entire passage is casual with some degree of formality. Choice B and D 'old-fashioned' and 'mom-and-pop' are too informal while choice C 'superannuated' is too formal.
Only choice A suits the tone of the passage.

Answer: A

37. 11 Deletion

To readers who do not understand what 'automated car' is the underlined sentence provides an important detail that explains the concept of automated cars. Also, without the underlined sentence, the readers can freely interpret the meaning of automated cars. Therefore, the sentence should not be deleted.

Answer: C

38. 8 Tense

The context clearly shows that the technology (automated car) has not yet been released. Therefore, choices B, C, and D can be eliminated since past and past perfect tense cannot be used to describe an action that has not yet taken place. Only choice A correctly uses the present perfect tense.

Answer: A

39. 2-1 Pronoun Agreement

The pronoun is referring to 'passengers' which is plural. Therefore, 'them' should be used instead of 'him or her'.

Answer: D

40. 11 Replacement

The relationship between the sentences before and after the conjunction must be clearly understood. Research must be conducted on the safety of cars with and without human control *because* people fear not having control when driving at high speed. The only answer choice that describes this cause and effect relationship is choice B 'so'.

Answer: B

41. 11 Insertion

Since the new sentence is talking about 'word of the companies', the previous sentence should mention different companies that talk about automated cars. Sentence 4 accomplishes this by stating that 'companies like Tesla and Google claim that…'. Therefore, the sentence should be added after sentence 4.

Answer: D

42. 11 Replacement

The relationship between the sentences before and after the comma must be clearly understood. The use of 'therefore' in 'might therefore increase' signifies that the increase in 'demand for vehicles of all kinds' is *the result of* 'increased availability and success of these vehicles'.

Answer: D

43. 11 Replacement

The relationship between the sentences before and after the transition must be clearly understood. Any conclusion about the effect of automated cars on the environment should be doubted 'until more data becomes available' *because* the effect is 'truly impossible to tell at so early a point'. The latter sentence is the conclusion, or the effect of the previous sentence. The correct transition is choice B 'Therefore'.

Answer: B

44. 10-3 Wordiness

Any further clarification on the nature of the questions is unnecessary as it is clear from the context that the questions are related to the effects of the automated car technology. Other answer choices can be considered too wordy.

Answer: A

Paul's SAT® Writing

지은이	김동현
발 행 인	김동현
발 행 처	엘티씨 (LTC)
출판등록	2008년 12월 24일
주 소	서울특별시 성북구 북악산로 831 201-504
대표전화	02-558-2715
홈페이지	http://www.paulacademy.net
	http://blog.naver.com/paulacademy
ISBN	979-11-86461-10-5

※ 이 책은 엘티씨(LTC)가 저작권자와의 계약에 따라 발행한 것이므로 본사의 허락 없이는 어떠한 형태와 수단으로도 이 책의 내용을 이용하지 못합니다.

※ 잘못된 책은 구입하신 서점에서 바꾸어 드립니다.

PaulAcademy
LEARN · TRY · FLY